In the Name of Reason

PATRICIO SILVA

In the Name of Reason

Technocrats and Politics in Chile

The Pennsylvania State University Press
University Park, Pennsylvania

Library of Congress Cataloging-in-Publication Data

Silva, Patricio.
In the name of reason : technocrats and politics in Chile / Patricio Silva.
p.   cm.
Includes bibliographical references and index.
Summary: "Explores the role played by technocrats in the political and
institutional evolution of Chile since the late nineteenth century until today, with
emphasis on the period from 1938–1973 as well as the period following
democratic restoration in 1990"—Provided by publisher.
ISBN 978-0-271-03453-9 (cloth : alk. paper)
1. Chile—Politics and government—20th century.
2. Technocracy.
I. Title.

F3099.S555   2009
983.06′4—dc22
2008036803

To the Memory of Norbert Lechner

Contents

Tables

Acknowledgments

Over the past two decades many people have helped me in one way or another in my endeavor to understand the role of technocrats in the political development of twentieth-century Chile. I would especially like to thank Verónica Montecinos, Eduardo Silva, Carlos Huneeus, and Miguel Angel Centeno, who share with me an interest in studying the technocratic ascendancy in Latin America and have become very helpful sparring partners. Their inspiring academic work and friendship have been for me an important source of motivation in the writing of this book. Over the years I have also benefited from critical observations made by many colleagues and friends to my work on the technocratic phenomenon in Chile. Among these, I would especially like to thank Frank Fischer, Alan Angell, Gerard van der Ree, David Hojman, Cristóbal Kay, Marco Moreno, Paul Cammack, and Kees Koonings. The Department of Latin American Studies at Leiden University and the annual conferences of the Society for Latin American Studies (SLAS) in the United Kingdom have been excellent places for academic dialogue and reflection.

Special thanks also go to Miriam Rabinovich, who translated some chapters from Spanish into English and corrected the entire manuscript. Joni Uhlenbeck was very helpful in the closing stage of preparing the final version. My thanks also go to the staff at Penn State University Press, especially to Sandy Thatcher, Cherene Holland, Patricia Mitchell, and Andrew Lewis for their constant encouragement and good advice. In this context, I acknowledge the helpful critique and useful suggestions put forth by anonymous reviewers. As the dictum goes, none of the colleagues and institutions mentioned before is accountable for the final version of my argument.

Finally, I want to express my immense gratitude to my wife Lia van Dijk, who continuously offered me the much-needed moral support to pursue this academic venture.

Acronyms

AD	Alianza Democrática (Democratic Alliance)
AHC	Academia de Humanismo Cristiano (Academy of Christian Humanism)
APEC	Asia-Pacific Economic Cooperation
CEO	Clima de Emprendimiento Organizado (Climate of Organized Entrepreneurship)
CEPAL	Comisión Económica para América Latina (United Nations Economic Commission for Latin America, ECLA)
CEPLAN	Centro de Estudios y Planificación Nacional (Center for Planning Studies)
CESEC	Centro de Estudios Socio-Económicos (Center of Socioeconomic Studies)
CIEPLAN	Corporación de Estudios para Latinoamérica (Institute of Latin American Studies)
CODELCO	Corporación Nacional del Cobre (National Copper Corporation)
COPROCO	Confederación de la Producción y del Comercio (Confederation of Production and Commerce)
CORA	Corporación de la Reforma Agraria (Land Reform Agency)
CORFO	Corporación de Fomento de la Producción (National Development Corporation)
COSACH	Compañía de Salitre de Chile (Chilean Nitrate Corporation)
CUT	Central Única de Trabajadores (Central Trade Union of Workers)
DESAL	Centro para el Desarrollo Económico y Social de América Latina (Center for Latin American Economic and Social Development)
ECLA	United Nations Economic Commission for Latin America (CEPAL)
FLACSO	Facultad Latinoamericana de Ciencias Sociales (Latin American Faculty of Social Sciences)

FPMR	Frente Patriótico Manuel Rodríguez (Manuel Rodríguez Patriotic Front)
IC	Izquierda Cristiana (Christian Left)
IDB	Inter-American Development Bank
ILET	Instituto Latinoamericano de Estudios Transnacionales (Latin American Institute of Transnational Studies)
ILPES	Instituto Latinoamericano de Planificación Económica y Social (Latin American Institute of Economic and Social Planning)
INDAP	Instituto de Desarrollo Agropecuario (Agrarian Development Institute)
INE	Instituto Nacional de Estadísticas (National Statistics Institute)
MAPU	Movimiento de Acción Popular Unitaria (Unitary Popular Action Movement)
MIDEPLAN	Ministerio de Planificación y Cooperación (Ministry of Planning and Cooperation)
ODEPLAN	Oficina de Planificación Nacional (National Planning Agency)
PDC	Partido Demócrata Cristiano (Christian Democrat Party)
PPD	Partido por la Democracia (Party for Democracy)
PS	Partido Socialista (Socialist Party)
SII	Servicio de Impuestos Internos (Chilean Internal Revenue Service)
SNA	Sociedad Nacional de Agricultura (National Society of Agriculture)
SOFOFA	Sociedad de Fomento Fabril (Society for Industrial Development)
SUR	Corporación de Estudios Sociales y de Educación (Institute of Social and Educational Studies)
UDI	Unión Democrática Independiente (Independent Democratic Union)
UNDP	United Nations Development Program
UP	Unidad Popular (Popular Unity)

Introduction:
Technocrats and Politics in Chile

Studies of the Chilean political system have historically been characterized by their strong emphasis on the role of political parties (Edwards and Frei 1949; Gil 1966; Garretón 1989; Scully 1992). This particular feature of Chile's political system has brought Manuel Antonio Garretón to claim that the political parties have constituted the "backbone" of Chilean society (1989, xvi). From a similar perspective Liliana de Riz concludes that "Chilean political history, unlike any other in the neighboring countries, developed with, and through, the political parties" (1989, 57). And finally, Larissa A. Lomnitz and Ana Melnick (2000) have argued that the political parties' influence on Chilean society has been such that they have permeated, and in a sense modeled, the country's dominant political culture.

There is no doubt that Chile has a solid system of political parties, a system that has, for many decades, made it possible for a relatively stable democracy to operate (see Valenzuela 1989). For this reason, it is not my intention to question the important presence and influence of political parties in the political and social dynamics of the country; nonetheless, I do not believe that they monopolized politics in twentieth-century Chile. As early as 1988, Alan Angell had expressed doubts about this reading of the political history of the country, rightly highlighting the strong antiparty feeling that has also been a constant in Chilean politics since the 1920s. The government of Arturo Alessandri (1924–25), the two administrations of Carlos Ibáñez (1927–31 and 1952–58), and the government of Jorge Alessandri (1958–64) all "flew the banner" of antipartisanship. To this list we should add the considerable citizen support received by General Pinochet with his "politics of anti-politics" (Loveman and Davies 1997) and, more recently, the support obtained in the 1990s by conservative leader Joaquín Lavín, who has also resorted to a clearly apolitical discourse (see P. Silva 2001b).

My analysis of the evolution of the political institutions of Chile has led me to conclude that, together with political parties, technocrats have also played a key role in the administration and ideological orientation of the different political projects that Chile has embarked on since the 1920s. A cursory overview of key historical milestones gives evidence of this. Thus, we can see how technocrats played a central role in the reforms launched in 1920 after Arturo Alessandri's victory, which were further reinforced in 1927–31 by the government of Colonel Carlos Ibáñez. These reforms not only implied the end of the oligarchic state, but also brought along with them a strong modernization of the state apparatus (see Ibáñez Santa María 1984 and 2003). Technocrats also played a leading role in the industrialization process promoted by the state from 1939 on after the foundation of the Corporación de Fomento (CORFO, the state development agency), which became the main tool to give shape and implement the industrialization-based developmental strategy (Pinto [1958] 1985; Muñoz 1986).

In the 1960s and until the military takeover of 1973—the period that Mario Góngora ([1981] 1988) so aptly called "the era of global planning"—the influence of technocrats increased together with the expansion of the state apparatus after the creation of new bodies such as the Land Reform Corporation (CORA) and the National Planning Agency (ODEPLAN) and the administrative structure that emerged as a result of the nationalization of copper in the late 1970s. During this period, technocrats also acted as the ideologists of developmental-style reforms through the United Nations Economic Commission for Latin America (ECLA) and the universities, advocating a purported structuralism that called for active action by the state (see Ahumada [1958] 1973, Pinto 1973a, C. Kay 1989, and Hira 1999).

After the military coup of September 1973, the so-called Chicago Boys were to become the main engineers of the neoliberal economic and ideological policy. One of them, Sergio de Castro, Pinochet's minister of finance, was to be for a long time their undisputed leader within the cabinet of the military government (C. Huneeus 2007; Arancibia and Balart, 2007). During the transition to democracy, in 1985–90, private institutes (such as CIEPLAN, FLACSO, and so on) and technical think tanks of the democratic opposition performed a crucial job of rapprochement to the technocrats of the regime, facilitating the agreements that preceded the changeover (Puryear 1994; Levy 1996).

Following the restoration of democracy in 1990, there was a strong expansion of the role of technocrats in the four administrations of the government coalition between 1990 and 2008, during which economists with a strong technopolitical imprint such as Alejandro Foxley, Eduardo Aninat, Nicolás Eyzaguirre, and Andrés Velasco were to become key figures in the first four governments of the Concertación. Finally, it is also possible to see that the project for the modernization and internationalization of the Chilean economy and society supported by the Concertación governments since 1990 has itself positioned technocrats to become key actors in future years (P. Silva 1997). Not only have these technocrats been the main executors of policies and programs, but they have also quite often supplied the political movements with the necessary instruments to articulate their political projects. One of the main characteristics of technocrats has been their continued presence within the state apparatus, providing administrative stability at times of strong political turmoil (1931–38); facilitating agreements and rapprochements (1988–90); or strengthening democracy through attainment of economic success and internationalization of the Chilean economy and society (1990–2008).

In the course of the twentieth century there has been a sordid struggle between political parties and antipartisan sectors. The latter have in general tended to give their support to solutions that are technocratic in nature. Nevertheless, political parties have also made use of technocratic models and projects conceived of mainly by technocrats, which have ranged from industrialization via CORFO to Eduardo Frei Montalva's "revolution in liberty," to Salvador Allende's "Chilean way to socialism," to Augusto Pinochet's "silent revolution" and the "growth with equity" project of the Concertación governments.

Identifying Technocrats

This study expressly seeks to make visible the importance that technocrats have had in the functioning of the Chilean political system since the 1920s.

Let it be said, however, that technocrats themselves are partly to blame for their relative invisibility and absence in studies on Chilean politics. In fact, the perception of their role in politics has been impeded by their tendency to distance themselves from political parties and mass media. Furthermore, technocrats do not identify themselves as such because of the pejorative connotation assigned to the concept by public opinion, since a "technocrat" is generally equated with a person who is cold, calculating, and lacking in social sensitivity.

In his classical study on technocracy, Jean Meynaud gives a minimal definition, namely, "the political situation in which effective power belongs to technologists termed technocrats" (1968, 29). On the basis of this minimal definition, Meynaud embarks upon an in-depth exploration of the different facets of technocracy and of the technocrats that constitute it. His analysis reveals the image of the technocrat as an individual with a clear technoscientific orientation who acquires political influence in the high government circles because of his (or her) specialized skills and expertise in the fields of economic policy, finance, and state administration. However, he makes it clear that the political power that technocrats may attain is not permanent and that it is always subordinated to the power of the politicians that steer the course of government. More than political power per se, it is "political influence" that technocrats exercise on the powers-that-be, by giving advice on complex economic issues and public policies (21–70). In turn, Giovanni Sartori (1984) rightly warns that the relative increase in the technocrats' power observed in modern societies does not have to mean increased power for technocracy itself. As he puts it, even when scientists govern, it does not necessarily mean that they govern like scientists (1984, 328–29). Frank Fischer (1990) stresses that technocracy is the *allegedly* apolitical adaptation of expertise to the tasks of governance. Thus, technocrats justify themselves by appealing only to technical expertise grounded on scientific forms of knowledge in order to find technical solutions to political problems (1990, 18). For the purposes of this study, I shall use David Collier's definition, namely, technocrats are "individuals with a high level of specialized academic training which serves as a principal criterion on the basis of which they are selected to occupy key decisionmaking or advisory roles in large, complex organizations—both public and private" (1979, 403).

Although most technocrats are trained as engineers, economists, financial experts, or managers, expertise in economic and administrative issues is not a necessary condition for the adoption of a technocratic outlook. As this study will show, individuals with formal training in sociology, political science, and the like can under certain circumstances become "technocratized" as they become influenced by the existing technocratic ideology and eventually accept the idea that decisions must be made by experts.

A recurring theme in the debate has been the existing differences among technocrats, technicians, bureaucrats, intellectuals, and politicians, and above all, the nature of their interaction within the political system. For Meynaud the difference between a technician and a technocrat was fundamentally one of degree, determined by the level of decision-making in which they take part and their influence on political leaders. As he put it, "The switch from technical adviser to technocrat is accomplished when the technologist himself acquires the capacity for making decisions, or carries the most weight in determining the choices of the person officially responsible for them. . . . The very large majority of technologists never *reach* the technocratic *stage*" (1968, 30–31; emphasis added). Later studies, which deal with the relation between technicians and technocrats, have paid more attention to the different public spheres in which both operate, and to their career patterns, as well as to their level and type of education (Camp 1980). Thus, Miguel A. Centeno and Sylvia Maxfield, when discussing Mexico, observe that *technicians* traditionally specialize in specific substantive areas such as health and agriculture and tend to enjoy job security and long tenure in traditional institutions of public administration. Besides, most of them have received their technical training in technological schools and universities in their home countries. As for technocrats, they usually operate in specialized planning institutions and think tanks that are more interdisciplinary in nature. These are experts who, more often than not, have postgraduate academic degrees from foreign universities, work both in public and private institutions, and frequently have some work experience in other countries (1992, 62–67).

The distinction between bureaucrats and technocrats appears to be less problematic, but here also there are gray areas with respect to their commonalities and differences. The most generalized opinion is that the bureaucrat only obeys and implements top-down legal guidelines, without questioning their legitimacy or effectiveness, according to the classical Weberian postulates. Besides, in the Latin American context, their level of professional training has traditionally been quite low, which in some cases may only include secondary education and practical experience acquired in years of service in public agencies (see Cleaves 1974). Technocrats consider bureaucrats limited in scope and old-fashioned, and likely to obstruct or even block the great administrative and economic reforms that they seek to implement. This may account for why they openly declare themselves the enemies of traditional bureaucracy, as well as why they often blindly attempt to reduce the number of government agencies, and to eliminate the largest possible number of bureaucrats, on the grounds of pursuit of efficiency (Camp 1983).

Despite their contempt of bureaucrats, however, many technocrats operate in bureaucratic environments (ministries, public agencies, and so on) and must work side by side with them, and are often forced to accept the bureaucratic rationale in an attempt to attain results in their policies. But also, the improved level of technical training in managerial methods reached by many bureaucrats in recent decades has made them somewhat approach the "cosmovision" of technocrats, which has even led them on occasion to adopt a stance that might be considered clearly technocratic, favoring the technification of decision-making and the assessment of personal merit (see Bresser-Pereira and Spink 1999).

Indeed, relations between technocrats and intellectuals in modern societies have been more complex and full of open conflict over hegemony than those between technocrats and bureaucrats (see Gouldner 1979). Currently, intellectuals in Latin America are generally sociologists, political scientists, and philosophers who have traditionally made it their job to formulate critical interpretations of the sociopolitical and cultural development of their respective countries, offering at the same time alternatives for change.[1] They criticize technocrats for their apparent detachment from social and cultural reality and from the needs of the population, and for their stubborn insistence on applying to developing economies rationalist-style economic and financial policies based on technical and theoretical guidelines generated in industrialized countries. In turn, technocrats generally look down on and distrust intellectuals, whom they identify as the main culprits of the process of political radicalization and economic collapse experienced by many Latin American countries in the 1960s and 1970s.

In the 1960s and 1970s, Latin American technocrats were largely subordi-

---

1. They represent the "intelectuales críticos y comprometidos," as they are called in Latin America, who following the Cuban revolution in 1959 flourished everywhere in the region. They criticize the status quo and demand profound socioeconomic and political reforms in their countries to meet the needs of the popular sectors.

nated to the intellectuals, whose map of the "road ahead" was based largely on political and ideological considerations. In those years, sociologists, rather than economists, exerted a greater level of influence within government circles. One can state that from the early 1960s until the mid-1970s intellectuals exercised a large degree of influence within the political elite of many countries, even when they took an oppositional stance. They were very visible actors who interpreted the national reality and defended particular ideological models through the universities and the mass media (Brunner and Flisfisch 1985).

The emergence of the military dictatorships of the 1970s was to produce a dramatic weakening of the traditional intellectual cadre, which became one of the central victims of repression. However, after the restoration of democracy in the 1980s, intellectuals—who, by definition, have the ability to come up with a critical view of the sociopolitical reality—have failed to make their voices heard with their past strength (Petras 1990). What can be observed instead from the 1980s on is that some intellectuals have adopted technocratizing attitudes. This can be seen, for instance, in the fact that in the last two decades intellectuals have been paying greater attention to the issues of government transparency and effectiveness. This concern, in my view, is connected to the increasing internationalization, academization, and professionalization of Latin American social scientists and intellectuals in general. During the last two decades, the meritocratic orientation of many intellectuals has been encouraged by a series of developments such as the growing dependence on foreign donors for financing their research, the increasing importance attached to postgraduate degrees obtained in U.S. and European universities, the participation in international congresses, and the growing acceptance of the tenet "publish or perish" (Brunner and Barrios 1987).

Finally, the relation between politicians and technocrats has also been plagued with conflict, in which the former have attempted to prevent the ascent of technocracy, which they consider a direct threat to their power within the political system. What we have witnessed is that the ascent of technocracy has been fostered by the decline of political parties in the new democracies emerging in Latin America since the 1980s. Political parties, which used to operate as the social mobilization mechanisms *par excellence,* no longer have the convening power and representativeness that they enjoyed in the past (Domínguez 1994). We should also bear in mind that in many countries, political parties used to be the primary recruiting ground for upper-level government officials. Their current decline has generated in some countries a greater space for the use of meritocratic criteria in the recruitment of cabinet members and candidates for other important government posts, who now simply define themselves as "independent" and even as "apolitical."

In the 1960s there was a tendency in academic discussion to stress the strong differences between technocrats and politicians, and the subordination of the former to the latter, who kept firm control of the government and the state bureaucracy (Vernon 1963). James Cochrane (1967) makes it clear that technocrats and politicians have different perceptions of how to preserve government legitimacy. So while the technocrats believe legitimacy is best maintained through a professional administration and the use of technical criteria for decision-making, politicians believe that the regime's legitimacy rests on the preservation of old national ideals and decision-making according to political guidelines.

Raymond Vernon's original dichotomy between politicians and technocrats no longer reflects the dynamics of the Latin American political elites; for since the early 1970s the dividing line between politicians and technocrats has become extremely fine. That is to say, over the years the rise of technocrats to the highest posts in the government has demanded that they acquire the technical and practical skills of both technocrats *and* politicians. However, this "new" type of technocrat—the "*técnico*-politician" (Grindle 1977), "political technocrat" (Camp 1985), or "technopols" (Domínguez 1994)—is actually not that new. As I show later, "technopoliticians" have been important members of the Chilean political administration since as early as the late 1920s.

Studying Technocracy in Chile: A Personal Journey

This book is the product of a long personal journey. I came across the technocratic phenomenon in Chile in the mid-1980s while I was writing my dissertation (P. Silva 1987). Although this study was not explicitly centered on the role of technocrats, each of its pages gave evidence of the significance of the group of technocrats popularly known as the Chicago Boys in economic policy in general and the agrarian strategy in particular. In fact, the Chicago Boys were the architects of the socioeconomic policies and were among the main ideologues of the military regime (see Rabkin 1993).

The Chicago Boys and their neoliberal economic policies were one of the elements most criticized by the opposition to the military regime, especially after the economic crisis of the early 1980s (see O'Brien and Roddick 1983). What I found striking was that once the military regime was over, the press and public opinion practically stopped talking about not only the Chicago Boys but the technocratic phenomenon in general. This prompted me to explore the question of whether technocracy had really lost its strength with the end of Pinochet's regime and the restoration of democracy. The first product of this inquiry was my article "Technocrats and Politics in Chile: From the Chicago Boys to the CIEPLAN Monks," published in 1991. In that article I suggest that the technocratic phenomenon in Chile, which had seen itself notably strengthened during the authoritarian period, seemed to have survived perfectly the transition from an authoritarian to a democratic regime and, in fact, there had already emerged initial evidence that made it possible to anticipate that technocrats would have an important role in the new democracy. Far from taking accusatory aim, my analysis intended rather to contribute with some political and sociological explanations related to the continuity of the technocratic phenomenon.

From then on, I concentrated on the search for an explanation of a phenomenon that I had already detected while writing my dissertation, the analysis of which became more and more urgent every day after the experience of the democratic transition and after the installation of the first democratic government in 1990, namely, which factors make the theme of the role of technocracy in Chile "appear" and "disappear" from political and academic debate in the country. What I had observed was that the theme of the existence of the technocratic phenomenon in Chile emerged fleetingly during the government of Jorge Alessandri (1958–64), and subsequently practically disappeared during the governments of Eduardo Frei Montalva (1964–70) and of Salvador Allende (1970–73). The theme reemerged strongly under the regime of General Pinochet (1973–90) and then, as already mentioned, disappeared again under the first three governments of the Concertación (1990–2006). All this was going on despite the fact that a serious analysis of the situation showed that since the late 1950s not only had there been no interruption in the importance of the technocratic phenomenon, technocratic influence within Chilean state institutions has been growing constantly (P. Silva 1993a).

It seems that the cycles of "death and resurrection" of technocracy as a subject of public discussion can be linked to whether or not the center-left intelligentsia is in control of the government. In retrospect we can see that the public discussion of technocracy only acquired political relevance during the Alessandri government (that is to say, before the advent of the Christian Democratic technocrats into government), and during the military government of General Pinochet (when the left-wing technocracy was removed from the state institutions). On the other hand, the discussion on technocracy petered out during the governments of Eduardo Frei Montalva and Salvador Allende (when center-left technocrats occupied influential positions), and following the restoration of democracy under the governments of Patricio Aylwin, Eduardo Frei Ruiz-Tagle, Ricardo Lagos, and Michelle Bachelet (when these center-left technocrats regained control of the state institutions).

The little acknowledgment until now of the role played by technocrats in the political and economic development of Chile is, in my opinion, related to the central position occupied by political parties. The parties, for ideological and electoral reasons, have systematically misrepresented the history of modern Chile as entirely the product of party politics, omitting all mention of technocrats and technocracy. Owing to the prevalence of the democratic regime, the eventual recognition of the technocratic element was considered to be problematic and not in keeping with the prevailing democratic ideology. This became even more marked in the 1960s and early 1970s because of the populist character of these experiments.

My next step was to carry out a historical study seeking the "origins" of technocracy in Chile—where was it born and under what circumstances? In this search, I came across a relatively little known technocratic project sponsored by the government of Colonel Carlos Ibáñez (1927–31) that is crucial to the understanding of the subsequent evolution of the technocratic phenomenon in Chile (see P. Silva 1994). Until the present, the Ibáñez period has always been a taboo subject among Chilean political scientists and historians. Because of its authoritarian nature it has been regarded as a disagreeable black spot in the country's long-standing democratic tradition. Hence, until recently no major aspect of the Ibáñez government, including its technocratic orientation, had been thoroughly studied by Chilean scholars.

In particular the many existing similarities, *mutatis mutandis,* between this early technocratic project and the administrative model adopted by Pinochet fifty years later moved me to carry out a comparative analysis of the nature of the alliance between the military and technocrats in both regimes (see P. Silva 2001a). I also found a strong continuity in the management of the state and of its institutions, starting with Ibáñez in the late 1920s until the late 1950s. In fact, the young cadre of engineers who were first hired by the state under Ibáñez years later were running CORFO (founded in 1939) and managing the main enterprises born from the process of industrialization of the state in the decades that followed (see Muñoz 1993). All of this gives evidence of the durability of technocratic action in Chile, from the 1920s until the present fourth Concertación term of office.

My most recent exploration has centered around the intellectual and ideological background to the formation of the first technocratic cadre in the 1920s. This research has led me to two great Chilean intellectuals whose influence was fundamental in the genesis of the pretechnocratic conceptions that would later materialize under the regime of Colonel Ibáñez. They are José Victorino Lastarria (1817–88) and Valentín Letelier (1852–1919), who proclaimed the need to adopt "scientific politics" in Chile (see P. Silva 2006a). The study of the life and work of both authors reveals the positivist, middle-class, democratic, and liberal origins of technocratic thought in Chile, which explains much about the evolution of Chilean technocracy in the twentieth century. I have also discovered a connection between the ideas of Lastarria and Letelier, and the formation of Ibáñez's technocratic team in the late-1920s. In fact, Valentín Letelier, Lastarria's most important disciple, inspired within the Radical Party (Partido Radical), partly through the Freemasons, the emergence of quite a cohort of young politicians, among them Armando Quezada, Luis Galdames, and Pablo Ramírez, who were later to play an outstanding role in the government of Ibáñez. Ramírez in particular was to encourage the promotion of technocratic engineers to strategic positions of power (P. Silva 1998, 2006b).

This book represents a synthesis of my recent research on the technocratic phenomenon in Chile. Most of the material used in it comes from different articles, chapters of books, and unpublished manuscripts, which have been thoroughly reformulated and placed within the context of a larger historical and analytical perspective. This book does not seek to become "the history of technocracy in Chile," but rather to present a series of theses on the evolution and importance of this actor. For this reason, and depending on their significance for understanding the technocratic phenomenon in Chile, some historical periods will receive more attention than others. By the same token, sometimes the analysis will be focused on the important role played by some specific individuals, such as Lastarria, Letelier, and Ramírez.

Most of the arguments presented in this study will be arranged along the following three analytic and thematic axes, which have been central to the general debate that has been taking place in the last forty years on the relation between technocracy and politics, namely, technocracy and industrial society, technocracy and social class, and finally, technocracy and political regime.

Technocracy and Advanced Industrial Societies

Many classical studies on the technocratic phenomenon either assert or imply that technocracy and its incursion within the realm of politics is directly connected to the consolidation of advanced industrial societies (Galbraith 1967; Meynaud 1968; Putnam 1977; Gouldner 1979; Fischer 1990) and even postindustrial societies (Ellul [1954] 1964; Bell 1973; Lindberg 1976). This argument highlights the fact that the industrialization process and the growing social, political, and technological complexity of the industrialized societies have led to the increased importance of assigning the decision-making process to people with technical credentials, rather than to those with traditional political aptitudes. Thus, for example, Fischer points out that "historically, the theory and practice of technocracy have been political and ideological *responses to* industrialization and technological progress" (1990, 17; emphasis added).[2]

As I shall suggest in this study, this has not necessarily been the case in Latin America, where the importation of ideas, doctrines, ideologies, and social projects originating in the core countries has been a constant since the emergence of the Latin American republics in the initial decades of the nineteenth century. Otherwise, it would be impossible to explain, for instance, the case of the so-called Mexican *científicos,* who as early as the end of the nineteenth century were advocating positivist proposals of a technocratic nature within Porfirio Díaz's regime (Zea 1970). In the case of Chile, as we shall see later, the technocratic cadre began to take over the state apparatus as early as the 1920s, with the emergence of a mesocratic regime, preceding by over ten years the creation of CORFO, which would later give shape to the

---

2. Max Weber had already suggested the connection between modern society and the need for expertise. As he put it, "The more complicated and specialized modern culture becomes, the more its external supporting apparatus demands the personally detached and strictly 'objective' *expert,* in lieu of the master of older social structures, who was moved by personal sympathy and favor, by grace and gratitude" (Gerth and Mills 1946, 216).

state-led industrialization process. What is more, these very same technocrats were to set in motion the process of industrialization and modernization that would characterize the decades to come.

The thesis that I shall attempt to develop throughout the book is that political factors contribute more to emergence of technocratic regimes than the systemic needs inherent in modernization and the growth in complexity of society resulting from the industrialization process. This is why in countries with comparable economic, social, and industrial development it is possible to observe different degrees of technocratic influence within the governments and administrative structures of the state. What is more, the forces that stimulate the rise of technocratic groups can be found not only within the circles of power but also in society at large. Often, in such cases, there emerges in society as well an intense uneasiness about traditional politics and politicians, which may lead to a cry for "apolitical" leadership. This, in my opinion, was evident at the time of Ibáñez's regime in the 1920s, during the Estado de Compromiso of the Radical governments in the early 1940s, Pinochet's dictatorship, and to a certain extent, also during the governments of the Concertación since 1990.

Technocracy, Ideology, and Class

Another central aspect of the general debate on the technocratic phenomenon has been the effort to establish the existing relation between technocracy, political ideologies, and social classes. The actual question is how "apolitical" and ideology-free are these technocrats, as most of them define themselves. From the classical study by Meynaud, a (not quite inaccurate) image emerges about technocrats being no more and no less than policy executors, whose only aim is to reach the objective set by the groups in power. By definition, they are in favor of industrialization and state interventionism in economic matters.

What we do know is that technocracy is a phenomenon that has already achieved universal presence in governments and political regimes ranging the full political spectrum: in German Nazism and the famous French technocracy; in the countries from the former Eastern European communist bloc; and more recently, in the People's Republic of China. In other words, there have been technocratic groups at the service of the most varied ideologies and doctrines since the early twentieth century up till now. In the specific case of Chile and regardless of the right-wing or left-wing orientations of the techno-crats, in my opinion, they have often been revolutionary in the sense that they have defended economic, administrative, and social proposals that implied profound transformations in their respective areas. If the Chilean technocrats have one ideological feature in common, this has been their idolatrous regard for progress and modernity (seldom defined by the technocrats themselves) and their attempts to achieve them at all costs (see Van der Ree 2007 and Correa Sutil 2004). This may perhaps be a mere reflection of the shared fasci-nation with modernity shown by every government of Chile since the early 1920s.

The second aspect of technocracy under discussion has to do with the social class or background of technocrats. If technocrats form a group whose roots and class identification are somewhat vague, can they then be defined as an elite of "socially unattached intellectuals," or the *Freischwebende Intelligenz* referred to by Karl Mannheim ([1936] 1976)? Meynaud, once again, who focused on the case of France, clearly presents an image of the technocrat as a member of the social elite at one of the prestigious and exclusive *grandes écoles*. According to other scholars, rather than being the representatives of a particular traditional social class, technocrats may be about to give shape to a "new class" that is challenging the power of the traditional industrial and political elites (see, for example, Gouldner 1979 and Kellner and Heuberger 1992). This perspective hints at a possible takeover of power, to be followed by a literal conversion of government into a techno*cracy,* that is, a new politi-cal order dominated by a minority of technocrats. It is my opinion, on the contrary, that the technocratization of the political system should not be con-ceived of as technocrats as such taking power, but rather as technocratism becoming the legitimate basis of power. In other words, I agree with Sartori (1984) when he says that technocrats do not rule directly, but via politicians.

Despite the fact that access to higher education and postgraduate studies in Latin America are luxuries within the reach of just a select few, one cannot conclude that the majority of technocrats in the region proceed from, or are part of, the upper classes of their respective countries. As we shall see in the case of Chile, ever since the early years of the republic, the middle class has always had some access to enlightened circles. For instance, Lastarria, Letelier, and many other Chilean professionals came from middle-class milieus, were educated at public schools, and through their talent and personal effort, managed to reach top positions in the world of politics, culture, and the academy, and came to be senators, ministers, ambassadors, university authorities, and so on. This penetration of middle-class sectors into the circles of political and intellectual influence occurs in Chile even now. For instance, former president Ricardo Lagos constantly stressed the fact that he was from the middle class, had studied at state-run schools, and had needed a scholarship grant to continue his education.

My contention throughout the whole of this study is that, rather than a class in itself, Chilean technocracy has constituted itself *around* the middle class. As Patrick Barr-Melej indicates, the emergence of the Chilean middle class since the mid-nineteenth century is indelibly linked to capitalist modernization and "classical liberal" projects that stimulated international trade, domestic commerce, and internal migration, factors that, as he points out, "created the necessary conditions for the proliferation of middle-class professions in such areas as governmental bureaucracy, accounting, small business, teaching, journalism, and so forth" (2001, 5–6). He also stresses the important fact that the members of the Chilean middle class also shared common cultural features which shaped their class identity. In his words,

> [A] mesocrat's being in the world, then, was not solely the function of economic activity and a comparable social standing; it also was tied to cultural norms and a cultural outlook. . . . In short, it may be argued that locating and identifying a mesocracy during this period by, say, examining employment data or breakdowns of occupations in census reports would not take into full account the pliability of "class" and, for that matter, the significance of culture and cultural practices in the elaboration of classes and identity. (6)

Thus, the main exponents of the technocratic ideology to be found in Chile agree in general terms with the central principles of the middle class, which has a strong meritocratic and anti-oligarchic character, in which education and the attainment of scientific knowledge take pride of place (Cerda Albarracín 1998). This connection between the middle class and the tenets of technocracy becomes distinctly manifest when we explore the legacy of Lastarria and Letelier, the adoption of their main proposals within the ideological bosom of the Radical Party (the Chilean middle-class party *par excellence*) and the subsequent emergence since the 1920s of a Chilean technocracy operating in the state sector. As we shall see in the following section, the fundamentally mesocratic character of technocracy will also be reflected in its positioning vis-à-vis authoritarianism and democracy.

Technocracy, Authoritarianism, and Democracy

The third and last discussion, which will cut across the different chapters of the book, has to do with the conflicting relation that technocrats have always had with democracy. This was already evident in the first promoters of technocratic ideologies, such as Henri de Saint Simon and Auguste Comte in the early nineteenth century, who advocated the installation of an "administrative state," in the hands of an elite of scientists, experts, and entrepreneurs. Their writings give clear evidence that they valued the preservation of social order and the "positive" or scientific administration of the affairs of the state above individual freedom, participation of the people, and democracy (see Jones 1998). A series of technocratic experiences in Europe and the United States during the twentieth century have also contributed to reinforce the close relation between technocrats and authoritarian ideologies and regimes. Among these experiences are those of Nazi Germany (Herf 1984); the short-lived technocratic movement of the 1920s in the United States, which in the early 1930s was to lead into a movement with a fascistoid bias (Bell 1960; Veblen 1965; Akin 1977); and the experience of "really existing socialism" in Eastern Europe and the Soviet Union (Konrad and Szeleny 1979; Rowney, 1989). Another case that is particularly relevant for Latin America in general and Chile in particular, is the dictatorship of Francisco Franco in Spain, whose policies of industrialization and modernization were supported by a select group of Opus Dei technocrats (see Fernández de la Mora 1986).

In the Latin American context, the image of an alleged "elective affinity" existing between technocracy and authoritarian regimes became markedly patent during the 1960s and 1970s as a series of "bureaucratic-authoritarian" regimes were established in the Southern Cone countries. In his seminal work on this new type of political regime, Guillermo O'Donnell (1973) identified the civilian technocracy as one of the military's principal allies in the "procoup coalition," and as key figures in the execution of the military regime's economic policies. Under the military governments of Argentina, Brazil, Chile, and Uruguay, a select group of economists and financial experts

acquired unprecedented discretionary powers in the formulation and implementation of radical financial and economic reforms (Ramos 1986; Malloy
1979). But in practice, it was the paradigmatic case of Pinochet's Chicago Boys
that was to raise awareness of the existence of an alliance between technocrats
and the military in Latin America (see Vergara 1985 and Valdés 1995). Finally,
many have insisted that an antidemocratic tendency is inherent in technocracy, since technocrats firmly believe that erratic policies formulated in reaction to massive popular pressure on the state apparatus can never solve social
problems, but that only they are capable of formulating and implementing
the correct, technical solutions to such problems (Meynaud 1968; Putnam
1977; Fischer 1990).

As I attempt to show in this book, technocracy may play very different
and even opposing roles under different historical and political situations.
Although at certain times in history technocrats have indeed given their support to authoritarian solutions, it can also be proved that, under other circumstances, they become directly or indirectly the key actors in the
preservation and operation of a democratic regime. In my opinion, the positioning of technocracy vis-à-vis democracy and authoritarianism during the
twentieth century in Chile has somewhat followed the classical patterns of
political behavior of the middle class. Thus, it has been conditioned by the
permanent middle-class fear of the masses and chaos, and its desire for order
and, at the same time, by its wish for social justice and the value it assigns to
personal effort. Thus, when the oligarchic regime was on its way out, technocrats became a strategic force in the emancipation of the emerging middle
class, with its strong rejection of inherited privilege and its strong advocacy
of rewarding merit and personal effort.

From the late 1930s on, when the middle-class sectors had already settled
down to power, technocracy became a balancing factor between, on the one
hand, the weakened oligarchic groups and, on the other, the emerging popular sectors. Technocracy not only gives the latter no preference, but also guarantees to the former that the businesses of the state will be well administered
and that economic policy will not be politicized. This was particularly the case
under the Radical Party administrations between 1938 and 1945. As I shall
suggest in this book, the state technocrats became a sort of mediating group
between a frightened and mistrustful Right and the forces of the Center-Left,
who were in charge of administering the funds of the country and the state
enterprises.

Chilean technocrats have had to operate within a highly politicized polity, despite the existence from 1938 to 1973 of an "Estado de Compromiso." It can be argued that the very existence of the compromise upon which Chilean democracy was built was in part the result of polarization and the inability of any one political sector to impose its will on the rest (see Valenzuela 1978; Scully 1992). This is why, for many decades, a marked three-way ideological split between the Right, the Left, and the Center permeated the Chilean political system, each of these sectors controlling almost one-third of the electorate. This is what scholars have referred to as the three-thirds pattern (Gil 1966; Drake 1978). Political polarization reached high levels, particularly during electoral periods. This polarization became very visible during the presidential elections in 1958, 1964, and 1970. Marcelo Cavarozzi concludes that "the consensus that Chilean elites reached during the 1930s and the 1940s was quite tenuous. . . . The fragility of the Chilean political consensus became progressively more obvious beginning in the early 1950s" (Cavarozzi 1992, 214). Eduardo Boeninger assesses the fragility of the Estado de Compromiso in similar terms. "It is paradoxical that the Estado de Compromiso existed in a climate of strong political instability and discontinuity. This produced an increasing loss of prestige by the political parties, politics and the practices of negotiation to achieve agreements between party leaders and members of the Parliament. This became even more evident as the economic malaise became more accentuated. To put it in present-day terms, the Estado de Compromiso was characterized by its unsatisfactory conditions of governability" (1997, 114).

In this polarized political environment, Chilean technocrats have since the late 1930s mainly operated as a moderating force. As a result of constant changeovers between center-left and center-right governments, the state apparatus was forced to seek support in a relatively stable body of technocrats. This was also the result of the lack of confidence between several social sectors and the politicians. In this context, technocrats have constituted, as it were, a sort of buffer or intermediary zone between contenders for power because of their technical capacity, their apparent neutrality, their lack of overt political affiliation, and so on. They also provided much needed continuity in state policies between different administrations because they were not easily replaceable. One of the most striking features of the permanence of technocrats in state agencies from 1927 to 1973 was their ability to survive from one government to the next. With perhaps the sole exception of the Alessandri Rodríguez period (1958–64) and the military regime (1973–90), most of the period under consideration shows an exceptional degree of continuity in the pool of technocrats in charge of specialized state agencies. As I show later in this book, the same young engineers who came into the state agencies in 1927 under Ibáñez "survived" all the different governments until 1958. The same happens later on. A good example is Sergio Molina, a technocrat who served as a minister in three different and even antagonistic governments (under the second administration of Ibáñez, under Alessandri Rodríguez, and under Frei Montalva). A similar degree of continuity can be observed between Frei Montalva and Allende. Following the victory of the Unidad Popular (Popular Unity, or UP) coalition in 1970, many Christian Democratic *técnicos* kept their positions at different state institutions (such as CORA, INDAP, ODEPLAN, CODELCO, and so on) because the Allende government did not have sufficient technical staff to run all those specialized agencies. Furthermore, many Christian Democratic technocrats became members of the left-wing MAPU and IC parties that finally became part of the governmental coalition supporting Allende. A clear example of this was Jacques Chonchol, who possessed marked technocratic credentials: he became director of CORA under Frei Montalva and later minister of agriculture under Salvador Allende.

When the mesocratic system encountered crucial survival problems like those in the late 1950s, technocrats (like those working at ECLA) went on to formulate economic and social reforms (particularly, the agrarian reform) that had an emancipatory impact on the neglected sectors of society, such as the peasantry and the urban poor. The technocrats also became the main agents in favor of the regional integration and later of globalization. There were, of course, clear political goals behind these policies, such as the active integration of the marginal social sectors into the political system in order to win their support at the polls. However, by making use of a technical and depoliticized discourse, these technocrats were able to present their policies as efficient instruments to transform the popular sectors into new consumers and strengthen the national economy.

The fact that technocrats have been kept on in key positions has been seen as typical of the new democracies emerging in the 1980s. In the case of Chile, technocracy offers guarantees to the powerful economic sectors, to the political Right, and to the military. The economic domain (particularly given the trauma of the early 1970s) has largely become "depoliticized," while the economic policymakers are isolated in a cocoon that protects them from direct pressures by the political and social sectors (see Haggard and Kaufman 1992).

It is obvious that the mere presence of technocrats is not sufficient to guarantee political and social stability. By the same token, prosperity alone is not sufficient to legitimize the political class. What we have seen in Chile since the mid-1990s is that the mere attainment of economic development and the use of an apolitical discourse have not apparently provided a solid and permanent solution to the need for political legitimacy. The people seem to be somewhat weary of the cold and colorless technocratic discourse, which became apparent under the government of Eduardo Frei Ruíz-Tagle in the late 1990s and has reached its peak under the Bachelet administration. What is interesting about this new situation, though, is that it by no means implies that the people should come to adopt politicized formulas. What we rather see is that the (consuming) mass consumption society, produced by the neoliberal model in Chile has created a public demand for a more marketized political message, in which apoliticism is combined with issues having to do with values and participation (Tironi 2005).

Thus, my central argument is that rather than having constituted a threat for democracy, technocrats have played a leading role in the consolidation of the democratic regime ever since the crisis of the 1930s, particularly in the generation and functioning of the so-called Estado de Compromiso from the end of the 1930s up to the early 1960s. The technocrats were also key actors in the economic and social transformations of the "decade of reforms" under the governments of Frei Montalva and Allende (1964–73).

So whereas during the Estado de Compromiso the Chilean governments pursued clear political and social goals with their policies, this, however, went hand-in-hand with the presence of technocrats who were supposedly defending technical and apolitical approaches to the problems of the day. Their very presence in the highest positions of the state agencies inspired confidence among the right-wing opposition forces. By providing that buffer zone to the system the technocrats indirectly made a very important contribution to the functioning of the Chilean democracy from 1938 to 1970. This constitutes in my view one of the main paradoxes about the political role played by technocrats in Chile, namely, that people who detested politics and politicians, at the end of the day were among the main facilitators—not deliberately but *de facto*—that made it possible for the pre-1973 Chilean democracy to function.

During the military government the neoliberal technocrats were part of what was known as the "soft" sector (O'Donnell, Schmitter, and Whitehead 1986) within the regime. They urged the military authorities to draw up a constitution and operate according to a rule of law. The Chicago Boys were particularly concerned about the mounting threats of boycott for Chilean products by the dockworkers' confederations in the United States and Europe because of the continuous violations of human rights in the country and were aware of the need for some form of legality, including respect for international agreements.

In the final phase of the Pinochet regime, the neoliberal technocrats seemed more preoccupied with the continuation of the economic model in the future democratic era than with putting up a fight for the continuation of the authoritarian regime. Thus, for the 1989 general elections, Hernán Büchi, Pinochet's successful minister of finance, was put forward as presidential candidate by the right-wing forces for the 1989 general elections. Büchi, however, showed an erratic position by declaring that he was tormented by "vital contradictions" when accepting that candidacy because he had no affinity whatsoever for politics (Angell 2007, 41). The rather passive attitude adopted by Büchi during his presidential campaign—he neither firmly criticized the democratic opposition nor convincingly defended the military government's achievements—indicates in my view that he, like many other Chicago Boys, no longer considered the Pinochet regime necessary to the survival of the new economic model. In fact, the neoliberal technocrats were convinced that once the masses had accepted the main tenets of the neoliberal postulates (reduction of the state, sacred respect for private property, consumption as the reward of individual effort, and so on), the restoration of democratic rule could be possible. It was evident that in the late 1980s the neoliberal economic model had became consolidated in Chile. In addition, many opposition leaders had already declared that they were not considering introducing fundamental changes in Chile's market economy in the near future (see Ominami 1991).

The positive relation of technocracy and democracy in Chile becomes more evident both during the period of transition and during the era of Concertación governments since 1990. My argument is that the technocratic groups (both of the government and the opposition) constituted themselves as spokespersons and mediators by becoming a channel for the dialogue between sectors of the military government and the moderate sectors of the opposition. It was in this that the private research centers and think tanks played a role of unique importance. They allayed the misgivings of politicians and translated the points of agreement and disagreement into technical language (see Puryear 1994). Indeed, the use of similar professional languages (Gouldner 1979), in the mutual relating of "comfreres" (particularly among economists such as Foxley, Büchi, and so on), facilitated the necessary reduction of the fear and feelings of mutual threat between the regime and the leaders of the democratic opposition.

My last contention here is that since the late 1990s technocratic ideology has mixed with the democratic idea in Chile, and that this has shaped an increasingly "technocratized" *and depoliticized* democracy, in which social problems are translated into technical terms.

1

Scientific Politics in Chile:
The Positivist Design

This chapter explores the intellectual foundation for the creation and expansion of technocratic groups within the Chilean government and state since the late 1920s. I intend to show that the technocratic boom experienced in Chile since the first government of Carlos Ibáñez (1927–31) was the result of an evolutionary process. This process was set in motion in the 1840s and began to mature throughout the second half of the nineteenth century.

As has been stated in the previous chapter, the ascendancy of technocracy in some Latin American countries was not the consequence of technical and organizational requirements posed by complex industrial societies, as the literature on technocracy generally suggests. Technocratic thought in Chile had already begun to emerge in the second half of the nineteenth century as a powerful tool for social and political emancipation. Some Chilean middle-class liberal intellectuals adopted some of the postulates of Comtean positivist philosophy and waved the banner of scientific reason against the suffocating oligarchic order of Chilean society. So in contrast to prevailing visions about the intrinsically authoritarian nature of technocratism, in Chile technocratic positivism has been instrumental in the emancipation of Chile's middle class and the spreading of civil and political liberties since the late nineteenth century. This chapter also aims to underline both the importance of intellectual leadership and the existence of a suitable institutional basis for the successful spreading of ideas. For almost half a century, two individuals exerted an indis-

putable intellectual hegemony within Chilean liberalism, facilitating by this
the relative ideological homogeneity one finds in the formulation of technocratic thought in the country. The ideas of emancipatory technocratism
spread through the influential sectors of the middle class via powerful organizations such as the Radical Party and the Freemasons.

As I mentioned in the previous chapter, my historical explorations led me to
the life and work of two great Chilean intellectuals—José Victorino Lastarria
and his main disciple, Valentín Letelier, whose influence has been crucial in
the gestation of the technocratic project that would subsequently be translated
into concrete policies during the government of Colonel Ibáñez. These men
insisted that the political class had to rule the country using scientific methods. Their starting point was the idea that scientific knowledge of the nature
and workings of society (based on Comtean and Spencerian readings) should
constitute the basis of the decision-making process at the nation's politico-
administrative level. The work of both authors reveals the positivist, middle-
class, democratic, liberal origins of technocratic thought in Chile, which will
help us to understand the subsequent evolution of technocracy in the twentieth century.

I suggest in this chapter that the generation of technocratic ideas in Chile
is closely related to local liberal thought and the struggle of liberals against
the conservative order established by Diego Portales in the 1830s, the oligarchy, and the religious hegemony of the Catholic Church during the nineteenth
century. In other words, it was related to an ideology that aimed at expanding
the citizens' individual and collective freedom, promoting the modernization
of the political and administrative structures, and putting an end to a political
and social regime they regarded as the continuation of a rigid order that was
colonial in origin.

The technocratic project fed particularly on the expectations and longings
of the nascent middle sectors emerging since the mid-nineteenth century. The
middle class developed subsequently under the wing of the booming nitrate
economy and would finally attain political power in the hectic decade of the
1920s. Despite being a social class in the initial phase of development, some
middle-class-born-and-bred individuals were to obtain a strong presence in
the political and intellectual debates of the second half of the nineteenth century. Such mesocratic principles as the valuing of merit, personal effort, and
study over ancestry would be instrumental in the generation of technocratic

proposals defending similar principles. The Radical Party, the Freemasons, and the university lecture rooms would be the channels to spread these mesocratic principles, which would be translated into concrete state policies beginning in the 1920s.

Comtean and Spencerian positivist thought, traditionally associated with the technocratism of Saint-Simon, turned out to be fundamental for Lastarria and Letelier in the articulation of their criticism of the prevailing system and in the formulation of alternative reformist proposals. However, as we shall see, it is evident that they used this philosophic stream in a way both critical and utilitarian in the pursuit of their own principles and agendas, which were consistent with the middle-class project generated since the 1840s. In other words, in my opinion, it was not positivism that led both thinkers to a pro-technocratic stance: positivism only contributed a more scientistic dressing to positions that had already long been espoused by local liberalism and radicalism.

The differences observed in Lastarria's and Letelier's approaches to a series of issues, such as the role of the state in the national economy and organization, the importance assigned to the principle of individual freedom, and so on, correspond to their personal reactions to the political and social changes of the latter half of the nineteenth century. However, both thinkers were of and from the middle class and promoted middle-class values and aspirations both politically and intellectually.

Lastarria and Liberal Positivism

In 1878 José Victorino Lastarria published his *Recuerdos Literarios*, in which he undertakes a historical review of the political and cultural history of Chile between the 1840s and the late 1870s. Possibly no other Chilean of his generation could have written this book in which the personal testimonies fully merge with the political and cultural history of the country. Lastarria was indeed a privileged actor in each of the major political and cultural events that took place between 1840 and 1880. Thus, man and work form an obligatory reference point from which to understand the intellectual evolution of Chile in the nineteenth century (J. Huneeus 1910). Lastarria's personal history is a clear example of a middle-class Chilean who through much difficulty, effort, and study managed to climb up to a respectable position in the social ladder.

Lastarria was born in 1817 in the city of Rancagua, when Chile was about to achieve the definitive consolidation of its independence from Spain.[1] The son of an impoverished middle-class small tradesman, at an early age Lastarria was sent to Santiago to get an education. In the words of Bernardo Suberca- seaux, "This boy from the provinces arrived in a stratified world, lacking all social support. In view of this adverse environment, study would be the only means to transcend his humble social origin" (1997, 1:37–39). The great Puerto Rican thinker, Eugenio María Hostos, said of Lastarria, "He is one of those self-made men who have most victoriously fought with all his might for his personal development and that of the social milieu in which he was formed."[2]

The difficulties Lastarria faced notwithstanding, it is only fair to point out that unlike other Latin American aristocracies the regime in Chile did make room for Lastarria and many others like him, who were to go far in the political and social spheres.[3] In fact, Lastarria was to become not only one of the most respected intellectuals of the second half of the nineteenth century, but also held outstanding positions as lecturer, member of Parliament, minis- ter of state, and ambassador of the Republic. As Frederick Nunn put it,

> Of reputable origin, but not wealthy by any means, he was proud of his accomplishments from his early years and rarely missed an opportunity to affirm them. "I have talent and I show it," he is reputed to have said, establishing him among the many of modest origins who have not been able to contain their pride at having made it to the higher rungs of society or intellectual circles. . . . Lastarria's origins proved no disadvan- tage at all in early nineteenth-century Chile, owing to the socio-political flexibility that prevailed in a polity and society in formation. Neverthe-

1. For a good account of his life, see Fuenzalida 1911.
2. Letter sent from New York in 1875, cited in Fuenzalida 1911, 1:5. His social origin was even used by his adversaries to scorn him. In 1849, for example, there was an article in the conservative newspaper *El Corsario,* in which Lastarria was referred to as "huacho, roto y pícaro" (a bastard, a pleb, and a rogue), and the author regretted that he had had access to such a good education.
3. As Aníbal Pinto points out, the Chilean oligarchy has characterized itself as having a "proverbial flexibility, with no closed registers; which instead of resorting to open warfare in general appears to give in, just like quicksand, in order to grab its enemies or cut them down to size, so as to at least reduce the losses that they want to inflict upon it" (1973a, 196).

less, he made no significant references to his family in any of his writings. It was as if he believed his life had begun only at the moment his intellectual ability manifested itself. (2000, xxv)

At the age of twelve, he began his studies at the Liceo de Chile, founded in 1829 by Spanish liberal José Joaquín Mora, author of the short-lived Liberal Constitution, which had been ratified the previous year. Lastarria became one of Mora's favorite disciples by demonstrating the ample intelligence and capacity for work that made him unique from the very beginning. Mora's influence was to be determinative in the formation of Lastarria's liberalism. However, this Spanish liberal soon came under harsh criticism from the conservative and clerical sectors, which hated the slant of his teaching methods and the contents of his lessons. After the victory of the conservatives over the liberals in the civil war of 1830–31, Mora was expelled from the country. When the Liceo de Chile closed down, Lastarria went on to study philosophy and law at the Instituto Nacional, where the Venezuelan scholar Andrés Bello was teaching. Although they developed a good mentor-pupil relationship, Lastarria eventually rebelled against his teacher, who had conservative ideas and was quite close to the sectors and social groups in power.

In order to pay for his studies, Lastarria began to do some teaching in 1836. In December he was awarded the degree of bachelor of law; in 1837 he graduated as a teacher of universal law and the following year as a teacher of geography at the Universidad de San Felipe. In 1839 he started teaching at the Instituto Nacional, where among his pupils were many figures who would later make names for themselves in the world of politics. That very same year he got his professional qualification as lawyer from the Universidad de San Felipe.

Now barely twenty-five, Lastarria was to become one of the architects of the so-called generation of '42, a literary and intellectual movement originating in 1842 that opposed the arrogance of the power represented by the Pelucones (the Chilean conservatives) and the church, and the institutions inherited from the colonial period (Jorrín and Martz 1970, 125). Another central figure of this movement was young Francisco Bilbao, a disciple of Lastarria's, whose anti-oligarchic writings and pamphlets conferred celebrity upon him among the liberal and radical young, but aroused the wrath of conservative and religious sectors. Bilbao was later persecuted by the powers that be for the remainder of his short life (Crawford 1971).[4] In addition, the presence in Chile of two great Argentine thinkers in exile, Domingo Faustino Sarmiento and Juan Bautista Alberdi, provided enormous stimulus to intellectual debate in those years (Gazmuri 1999, 29). An even more important event for the intellectual development of the country and for Lastarria's professional life was undoubtedly the inauguration of the University of Chile, with Andrés Bello as its first rector. Lastarria joined the cadre of teachers of this institution of higher education in 1846 and developed a fruitful teaching career. In the last decades of the nineteenth century, the University of Chile was to become an academic and intellectual crucible for liberal and positivist thought.

Circles Versus Parties

Lastarria, a liberal *pur sang*, never felt at ease in liberal political organizations or in any other. He blindly protected both his personal freedom and the freedom to criticize any aspect of Chilean politics that he considered to be wrong. In fact, he always expressed his dissatisfaction with the existing parties and their performance and dreamed of creating a "progressive" party cutting across the political spectrum, a dream he never realized. What Lastarria said in 1849 about his position vis-à-vis political parties and politics is, in my opinion, almost identical to the position adopted by many technocrats in the twentieth century:

> I have always regarded myself as a liberal, never a *pipiolo* or a representative of any political party. My role as opponent of the government and my reserved conduct toward its enemies have made me appear as a man suspect to parties. My independence, my attachment to my own convictions, and my disdain of proselytism could not be appreciated by men bent on fighting. However, I have always been content thus, and

4. In 1844, his controversial essay "La sociabilidad chilena" was published in the newspaper *El Crepúsculo*. In it Bilbao openly criticizes the Catholic Church and the Chilean aristocracy, denounces the large social inequality existing in the country, and demands increased freedom. Bilbao was tried on the charges of sedition, immorality, and blasphemy, and there was an order to destroy his essay. Soon Bilbao was forced to flee the country. This demonstration of the pride and power of the Chilean oligarchy and its merciless treatment of Bilbao would leave a mark on Lastarria and a whole generation of young Liberals and Radicals who persevered in their struggle against and criticism of the regime inspired by Portales. Bilbao literally died in the arms of Lastarria in 1865 in Buenos Aires, where the former was leading a life of self-exile and the latter was serving as Chile's ambassador to Argentina.

have never sacrificed my principles or my independent judgment to any party political interest. I opted as more convenient to devote myself to studying and to the education of the young; I have renounced politics and confined myself to schools.[5]

In fact, Lastarria shunned open political demonstrations and party caucuses and would rather lock himself in to write short stories and essays in political philosophy, which he discussed in small literary circles. It was precisely within these literary circles that Lastarria managed to inspire several generations of young liberals, instilling in them a love of history, Chilean and world literature, philosophy, and intellectual debate.

Thus, in 1859 he was one of the creators of the Circle of Friends of Belles Lettres, which held well-attended meetings at his house until 1864, at which there were literary contests and lectures of all kinds and discussion of the literary and scientific novelities newly arrived from Europe. In 1873, Lastarria created the Academy of Belles Lettres, which was better organized and had more links with political parties and national figures of renown (such as Benjamín Vicuña Mackenna, Diego Barros Arana, Miguel Luis Amunátegui, and so on). Valentín Letelier was one of the many young men who would enthusiastically attend the talks given by Lastarria and a large number of intellectuals.

Positivism and Freedom

As Allen Woll (1976, 496) pointed out, the foundation of this academy constitutes the turning point in the development of positivism in Chile. It is well worth looking into Lastarria's inaugural speech and the bylaws of this new intellectual initiative, which were imbued with positivist, scientific, and modernist principles. The first of its Articles of Association reads as follows: "The Academy of Belles Lettres seeks to cultivate the literary art as an expansion of philosophic truth, adopting as a rule of composition and criticism, in scientific works, its adherence to the facts demonstrated in a positive way by science, and in sociological works and works of serious literature, its adherence to the laws of the development of human nature . . . and to mold it to the social, scientific, and literary advancements of the age" (Lastarria [1878] 2000, 328–29). In his inaugural speech, Lastarria reasserted his support of positivist

5. *Revista de Santiago* 3:61 (1849); quoted in Fuenzalida 1911, 1:51–52.

principles, but made it clear from the outset that he did not espouse them in an acritical and submissive manner, but rather adapted them to his commitment to democracy and individual freedom, and even took the liberty of reformulating the Comtean "Order and Progress" motto:

> Our association . . . embraces as a rule of composition . . . its agreement with the facts proven in a positivist way by science, in conformity with the laws of the development of human nature, which are *Freedom* and *Progress*. . . . The study of letters and science . . . can definitely not have any other basis for investigating the truth than the independence of the spirit, and independence that constitutes one of the most valuable rights of man, one of the rights or freedoms that make up the essence and substance of democracy. (334)

In his *Recuerdos Literarios,* Lastarria reminisces that he had only become aware of the work of Auguste Comte and the existence of his *Course de philosophie positive* (1830–42) in 1868 through Émile Littré's book *Auguste Comte et la philosophie positive* (1864). Littré was to become one of the favorite writers of the followers of Comte in Latin America. According to Lastarria, his encounter with Comtean positivist thinking was quite a revelation. His surprise was due not so much to the novelty of the conception, but to the similarities of this doctrine with his own ideas, which he had been developing since 1842. In other words, Lastarria saw in Comte's work only a reaffirmation that his vision of history and politics had been the right one and that it ran abreast with the scientific and academic positions being articulated at the same time in Europe. As José Joaquín Brunner (1988a, 62) explained, Lastarria immediately accepted Comte's law of the three stages of societal development (the theological, the metaphysical, and the positive), which he applied to his permanent controversy with the conservative sectors to criticize the Portales-inspired state and the oligarchic regime in a more scientific-sounding tenor. When applied to the Chilean reality, the Catholic Church and all the legacy of the colonial era represented the theological stage, whereas idealism and materialism represented the metaphysical stage. Progressive liberals like Lastarria were the self-proclaimed promoters of the positivist or scientific state and sought the elimination of conservative laws and institutions originating in colonial times and the moral and cultural regeneration of the nation.

Although Comte's ideas corresponded to the European reality and were the response to the social and political dislocations of modernization and the growing industrial society, they were adapted to the national realities of not only Chile, but also Mexico and Brazil (see Zea [1965] 1976 and Hale 1996). There is, however, a fundamental difference between the Chilean case and that of the other two countries: in Brazil and Mexico positivism was used by the ruling elites to legitimize their power and their alleged ethnico-cultural superiority, but in Chile positivism became the doctrine of middle-class forces to criticize the status quo and attempt to force a major social renovation. In addition, in Chile positivism was to be embraced not only by the middle-class intellectual sectors but also by an emergent bourgeoisie from the provinces, particularly Copiapó. This province had been getting rich with the mining of silver and promoted progress and change and, in addition often funded scholarly programs and intellectual contests of all types.[6]

Therefore, Lastarria adopted positivism as a liberal philosophy but only accepted its ideas to the extent that they did not clash with his own liberal principles. It is only thus that we can understand why Lastarria rejected Comtean authoritarianism, which was reflected, among other things, in the open support that Comte gave to the installation of the *régime d'exception* of Napoleon III in 1851—which claimed to guarantee order and be a driving force of progress—or in Comte's praise of the tsar of Russia, whom he called "the only statesman in Christendom" (Zea [1965] 1976, 228; G. Vial 2001, 1:111). Lastarria clearly did not share Comte's concern for order, because the preservation of "order" was precisely the justification Portales and the conservative constitution of 1833 used to legitimize its campaign to restrict civic freedom, to expel the liberals from the public administration, and to endow Chilean presidents with quasi-dictatorial powers. It goes without saying that for Lastarria progress had to tread the path of freedom.

Even less support was to be expected from Lastarria and the Chilean liberals for the so-called religion of humanity proposed by Comte in his mature stage (Woll 1976, 495). Somebody like Lastarria, who, together with many other liberals, had fought all his life against the dogmas of the Catholic Church and its abuse of power, could not end up by accepting another reli-

---

6. Such was the case of Federico Varela, a mining entrepreneur from Copiapó, who subsidized not only many of Lastarria's publications and activities but also those of many other positivist liberals. In addition, for a long time the city of Copiapó was the seat of local positivism, the home of positivist discussion groups, and the source for many publications dealing with the work of Comte.

gion (Fuenzalida 1911, 2:52). Lastarria referred to Comte's religious proposal as follows: "Auguste Comte . . . after having studied human progress and understanding its laws with the whole truth, has failed in his attempt to formulate the new synthesis in an absurd religion and in a political system that revolts good sense, because its bases are belief and spiritual power."[7] These and other differences with Comtean thought would once again become manifest with the publication of his main politico-philosophical work, *Lecciones de política positiva* (1875), based on the series of talks and lessons delivered at the Academy of Belles Lettres.

Lessons on Positive Politics

Lecciones constitutes a true critical liberal and positivist manifesto. In it Lastarria formulates a series of ideas of technocratic nature that would later be once again taken up in the work of Valentín Letelier. As Charles A. Hale suggests (1996, 154), this book seeks no less than to establish a science of politics in Chile.

In this work, Lastarria identifies politics as "the science of the government of society" ([1875] 1891, 2) and points out that Latin America is undergoing a moment of transition in which the old oligarchic order has begun to crumble and there is a need for new government formulas. After expressing his disappointment with the resurgence of reaction in mid-nineteenth-century Europe, Lastarria turns his attention to the North American reality for a new source of inspiration. In *Lecciones* he analyzes the U.S. political system, paying special attention to the politico-institutional apparatus that makes democracy work at local level. Thus, he proposes the adoption in Chile of what he calls "semocracy" or self-government, in which individuals would have a valid voice before the local and national political authorities. As Subercaseaux (1997, 2:157) rightly points out, however, the problem with Lastarria's analysis is that it is too theoretical and has no further concrete information on how the system operates in real life. This is a characteristic of Lastarria's turn of mind: he was carried away by ideas, not the practical and actual experiences arising from them. Because of this, Woll's criticism of Lastarria and the rest of the Chilean positivists is quite valid when he points out that although they proclaimed the need to make all ideas and facts undergo scientific critical analysis,

---

7. J. V. Lastarria, *Miscelánea histórica y literaria*, vol. 2, 1868; quoted in Zea [1965] 1976, 227.

they seldom turned this analysis on their own work (1976, 1982). Even Alejandro Fuenzalida Grandon, his biographer and admirer, could not but voice his criticism because of this.

> Should there be any reservation about *Lecciones,* it would certainly be Lastarria's love for political ideology that made him induce as true what was but a noble mirage of his spirit; because in relation to Chile, could his observations be considered as the fruit of experimental study? Did we by any chance have a political science tradition to be able to deduce laws, formulate principles? Not at all. Lastarria used to build on air and so, when he found no solid ground on which to stand, he had to resort to foreign theory and bring it into the country. (1911, 2:49)

In *Lecciones* Lastarria also pays attention to two issues that will later resurface in the technocratic criticism of the administration of the state, namely, bureaucratization ("oficinicracia," as he called it) and administrative centralization. These issues, as we shall see in the next section, will return even more strongly in the work of his disciple, Valentín Letelier. Lastarria criticizes the adoption by the Chilean authorities of public policies that have made bureaucracy proliferate and have tended to strengthen the power and control of the state. As he says, "Herein has been born the poisons of administrative centralization and bureaucratic organization, that is, the discipline of the power of the influences of the government offices and agents to stifle the rights of man and society" ([1875] 1891, 18). He also rejects the practice of the ruling Chilean aristocracy to grant privileges and immunity to state officials and members of some public professions, as this inexorably leads to abuse of power (177).[8] It is these privileges that "turn civil servants into a class of irresponsible mandarins" (196). Lastarria makes an appeal to the Senate to ensure that such abuses do not occur and bureaucracy does not expand unrestrained. In addition, in his opinion the executive branch of government should only have the power to appoint the central government administration personnel, but not the local government officials (405), because according to him "the independence of the township is the basis of free government" (426). He refers to administrative decentralization as one of the needs of mod-

---

8. "In the public services of the state, the personal interest of the official, far from being a guarantee of his responsibility, is a danger of abuse" (Lastarria [1875] 1891, 277).

ern nations that should be accomplished as a merely political reform that does not call for the "social preparation" of the population, given that this is a reform that affects above all the high circles of power (443–44). According to him, this reform would be easier to carry out in Latin America than in Europe because in the new continent "vices are less resistant and less powerful than the interests that nurture them" (56).

In *Lecciones* Lastarria also fires some shots against the ruling aristocracy and the regime established by Portales that he had battled against all his life. He regrets that the ideals of social and political regeneration that inspired independence and subsequent period should have been stifled in Chile after the revolution of 1829–30. "In Chile," he said, "there still prevail in social life the theological and metaphysical ideas of the Middle Ages" (64). In his analysis of the aristocratic regime he acknowledges its strength and its capacity to exercise its hegemony over the population. The changes brought about by the conservative regime "have been so profound and enduring that they have been able to educate one generation and modify society in the counter-revolutionary sense. Here, moral progress has been thwarted; here neither the past has been corrected nor the future prepared: instead, the past has been rehabilitated, instilling it with new life, new vigor, under different forms, in a different mold" (67).

As a good liberal Lastarria also points to the need for the state to guarantee the autonomy of universities, so that scientists may be free from political pressures. Because they were civil servants, university professors were forced to submit to the political interests of those who do or do not guarantee continuity of employment and possible promotion. This generated a "climate hostile to the progress of sciences and letters that have a seal of originality and daring, and are able to escape routine or the order of convention. It is necessary to acknowledge the principle that the fundamental idea of sciences should be in a society independent from the power of the state and of any other spiritual power" (132). Saying so, Lastarria was also throwing some darts against the intervention of the Catholic Church in education, and its permanent rejection of academic freedom in the university lecture halls.

A Government of the Best?

However, what constitutes the most interesting and revealing aspect of *Lecciones,* from the viewpoint of the discussion on technocracy, is Lastarria's resolute rejection of Comte's views on who should rule at the positive stage. Comte left no doubt about his faith in the French aristocracy, from where the "government of the best" should emerge. Here we can see mesocratic, meritocratic, and democratic Lastarria openly rejecting what is a clearly elitist proposal. He accepts that in modern societies there are hierarchies founded on social and economic activities (183) but this does not change the principle that there should be equality of rights for all and that the government should also be of all. He reasserts his democratic spirit when he says:

> Government, according to the conditions and trends of modern society, is not of the best, or of the worst, or of nobody, but of everybody. . . . Some positivists aspire to seek in one class of society the best conditions of aptitude for the functions of government. This theory is dangerous because, without intending to, it gets to the problem of having to acknowledge a ruling class, out of the wish to find the government of the best. What they do not perceive is that in the government of all, mistaken ideas are corrected by freedom and not by the impediments and exclusions with which they intend to avoid them. (185)

In my opinion, these words should not be interpreted as representing an antitechnocratic attitude, but rather as a reflection of Lastarria's strong meritocratic, mesocratic, and anti-aristocratic inspiration, which rejected the idea of establishing a "mandarin class."[9] According to Lastarria, this would lead to a "government by castes, whose irremovable and irresponsible officials are prone, among other vices, to routine, sloth, irreflection, and apathy, which characterize to such a large extent all the cadres of life officials" (185–86). In other words, he feared that this attempt to attain a "government of the best" might become an inefficient bureaucracy advocating a greater degree of administrative centralization of the state. And it is precisely his antibureaucratic stance that makes him consistent with the technocratic discourse that we find in present-day Chile. From a mesocratic perspective, Lastarria challenged the values of the aristocracy with values that have been traditionally upheld by the middle class, such as "probity, doing one's duty, morality, patriotism, and a disinterested cooperation to social development" (184).

9. "Public opinion in modern society revolts against all aristocracy, a word which is nowadays a synonym for unjust and antisocial privilege. . . . The superiority of aristocracy is not a [matter of] personal merit but one of wealth and power" (176, 182).

Although Lastarria was a staunch advocate of equality before the law, his meritocratic spirit and his own condition of being a self-made man led him to accept without further questioning the existence of social inequalities attributable to "natural" factors. Thus, in his opinion:

> Inequalities are brought about by the fact that not everybody has an equally vigorous and illustrated intelligence, or an identical sensibility, and so on. In terms of action of these diverse qualities, men develop in an unequal way according to the peculiarity of their character, and using their rights respectively, that is, their freedom. This is a general fact in the mode of procedure of human forces, a law from which unequal conditions of wealth, talents, social position, derive: this inequality is invincible as it is natural. (174)

Yet this does not imply that Lastarria was in favor of a savage free trade system where only the rule of the strongest would prevail. As Leopoldo Zea has pointed out, Lastarria saw in industrial wealth a way toward a solution to the problem of the mental emancipation of the Latin American nations, but rejected the proposition that individual labor for one's own welfare would be sufficient for the attainment of a true liberal order or an authentic morality ([1965] 1976, 195). Thus, Lastarria asserted in his *Recuerdos,* "we had to reject the perverse doctrine that made material progress and the prevalence of wealth the sole elements of political order." There is a civic and moral obligation to help others and to educate the people. Lastarria, like Letelier in later years, did place a strong emphasis on the need to extend access to primary and secondary education to the masses in order to improve their level of knowledge and make them fit for modern society. As he knew perfectly well from his own experience, had it not been for the education that he had received, he would never have had the chance to develop all his intellectual aptitudes and to gain access into the cultural elite of the country.

As Hale rightly points out, in Lastarria as in other Chilean liberals there is a tension between his appeal to set limits to the authority of the state and the need for that very same state to launch a series of reforms to increase public freedom and improve public education (1996, 155). Personally, I have the impression that Lastarria's rejection of action by the state and his negative vision of the role of the state are directly related to his explicit struggle against the conservative forces in power. How could he trust in the action of a state that he considered unfair, repressive, and reactionary, controlled in his view by a mediocre oligarchy? Chile was obviously in need of a political science to be applied to the matters of state, but Lastarria doubted that the ruling elite would accept the regulation of political activity by means of scientific principles out of sheer fear of losing their privileges. Lastarria expresses some kind of resignation at the end of his book: "The nations that are most in need of political science are the ones that most disdain it, dominated as they are by oligarchic governments and parties, for which the positive thing about politics lies in personal interests and not in the emancipation of man and society. What is there to wonder if an enormous disdain should relegate such lucubration as this to oblivion, as it does not satisfy the needs of the moment? We know it only too well" ([1875] 1891, 452). He was correct. In Chile modernizing the structures of the state in a radical way did not begin until the early twentieth century. However, it would be mistaken to believe that Lastarria's permanent and life-long effort to realize his liberal and positivist ideology was in vain. As Gonzalo Vial states, "Positivism had truly colored the whole of our 'nonconfessional' thought by the end of the century and we can accurately say that none of the followers of such thought escaped being influenced by Comte to some degree" (2001, 1:111). What is more, positivism, the same as liberalism, was in fact gradually integrated into the public and social policies of the "fusion" governments of Chile (liberal and conservative) beginning in 1861 (Jorrín and Martz 1970; S. Collier and Sater 1996; S. Collier 2003). This reality led Zea to conclude that positivism mixed with Chilean intellectual life during the second half of the nineteenth century ([1965] 1976, 234).

After Lastarria's death in 1888, his favorite disciple, Valentín Letelier, was to become the undisputed spokesman of Chilean liberal positivism and the leader of a second generation of positivists, who would carry on with Lastarria's fight against the oligarchic state.

Letelier and State Reformism "from Above"

After the death of Lastarria, the master, positivist thought was already deeply rooted in the country's political and intellectual scene. Many of his disciples held important positions at the university, in the *liceos* and institutes of higher education, and in the government and Parliament. In the 1890s Chilean society was also experiencing remarkable political and social changes. After the civil war of 1891, which led to the fall of the government of José Manuel Balmaceda and the installation of a parliamentary system, Chilean politics sailed into manifestly more troubled waters. The constant and growing tensions between government and Parliament, which characterized the period from 1890 to 1920, visibly weakened the legitimacy of the national political institutions. What is more, the annexation of vast territories that had belonged to Peru and to Bolivia after the War of the Pacific (1879–83) had brought a strong increase in fiscal revenue and the consequent growth of the state bureaucracy and the middle class in general (Góngora [1981] 1988, 64). As Subercaseaux points out, by the end of the nineteenth century the middle class had already become an important social actor that even at that time aspired to exercise power by itself, on behalf of and for the benefit of the whole of society (1997, 2:66).

However, not all classes benefited equally from the new prosperity, and the social sectors that had been passed over began to protest and demand improvements in their living conditions. At the turn of the century most Chileans felt that the country was stagnating and that there was a need for a strong political social and institutional renewal (see Venegas 1910 and Encina [1911] 1981). In this climate of growing social unrest, those who upheld positivist and rationalist worldviews became more radical in their positions and adopted a more active and militant attitude in the national political battle. Consequently, the Radical Party became the chief political organization formulating criticisms of the current system and proposals for profound transformations in the spheres of labor laws, education, and the public administration of the state.

Like Lastarria, who played a central role in most of the political and social debate of the 1850–80, his disciple Letelier was to be an undeniable key figure in the political and cultural evolution of the country in the period that followed, until his death in 1919. Their lives ran along similar courses on many occasions, and their political and philosophical positions also showed some points of convergence. However, as we shall see, partly as a result of the new political conditions, partly because of his pragmatic temperament and orientation, Letelier was a man who combined intellectual reflection and political action in a successful way. He put much more energy into, and was to be more effective than his mentor in, his attempts to transform the structures of the state and to facilitate social transformations in the country.

When we look at their social backgrounds, their childhoods, and subsequent patterns of education and intellectual development, we cannot but conclude that both thinkers had quite similar personal trajectories. Letelier was born in 1852 in the provincial city of Linares, the child of an impoverished middle-class family.[10] After the death of his father, his mother was unable to bring up her children unaided, and thus, several relatives shared looking after them. Young Valentín was placed in the care of a close relative, who owned a school in the city of Talca, and who took over his primary education. After this, Valentín Letelier was sent to other relatives in Santiago, to proceed with his studies at the Instituto Nacional, whose headmaster at the time was the great historian Diego Barros Arana. Like Lastarria, Letelier very soon began to do some teaching in order to pay for his studies and earn a living. He studied law at the University of Chile, where he came into contact with Lastarria and positivism, and where he would become a regular participant in the talks and discussions held at the Academy of Belles Lettres. At the same time, Letelier also attended regularly the circle of positivist young men chaired by Jorge Lagarrigue, where the works of Comte and Littré were analyzed. The subject of his licentiate's thesis in law and political science was administrative decentralization. In this early work it is already possible to find his main criticism of the operation of public administration—a topic to which he would devote much of his energy in the course of his academic work.

In 1875, once he had his diploma, he set out for the northern city of Copiapó, the cradle and nerve center of Chilean radicalism. It was in this city that he was appointed a professor of literature and history, and continued to spread the positivist word through his classes and publications in local newspapers. He also became an active member of the Radical Party and of the local Masonic lodge. During his stay in Copiapó, he studied the European positivist authors in greater depth and produced translations into Spanish of his much admired Littré, among others. In 1878 he returned to Santiago and took active part in the Club del Progreso, which had replaced the Academy of Belles Lettres, in which he gave some talks and readings.

The Social Question and the State

Even at that time the philosophical and political differences between Lastarria and his disciple, which in later years were to become more evident and pro-

---

10. The source of these and other personal data is Luis Galdames's *Valentín Letelier y su obra* (1937).

nounced, were noticeable. Unlike Lastarria, for whom the defense of individual freedom had practically become his leitmotiv, Letelier showed himself to be more interested in catering to the social needs of the masses, seeking social justice and the progress of humankind within a climate of order. In an article that he wrote in 1881 we can read, "Preserving order without hindering progress, favoring progress without upsetting order: such are the two fundamental topics of all positively scientific policy.—The preservation of order at the expense of progress generates despotism and restricts the free development of human faculties. The stimulus of progress without paying attention to order engenders revolution and disturbs the harmony of the social elements" (quoted in Galdames 1937, 68). It was only after Lastarria died that Letelier began to criticize his teacher's doctrinaire liberalism explicitly. Thus, in his book *La lucha por la cultura* (1895) he termed as "antiscientific" the idea that personal freedom and freedom of thought should constitute inherent and inalienable rights in human nature (a view, in fact, upheld by Lastarria). For Letelier, out-and-out liberalism that neglects the social needs of masses can only lead to the breakdown of institutional order and end up in anarchy or communism. But on the other hand, Letelier also claimed that "scientifically, freedom is just as indispensable for the development of human faculties as is authority to satisfy social needs" (1895, 4). It is not that Letelier abandoned the principles of freedom and democracy of his teacher, but he was simply aware that liberty alone was not enough to ensure social order and the progress of humankind. Also, he feared disorder and anarchy precisely because he saw in these social blights a direct and serious threat to personal freedom.

Moreover, Letelier did not share Lastarria's pessimism about the role of the state in the social development of the country. For Lastarria, the state constituted a threat to individual freedom almost as great as the Catholic Church and the aristocratic sectors. On the contrary, for Letelier the state might become an ally in modernizing efforts and was the only political entity that might manage to reduce the permanent interference of the Catholic Church in the social and cultural life of the country. Therefore, the state should be ready to fall back on its authority to impose the political and social reforms that the country needed. In *La lucha por la cultura*, Letelier expressed this idea in no uncertain terms:

> Let us not hesitate to adopt an authoritarian policy out of the idle fear that we may be considered authoritarian. Whenever we deem it to be

indispensable, let us compulsorily impose education, vaccination, saving, insurance; let us ban the employment of children who have not finished their schooling; let us fix working hours and working days; let us regulate prostitution, drunkenness, examinations. Let us have the authority of the state always prevail over the authority of the church; and let us not care that we are called authoritarian if through such means we can increase man's capabilities, make him more in command of himself and endowed with more vigor and originality. . . . Let us be men of science and as such, let us always bear in mind that the end of politics is not freedom, nor is it authority or any principle abstract in nature, but to satisfy the social needs of man and the development of society. (Quoted in Subercaseaux 1997, 1:214)

Letelier wrote these words in 1886. In them he demonstrates a strong conviction that the state must intervene more forcefully in the execution of social reforms. His political and philosophical ideas about the role of the state in the search for progress and social stability were to consolidate to a visible extent during his stay in Germany in 1881–85. During these years he worked as a secretary to the newly created Chilean Delegation in Berlin, and this gave him the chance to be a direct observer of the political, social, and cultural reality of Prussia at the time of Bismarck.

Among other things, Letelier studied what went on behind the scenes of the so-called *Kulturkampf,* into which Bismarck had resolutely engaged to reduce the influence of the Catholic Church in Germany. At the same time, he kept an attentive eye on the politico-religious struggle taking place in neighboring France. His stay in Berlin increased his admiration for Bismarck and his social pacification policy by means of resolute labor and social reforms aimed at the express objective of putting a brake on the rise of the revolutionary socialist movement (G. Vial 2001, 1:84). The German experience also convinced him that the threat of revolutionary socialism might soon come to Chile. In his opinion, this danger "from below" for the attainment of progress and social order would be just as serious if not more so than the imbalances provoked by the conservative forces and the aristocracy in general. In Germany, Letelier learned how effective action by the state could dismantle the destabilizing elements generated both within the elites and the masses. All this was to convince him that the so-called state or chair socialism constituted a political option for Chile to deal with the growing social unrest in the country. As Julio Sepúlveda Rondanelli rightly observed, "Letelier favored a socialism that was neither Marxist nor revolutionary, but rather à la Bismarck" (1993, 77).

The "Estado Docente"

One of the explicit tasks that the Chilean government commissioned Letelier to do in Berlin was study the Prussian educational system, which was considered to be one of the most advanced and effective in Europe. Letelier enthusiastically addressed himself to this task, since he was particularly interested in education and had been for quite a few years. He considered education to be one of the main tools to achieve the social and moral regeneration of Chile. According to Luis Galdames, in Copiapó in the late 1870s Letelier was already carefully studying the Spanish translation of Herbert Spencer's *Education: Intellectual, Moral, and Physical* (1861). He was especially impressed by Spencer's views on the importance of the natural sciences and history in education in general, his views on the culture of nations, and his critique of the classical approach to teaching history (1937, 56). In a series of reports, Letelier analyzed German preschool, primary, secondary, and university education and made several suggestions for incorporating German ideas and experiences into the Chilean educational system, some of which were actually accepted and implemented. Letelier was of the opinion that the general intellectual level of the country could only be raised if the teaching of scientific knowledge began in primary school. Letelier was confident that the expansion of education in Chile would generate a vast upward social mobility, based on individual merit and effort (Barr-Melej 2001, 148).

Letelier returned to Chile in 1885 and immediately began implementing his educational reforms. He started from the premise that the establishment of a modern, science-based educational system would contribute to a greater unity of purpose in the whole nation. As he put it, "In the midst of the moral disturbance of contemporary societies, in which everything divides us, religion, politics, art, we could see just one single thing that unites us: science" (Letelier 1886, 183). Brunner points out that Letelier was convinced that only a public educational system based on a positive and liberal philosophy could ensure the intellectual development of the nation in spite of the existing political turbulence (1988a, 72–73). For Letelier education should play an essential role in national politics. In 1888, he wrote: "Every good system of politics is a true system of education, just like every general system of education is a true political system" (quoted in G. Vial 2001, 1:119).

In his vision, the Chilean state had to become an "estado docente" or "teaching state," which would have the obligation to offer a secular and scientific education to be supervised by the university, which would in turn become an "universidad docente." In this new role, the university would not only watch over higher education but also contribute with analytical and scientific tools to the improvement of primary and secondary education. As a matter of fact, in the reforms carried out in the late 1880s, the university would come to play the role of superintendency of the country's education.

Obviously, not everybody shared Letelier's enthusiasm for radical reform. His plans met with harsh resistance from the conservative and religious sectors, which saw in them an attempt to impose a "lay" ideology as the national model. Thus, from the late 1880s until the early twentieth century, Chile was to undergo a sort of *Kulturkampf* of its own between radicals and liberals on one side and conservatives on the other, brought about by the educational reforms.

The next issue was how to set up a modern, science-based educational system if most school teachers lack the necessary technical and professional training to meet a challenge of such magnitude? In order to tackle this essential problem, Letelier set about establishing a teacher-training institution that highlighted modern pedagogical methods and instilled a scientific mentality in teachers-to-be. With the support of President Balmaceda, the Instituto Pedagógico was created by decree in 1889. Letelier hired a group of German educators to run the newly created educational center. The presence of these German pedagogues in Chile and their use of revolutionary teaching methods for mathematics and the physical and natural sciences were to stamp a scientific seal on this new form of training teaching cadres. The first graduates from the Instituto Pedagógico included Enrique Molina, Alejandro Venegas, the brothers Pinochet le-Brun, and many others who would later play a leading role in public and university educational policies and in the intellectual world of the first decades of the twentieth century.

For Letelier, the so-called teaching cadres were meant to lead the great modernization of Chile. Thus, both in his *La lucha por la cultura* (1895) and in his magnum opus *La filosofía de la Educación* (1892) he refers to teachers as the moral foundation for the regeneration of the country and the education of national political elites. It should be borne in mind that a large number of teachers were middle class in origin and that a not insignificant number of them sympathized with the Radical Party or were members of a Masonic lodge. In other words, this project for change was clearly conceived from a mesocratic perspective that benefited middle-class sectors and made them become important actors in the ongoing process of transformation. What can be seen is that little by little the idea that those in a position of authority should have a good education with some kind of scientific slant spread and became generally accepted. These innovations represent the initial stages in the development of a distinctly technocratic ideology, which was to become even more visible in the first decades of the twentieth century. Gonzalo Vial sums up this phenomenon as follows:

> In short, the *imago mundi* proposed to Chile by scientists was that pro-
> vided by contemporary science. . . . The unifying road that was being
> offered was the dissemination of such *imago mundi* through education.
> The goal aimed at was government handed over to a new class, which
> would be the repository of scientific knowledge, created and inspired by
> the "teaching cadres," whose "spiritual power" would float over the
> whole of society and would replace the power of the church. (2001,
> 1:121)

Letelier, however, knew perfectly well that the idea of the Estado Docente would not be consolidated by just raising the level of primary- and secondary-school teacher training and by improving the quality of public education in general. In his long "struggle for culture" there was still one much more difficult battle to fight: the implementation of a deep reform within the University of Chile. Letelier saw as urgent the task of reinforcing even more so the objective of the scientific training of university students, thus going far beyond what was the rule in that university until the late nineteenth century. Up to that time, the majority of university studies provided a very limited professional training in academic terms: indeed, the curriculum was oriented almost exclusively to the acquisition of practical skills to be applied in the graduates' profession. Fully aware that the university was the cradle of the political and administrative elites of the country, Letelier saw the moderniza-tion of the teaching programs of the university as a *conditio sine qua non* to improve and increase the technical capabilities of the elite in charge of the state. In this manner, as Nicola Miller concludes, "The university was expected both to create a modern scientific and academic tradition in Chile and to oversee the creation of the professionals it was believed Chile needed in order to modernize" (1999, 77).

Teaching the Administrative Elite

Letelier focused his criticism of the university curriculum on the Faculty of Law and Political Science. This choice of target responded not only to his own profession as a jurist, but also to the fact that this faculty educated the vast majority of the political and administrative elite of the country; a significant number of the then top civil servants, ministers, diplomats, and members of Parliament had read law. In 1887 he published in the press an extensive syllabus addressed to the renovation of the study of legal sciences in the country. In this document, he made a devastating diagnosis of the quality of legal training in Chile. Besides clarifying that "Political Science" was just part of the name of the faculty and definitely not part of the curriculum, he declared that the faculty, "founded to provide special instruction in the law, in fact did not supply the proper grounding for any professional career; and although it was meant to form citizens and statesmen—because the relevant disciplines coexisted—it was impossible to acquire there the most indispensable knowledge for the performance of public functions" (quoted in Galdames 1937, 124–25). Letelier suggested that an education in law should start with sociology and should also incorporate other social science subjects to expand the analytic capacity of the future lawyers. In the words of Galdames, "It was indispensable to aim at the creation of a new class of leaders to free society from the exclusive tutelage of lawyers, whose diffuse banality and narrow-mindedness in the face of any issue, had already shown their ineptitude to perform such functions. . . . It would therefore be necessary to organize special courses of politics and public administration . . . with the manifest plan of preparing the ruling elite" (1937, 127). What Letelier ultimately sought was the creation of an enlightened and scientifically disciplined bureaucracy, which after receiving an education at the Faculty of Law and Political Science, could devote their lives to public service. For these reforms to have a practical effect on the quality of the national bureaucracy, Letelier explained that it would be necessary to change the criteria for civil service appointments and listed the requirements that would make it possible to assume that applicants had the necessary knowledge. Only the setting up of a rigorous process of selection would guarantee the presence of the best in the public apparatus and do away with the old and harmful culture of distributing public posts among relatives and political cronies. Already in his reports from Berlin Letelier had made it clear that there was a great difference between Germany and Chile: in Germany, what prevailed was how well prepared a person was, whereas in Chile it was favoritism. Finally, Letelier proposed the creation of a Chair of Administrative Law to safeguard the scientific level of the education that the ruling class would receive.

In the concluding statement of his proposal for changes in the law curriculum, Letelier makes a strong appeal for change:

> It is already unbearable that in the current state of our culture ignorance should continue to assault the public administration jobs and get trained at the expense of the state and society. With as much reason as a tradesman demands applicants to the position of accountant to know their book-keeping, the state should demand from those aspiring to politico-administrative positions to prove that they have knowledge of the sciences of administration and government. (Quoted in Galdames 1937, 127–28)

However, most of the reforms proposed by Letelier failed to obtain the necessary support from within the Faculty of Law or among the political class. What did get created was the Chair of Administrative Law, whose first holder in January 1988 was no other than Letelier himself. From that moment on, Letelier made the most of his position to teach the subject according to his positivist principles, giving it a clearly sociological imprint. In his students, he sought to instill the idea that government and public administration are not the same thing and that although public administration departments were responsible to the government, civil servants were not subordinated to any political end. In a nutshell, public administration should serve society and the state, not a particular government or political regime (Galdames 1937, 145). With this, Letelier highlighted the need to guarantee the continuity of incumbents so that any change in government should not produce a disruption in public administration. As years came and went, Letelier's position within the faculty was to become stronger. This gave him the necessary influence to attempt once again to undertake the change in syllabus contents, but this time from within the university and in a more conciliatory spirit. The struggle was long and difficult because of the natural resistance to change and because of ideological opposition to the content of his reforms. These were ultimately agreed on at the turn of the century, in 1901. Letelier was about to reach the apex of his prestige as an academic and educational reformer with his appointment as rector of the University of Chile, a post he was to hold between 1906 and 1911. During his term as head of the University, he strove even further in his efforts to modernize university education and to generate scientific awareness in the students. By this time, it was evident that the liberal and secular sectors had won the *Kulturkampf* and that the idea of introducing into the curriculum a political science for the administration of the state was already widely considered a legitimate aspiration of good government.

On Political Science in Chile

The year 1886 saw the publication of Letelier's *De la ciencia política en Chile*. In it he expands and clarifies his ideas about establishing a science of politics in the country in order to create a government based on scientific principles. He initially argues that in Chile there is no political science, as proved by the fact that the different parties are reciprocally obstructive and carve up society, weakening it and making it impossible to embark upon radical reforms and great political undertakings (17). In his opinion, wherever strong political discrepancies materialize there is no science, as the latter always ends up by doing away with discrepancies. Thus, Letelier showed his blind faith in science as the way to resolve conflicts: "Politics has never been able to put an end to discrepancies. Whereas scientific discussions sooner or later have always ended up by generating an agreement among those involved, political discussions have never achieved anything but make animosity more intense, hinder concord further, and perpetuate division that was about to be healed" (16). The absence of political science was mainly due to the fact that it can only be constituted on the basis of the philosophy of history. This latter discipline, according to him, was not yet sufficiently developed in Chile (28). Since he felt obliged to refer to the views of his teacher Lastarria on the same issue,[11] Letelier pointed out that they would be unsuitable for the current reality of the country, particularly because toward the end of his life, Lastarria put forth

11. As expressed by Lastarria in his *De la ciencia política en Chile* (1876).

a project for a liberal political constitution that few would consider to be feasible.

In this work Letelier devotes many pages to what in his opinion should be the training of statesmen, giving free rein to his ideas on how to create a scientific mentality and a scientific approach to governing among the members of the Chilean political class. To eliminate politicking, it would first be necessary to exclude partisan politics from university lecture rooms.[12]

According to Letelier, the duty of any statesman is to carry out a rational analysis of the general factors that cause a problem and their interaction, avoiding the adoption of biased and reductionistic approaches that hinder the good understanding of matters of state (1886, 77). Full of the rational spirit that characterized him, Letelier gave this advice:

> The true statesman should find out the hidden filiation of events in order to discover the social causes that generate them and, without fear, be able to adopt radical measures that are no mere attempts, but the systematic application of the general knowledge of sociology to the government of states. The ruler who seeks inspiration in science knows, in fact, that positive politics is that which would rather prevent social ills than repress them or which, stated in other terms, seeks to change the social conditions that cause them rather than the will that executes them. (85)

In other words, if politics became an actual science, statesmen would have to be able to foresee the genesis of social conflicts and formulate the right policies to eliminate the social ills that generate them, and thus ensure social order. According to him, this was the great lesson of Bismarck in Germany, where social-democratic legislation was being adopted to prevent future problems (86).

In Letelier's view, the constant failure of noble and well-meaning citizens in Chilean politics was due mainly to their lack of scientific preparation to engage in the "art of government," since in order to rule the country in a proper way it is not enough to be inspired by patriotism or by a sound and fair idea (90). The problem, then is how to disseminate such scientific princi-

---

12. As he says, "We prefer it a thousand times that state-sector professors were not to turn into political tribunes, or the quiet lecture rooms into troubled meetings, or our children into passionate political zealots" (Letelier 1886, 35).

ples among the representatives of the political class. His solution was to teach these principles in university classrooms. Thus, the scientific knowledge of politics acquired at the university could later be passed on to the rest of the population by means of the press, books, conferences, and so on. But there was still a long way to go before reaching this ideal situation. According to Letelier, "Our political education is so ineffectual that there is no single graduate from our university with the necessary knowledge to solve the simplest governmental problems" (93–94).

From a distinctly technocratic perspective, Letelier launched a strong criticism of the inability of political parties to solve in a satisfactory way the serious problem of contemporary politics. It was precisely the failure of the established political parties to solve the problems of the people that had given rise to revolutionary alternatives, which, despite their claims, had no solutions either. He had such a deep mistrust of the masses that he rejected any program that included what he called the "dogmas" of equality and popular sovereignty, which he considered nothing more than attempts to use the masses to influence the decisions of the government and of the political parties in general. "The main cause of our political corruption is undoubtedly that our institutions, moved by a healthy yet premature idealism, have conferred by right upon the popular mass a political weighting for the exercise of which they were not and are not ready. . . . And by giving the vote to an uncultured crowd, without any notions of moral or right, we have placed the Republic in the hands of vile people, ready to sell it for a bowl of lentils" (108). Thus Letelier made a veiled criticism of Lastarria, who had assigned so much value to "preconceived" principles such as liberty, sovereignty of the people, and so on. In his opinion, these principles alone could not solve the political problems or meet the social needs of the nation. In his view, if implemented, the "dogma of absolute freedom" of the liberal school would overturn any attempt to influence individuals and society in general to generate the moral feelings of order and discipline and undermine existing political institutions. Therefore, "so as not to violate liberty, the liberal school does not prevent any of the social ills, hinders all measures to end them in a radical way and does nothing about the problems that contemporary times present to the mind of the statesman" (126). So, without mincing words, Letelier proposes as a solution the adoption of what he calls a "state authoritarianism," which in his view has to be a responsible government that will guide the political development of the country. There would be no alternative to this formula of a state determined to act with authority in the effective search for solutions to social questions. According to Letelier, the country was the breeding ground of a social volcano, which could blow up at any moment, seriously jeopardizing the social order and sociability in the country. But, as Zea rightly observes, this does not imply that Letelier is in favor of despotism. What he wants is a responsible liberalism, the limits of which are set by the responsibility of the individuals that make up society; he wants order, but responsible order, and freedom, but responsible freedom ([1965] 1976, 272–73). Góngora was to term this particular type of authoritarianism favored by Letelier "moderate authoritarianism" ([1981] 1988, 107).

According to Letelier the science of the state cannot be wed to a given ideology, since no ideology could be a true science of government. "The science of government cannot be conservative, liberal, or radical in the ordinary sense of these words. Regardless of its various applications, every science is one, everywhere in the world. Therefore, political science is not well served by denominations that correspond to local parties, whose mission is the pursuit of occasional ends" (127). On this note, the work concludes with an appeal to keep partisan-political ideologies apart from the formulation of universal principles based on scientific rationality, which should rule the running of the government and the state.

The Instrumental Party

It is undoubtedly difficult to understand that such antiparty positions should be voiced by one of the top leaders of a political party, the Radical Party, under whose platform he served two terms in Parliament. It is equally difficult to understand the ample support given to Letelier's opposition to political parties and his call for the depoliticization of the civil service. In order to do so, it is necessary to refer to the long struggle of radical sectors against the oligarchic state since the troubled 1840s. The founding roots of the Radical Party boast such figures as Francisco Bilbao, Santiago Arcos, Eusebio Lillo, and other radical liberals who in 1850 founded the Sociedad de la Igualdad, strongly influenced by the radical principles of the 1848 revolution in France, to which Bilbao was an eyewitness. With a rationalist, secular, and humanist seal, the Sociedad attracted the intellectual youth of those years under the motto "the sovereignty of reason as the authority of authorities, the sovereignty of the people as the basis of all politics, and universal love and fraternity as the moral foundation" (Sepúlveda Rondanelli 1993, 20).

The Radical Party as such was created in 1863 in the city of Copiapó, in the north of Chile, where the Radical Assembly was founded. The party leaders were prominent mining entrepreneurs such as Pedro León Gallo and Manuel Antonio Matta, who were strongly anticlerical and dreamed of the democratization and modernization of Chile and its political institutions. From the outset, Radicalism attracted the support of middle-class sectors such as teachers, artisans, civil servants, and so on, who saw in its tenets a way to social emancipation. Also from the very beginning, the Radical Party found itself strongly linked to the Masonic lodges, which, from the 1850s on, underwent a solid expansion all over the national territory. Thus we can observe that during the second half of the nineteenth century the large majority of the leading groups of the Radical Party were also active Masons. Freemasonry was to become an instrument of professional promotion for political and bureaucratic careers. By 1880, the Freemasons already had a strong presence in the academic bodies of the University of Chile and the Instituto Pedagógico. As Cristián Gazmuri has pointed out, at the end of the nineteenth century these institutions trained an important generation of teachers with a Masonic orientation who "imbued of a republican and rationalistic culture would become the backbone that would educate the generation that governed 'Mesocratic Chile' from 1925 until the decade of the 1950s" (1999, 171). Thus, both the Radical Party and the Freemasons adopted the secular liberal thought upheld by Lastarria and Letelier and other mesocratic leaders, translated it into a political platform for change, and played a crucial role in the reforms that began in the 1920s.

The Radicals adopted Comtean positivism from the start and were steeped in the rationalist discourse spread by figures like Lastarria and Letelier, who were considered by the members of the Radical Party as true icons of the national enlightenment. A political organization that looked to science as the ruling principle for its activities could not but value its scientists and academics of the stature and convictions of Lastarria and Letelier. In particular, Letelier's demands for thoroughgoing reforms in education and in the administration of the state are fully taken into account in the different documents and resolutions adopted by this party from the 1880s on. This was the case at the important Radical Convention of 1888, in which Letelier was one of the main speakers and had an outstanding participation in the debates.

Among others, the final conclusion was that "as science was the basis of independence of spirit, the education to be provided by the state should be essentially scientific and have a moral and social aim." On this occasion, the Radical Party presented its first political manifesto, which, among other points, demanded "the reduction in number of civil servants to the strictly necessary for the services of the administration and the application of rigorous competence tests for the appointment of candidates to positions in the civil service; and the setting up of a system of promotions in each of the administration branches" (Sepúlveda Rondanelli 1993, 62–65).

Letelier's influence within the Radical Party and indirectly on the course the Chilean political process would follow in years to come was to become fully manifest during the Great Radical Convention of 1906. It was in fact at this congress that there was a definition of the ideological course to be followed by the party in future decades. It was also at this congress that there was a final confrontation between two positions that had up to that time coexisted within the party. One of these was the liberal position supported by Enrique Mac-Iver, a respected member of Parliament and one of the party leaders, who advocated a free-trade liberalism in which the state should restrict itself to its basic functions. The main issue that he wanted to incorporate into the Radical agenda was the fight against administrative corruption and the expansion of education to make it possible for the social sectors bypassed by development to rise by their own efforts. Letelier appealed to Radicals to concentrate on solving the social problems of the masses, which in his opinion, called for a decisive and active action by the state. Mac-Iver pointed out that the alternative offered by Letelier would lead to an authoritarian socialism that was inconsistent with the libertarian tradition of the party. Although Letelier's position won the day within the convention, several of the points defended by Mac-Iver were incorporated into the final statement, in an effort to preserve the internal unity of the party (Galdames 1937, 378–81).

Among Letelier's supporters at the convention was a group of young Radicals, most of them lawyers, who had studied under him and shared his ideas about installing a sort of state socialism that would by means of advanced social legislation solve the problems of the masses, thus preventing their radicalization and alienation from the prevailing social system. Among his main supporters were some of his disciples, such as Armando Quezada Acharán, Enrique Oyarzún, and Fidel Muñoz Rodríguez, who would later play an important role in the Radical Party, Freemasonry, and the administrations of Arturo Alessandri and of Colonel Carlos Ibáñez.[13]

Thus, Letelier's position eventually became the core doctrine of the Radical Party. The Radical Party, which represented the interests and aspirations of the emerging middle class, was to play a leading role in Chilean politics during the first four decades of the twentieth century. The ascent of Radicals to government positions from the early 1920s on was to become a direct stimulus to the efforts for the technification of the state, which would materialize for the first time under the government of Carlos Ibáñez in 1927–31.

13. Armando Quezada Acharán was later to be deputy, senator, and ambassador and would hold different ministry portfolios. He was appointed rector of the University of Chile during the administration of Colonel Ibáñez. In 1930 he became Grand Master of the Chilean Freemasons. As for Enrique Oyarzún, he later became a deputy, senator, minister, and president of the Radical Party. Fidel Muñoz Rodríguez later became a deputy, ambassador, minister of state, and Grand Master of the Chilean Freemasons in 1935. All three of them at different periods headed the Ministry of Finance, where a large number of technocratically oriented economists and engineers concentrated. The name of Luis Galdames should be added to this roster of Letelier's followers. Galdames studied at the Instituto Pedagógico and later under Letelier. He was an active educational reformer both in Chile and in other Latin American countries. In his capacity as director of secondary education, Galdames carried out important educational reforms during Ibáñez's government (Castillo et al. 1999).

2

Pablo Ramírez and the "Administrative State"

After a long period of germination the intellectual and political legacy of Lastarria and Letelier found concrete expression in the turbulent 1920s when
middle-class sectors came into power and launched profound reforms of the
country's political and administrative structures. This chapter focuses on the
generation of a technocratic project during the government led by Colonel
Carlos Ibáñez. This particular case provides crucial insights into the role public opinion and society at large play in facilitating the emergence of technocratic regimes. This important aspect of the country's political mood has been
generally neglected in current discussions on technocracy. As this chapter
reveals, technocratic regimes can arise in situations of extreme political instability in which the prestige of politicians and political parties rapidly evapo-
rates and the people's demands for radical changes become generalized. Right
or wrong, many see young technocrats in the government as an assurance
of generational renovation and a sign that state affairs are being properly
administered. In this context, the people's support for replacing the traditional political class by technocrats can be seen as a form of public punish-
ment of the former.

The Ibáñez years also illustrate the readiness shown by middle-class sectors
to abandon their commitment to democratic formulas and to support authoritarian alternatives when motivated by fears of chaos and anarchism "from
below." After decades of having struggled against the oligarchic order and in

favor of the expansion of democratic rights, middle-class sectors and their representatives (particularly the Radical Party) embraced Ibáñez's authoritarianism out of fear of social upheaval. As we will see later in this book, *mutatis mutandis,* a comparable scenario emerged in the country in the early 1970s, with similar outcomes.

Leadership seems to be of crucial importance in formulating a technocratic project and in attracting and recruiting the required personnel to deploy it. A single person became fundamental for shaping Ibáñez's technocratic project. The charismatic Pablo Ramírez succeeded in assembling a formidable group of young technocrats with himself at the head who enthusiastically implemented a series of reforms that in a few years totally transformed the Chilean state. Later in the twentieth century we find figures such as Sergio de Castro and Alejandro Foxley fulfilling similar pivotal roles in providing inspiration and leadership to a group of technocrats in charge of the economic policies.

This chapter aims also to stress the importance of the existence of a common professional identity in the technocratic groups in charge of state policies. Most of Ramírez's technocrats were *ingenieros* with a strong generational bond and professional identity. In possession of an admirable "esprit de corps" they experienced the possibility of running several state institutions as a noble "mission" and as a historical chance to modernize the nation in a profound way. As will be shown later in the book, a similar professional cohesion and mystique can be found in the group of Chicago economists who administrated the reforms during the Pinochet regime and among the CIEPLAN economists who have been playing a decisive role under the current Concertación administrations.

Finally, this chapter illustrates how the state is envisioned by the middle class as the main instrument to satisfy their aspirations for more and better education, as the provider of order, and above all as the generator of employment for a fast-growing group of young professionals.

The rise of public technocracy in Chile in the late 1920s took place under very specific historical and political circumstances that proved decisive in facilitating its consolidation. The crisis and the final breakdown of the oligarchic state in the early 1920s had produced a deep feeling of discontent among Chileans about the parliamentary system, the politicians, and the so-called aristocratic frond (Alberto Edwards [1924] 1952). The general dissatisfaction with the existing order was reflected in the publication of several critical essays denouncing the social, political, and moral decline of the nation. A vivid expression of this particular state of mind is Francisco Encina's *Nuestra inferioridad económica,* published in 1911, in which he strongly criticizes the weak and inefficient parliamentary regime and calls for a stronger executive and modernization of government institutions. It cannot be denied that during those years the prestige of parliamentary democracy in general, and politicians in particular, had totally evaporated. As Góngora concluded in a reflection about this particular period, "Parliamentarism was morally, intellectually, and politically completely discredited, according to most testimonies" ([1981] 1988, 130).[1]

Following World War I, the crisis of the oligarchic order reached its final phase when the state's main financial basis abruptly disappeared as a result of the collapse of the nitrate economy. This produced a severe economic crisis, which led to a dramatic reduction in national revenue and to an explosive exacerbation of the social and political tensions in the country. The overall dissatisfaction with politics and politicians, combined with an all-embracing appeal for the modernization of the state, created a very propitious climate for the adoption of so-called technical and apolitical policies by the post-oligarchic governments. Indeed, the administrative reforms and the expansion of the state institutions initiated under the first government of Arturo Alessandri (1920–25) were mainly legitimized by arguments stressing the need to achieve efficiency and technical excellence in the conduct of state affairs.

Besides the general antipolitical mood existing in the country, the official emphasis on technical expertise was also motivated by the government's objective of eliminating traditional bureaucracy—an unwanted remnant of the oligarchic order—from the state apparatus. The government's initiatives in this direction led to a veritable *empleomanía* (employment binge), as large cohorts of new public employees from middle-class backgrounds invaded both the existing and the newly created state institutions (Urzúa and García 1971, 44–52). Furthermore, the decision to integrate people with technical backgrounds into the state apparatus had a clear-cut political objective; it was hoped that their professional competence and authority could function as a force for pacification in a polarized polity. The government hoped that the

---

1. In similar terms Collier and Sater (1996, 199) indicate that in those years "the Parliamentary Republic was decomposing fast. We need not fall into the old cliché of historians that the nation was 'seething with discontent.' Nevertheless, there were many indications by this point that Chile was approaching a conjuncture of sorts."

técnicos would be able "to solve the fundamental problems affecting national stability and harmony through technical planning and the successful execution of their administrative tasks" (Ibáñez Santa María 1984, 57).

The value assigned to technical expertise was to become even more explicit during the first government of Colonel Carlos Ibáñez (1927–31), who stressed the need to construct what he called a strong and efficient state. For this purpose, he attempted to "insulate" the public administration from political activities in order to avoid its subordination to parliamentary debates and party interests. Brian Loveman puts it in a nutshell: "Ibáñez rejected liberal democracy and blamed politics for Chile's decadence" (1979, 251).[2] By banning "politics" from the functioning of the state apparatus, Ibáñez gave the state activities a purely administrative character. The emphasis put by the Ibáñez regime on administration was such that Góngora could conclude categorically: "From May 1927 until July 1931 Chile had to live without national politics; there was only administration" ([1981] 1988, 170).

In this chapter I explore Ibáñez's attempt to establish an "Administrative State" in Chile that would operate on the basis of technical and scientific considerations rather than political deliberations. For this purpose I will focus my analysis on the enigmatic figure of Pablo Ramírez, who was Ibáñez's minister of finance and the main architect of this ambitious technocratic project. In my view Ramírez is part of Letelier's ideological legacy, for he attempted to address the main social and political tasks considered urgent by the old Radical leader: modernization of the state administration, consolidation of the Estado Docente, and the tackling of the social question. As a lawyer, as a Radical, and as a close associate of Senator Armando Quezada Acharán, Ramírez was to translate Letelier's ideas into a concrete technocratic project.

The Genesis of a Political Technocrat

Pablo Ramírez remains a relatively unknown figure in Chilean political history despite the fact that in the period 1912–29 he was a two-term national

---

2. Ibáñez's "allergy" to party politics and politicians should have been the common denominator that brought soldiers and technocrats together at the governmental level. They also shared the common goals of "efficiency" and "modernity," and possessed a meritocratic worldview. These values were introduced into the mentality of the Chilean soldier after a profound process of institutional modernization conducted by Prussian military advisers at the end of the nineteenth century (Nunn 1970).

deputy, minister of justice and education, the first National Comptroller of the Republic, and minister of finance.[3] In my view, Ramírez has to be regarded as an early example of a "political technocrat" (Camp 1985), for he successfully combined the technical and practical skills of both technocrats and politicians in his attempt to transform Chilean society. By focusing on his public life and political evolution, I have attempted to highlight the specific historical and political circumstances that strengthened his technocratic worldview and later facilitated the rise of Ibáñez's techno-bureaucratic project.[4] Through this exercise we can cast more light on the general conditions that have led to the rise to power of experts and the particular ideological orientation that guides their actions.

Pablo Ramírez Rodríguez was born in Valparaíso in 1885 to a comfortable middle-class family. He did his primary and secondary education at the MacKay School, the Seminario of Valparaíso, and Padres Franceses. Then he went to Santiago to study law at the University of Chile. He was a brilliant student and soon became well known in university political circles because of his skill in oratory and his highly combative debating style. In 1908 he obtained his law degree. In that year he presented a paper on matrimonial property law at the Scientific Congress of the Radical Party, which brought him into contact with members of the party leadership. The following year, he became a member of the Radical Party and began his rapid rise to political prominence. In 1912 he was elected as a national deputy for the Radical Party.[5]

3. The existing lack of literature and information about Pablo Ramírez undoubtedly has much to do with his service under the first government of Carlos Ibáñez. This period is still taboo among many contemporary Chilean political scientists and historians because they still do not know how to deal with this popular but authoritarian episode in Chilean political history.

4. Most of the rare works on Ibáñez were written directly after his fall in 1931. They were penned by both disillusioned former supporters and outspoken adversaries condemning his regime (see, for example, Vergara Vicuña 1931, Agustín Edwards 1931, and Melfi 1931). Some years later, clearly apologetic books appeared from the pens of Ibañistas (see Montero 1937). They are all characterized by their lack of objectivity and emotional distance in dealing with the subject. Some books on Ibáñez were published on the eve of his second administration (1952–58) or at the end of his government (see Montero 1952, Würth Rojas 1958, and Correa Prieto 1962). Since the early 1960s almost no study of the Ibáñez government has been made in Chile. Among the few exceptions we find the study by Patricio Bernedo (1989) on Ibáñez's economic policy and the book by Jorge Rojas Flores (1993) on labor organizations during his first administration. As Rojas Flores acknowledges in his introduction, this period has been almost completely abandoned by current Chilean historians (10). Nunn 1970 and Loveman 1979 are still the best sources on this turbulent period in Chilean political history.

5. As Nunn correctly indicates, the 1912 parliamentary elections represented a major landmark in the rise to political power of the middle class. In the wake of that election, "upper-

He became the *enfant terrible* of Parliament because he did not spare anything or anyone in his resolute criticism of the oligarchic regime. He soon became a well-known national political figure and in May 1919, at the age of thirty-four, was asked by President José Luis Sanfuentes to become minister of justice and education (Figueroa 1931, 602–5).

Ramírez's parliamentary and political speeches of this period not only display his political thought but also represent a vivid historical testimony of the breakdown of the oligarchic parliamentary regime.[6] This system came to an end with the rise of the middle class to power after the dramatic victory of Arturo Alessandri in the 1920 presidential elections. The speeches reflect Ramírez's growing disappointment with the governing Liberal Alliance as it became clear that Alessandri was not going to deliver the promised profound changes in Chilean politics and society. These speeches also show Ramírez's meritocratic and scientific-oriented weltanschauung, as well as his concern for the modernization of all aspects of Chilean society.

The Social Question

In the late 1910s, Ramírez was perhaps the member of Parliament most conscious of the profound political changes that were about to take place in the country. He was above all extremely aware of the very real danger that the country might slide toward a dramatic confrontation between the oligarchy and the forces demanding profound social and political changes. The Radical senator Armando Quezada Acharán presented Ramírez's thought as a moderating alternative "between the stubbornness of the reactionary forces, which are not disposed to give anything away to the new spirit, and the [left-wing] extremism which aspires to bring the social fabric down from its foundations" (Ramírez 1921a, vii–viii). As Ramírez pointed out, he condemned both "the tyranny from above and the anarchy from below" (1921b, 52).

Ramírez's main objective was the elimination of the oligarchic order. He was clearly less worried by the ascendance of the popular sector. As he once

---

middle-class provincial politicians had assumed positions of influence in Chile at the expense of the central valley oligarchs and their provincial allies" (Nunn 1970, 12–13).

6. The following analysis of Ramírez's political thought is based mainly on two books (Ramírez 1921a and 1921b) I found at the Biblioteca del Congreso at Santiago, which has a good collection of his parliamentary and political speeches of the period 1919–21. They seem to have been published by Ramírez's radical comrades to elevate his political figure in the new political era inaugurated by the 1920 presidential victory of Arturo Alessandri.

indicated, "It is necessary in Chile to facilitate the entry into Parliament of the largest number of workers' representatives possible. We must incorporate them into the political process in order to search for solutions to their problems within the bounds of constitutional norms" (1921a, 43–44).

His message to the ruling class was unambiguous: if it wanted to avoid a social revolution, it would have to enforce advanced social legislation like that recently passed by some European nations:

> I do not expect that by introducing the labor legislation we are going to solve the problem. No. As long as societies have not regulated the advent of the proletariat to economic power and have not admitted it to the intimacy of production; as long as it remains treated as an external, mechanical agent and it cannot participate in its deserved share, as long as economic relations are determined more by hazard and force than by reason and equity; the social question will persist. (1921b, 46–47)

Yet he refrained from saying that he knew that the adoption of an advanced social legislation could only provide a temporary solution, because solutions to social conflicts require real changes in societal relations.

Democracy and Efficiency

Another recurring concern in Ramírez's parliamentary interventions was the inability of the oligarchic regime to form a government that could actually rule the country. His persistent criticism of Chile's parliamentary system should not be immediately interpreted as evidence that he had adopted an authoritarian stance. It must be said that Ramírez, at least at the beginning, did not criticize democracy *per se,* but an oligarchic regime that was extremely conservative, socially exclusive, exceptionally inefficient, and in an advanced state of decomposition. However, from the very beginning he left no doubt about his support for the idea of a "strong" government. As he once stated, "In the government generated by the parliamentary regime, which is technically called 'cabinet government,' the cabinet lacks the most fundamental capacities to govern. . . . A government without the capacities to accomplish its objectives is just a nominal government" (1921a, 10–11). In fact, his plea in favor of a democratic system in which government and president would possess more power in the political decision-making was nothing more than a plea for the system that eventually came into force in 1920, namely, presidential democracy.

His attacks on the Chilean parliamentary system were primarily directed against the "parliamentary ordinance" (Reglamento de las Cámaras) that allowed endless debates, deliberately extended by those sectors interested in postponing the adoption of a particular item of legislation. This frustrated any attempt to modernize the existing legislation and even stood in the way of the functioning of the government. He understood that this was one of the most powerful political instruments of the oligarchic forces. In a speech to the youth of the Radical Party, Ramírez declared: "To reach the enemy, it is necessary to cross a point, an unassailable location; from that bastion, firmly entrenched, the church, capitalism, and all the vested interests offer resistance. There we find the entire reactionary forces forming a guard of honor. That impenetrable dug-out is called parliamentary ordinance" (1921a, 14).

This speech produced a strong reaction. The right-wing press accused Ramírez of having attacked private property, religion, and the family. In a later parliamentary debate, in which he defended himself against this wave of criticism, he used a series of technocratic arguments to support his opinions. He legitimized his attack on the "parliamentary ordinance" by referring to modernity, efficiency, and science: "When I asked for an improvement in our parliamentary system via the reform of its rules on the closure of debates—in order to permit the organization of a solid and efficient government that could adapt itself to the demands of modern progress—I did not do this as a revolutionary but as a man of order who is looking for a calm and scientific evolution of society" (1921a, 25). Time and again, he referred to recent experiences in European countries such as France, England, and Germany to support his arguments in favor of specific measures. It is evident that Europe represented the prime source of modernity for him: "In all modern countries new parliamentary reforms have been introduced, in order to strengthen the authority of the cabinet and reduce the length of the debates" (1921b, 31). After this, he gave a detailed description of the reforms introduced in England and France to achieve this purpose.

Finally, he linked the existence of this ordinance to the mediocrity of Chilean politicians. He claimed this ordinance had led to "the perpetuation of many mediocrities in the Cabinets" (1921b, 53). "This vicious ordinance is . . . the generator of moral cowardice, the godfather of the conceited mediocrities who have generally governed the country" (54).

Meritocracy as the Tool for Social Renovation

Ramírez could not mask his contempt for the Chilean traditional elite, the clergy, and the social forces and ideas that had contributed to the survival of the old oligarchic regime. He possessed a strong middle-class conscience, which led him to reject the privileges that the ruling class obtained and maintained solely because of the social origin of its members. The mesocratic spirit that inspired Ramírez in his parliamentary life clearly emerged in a speech commenting on the results of the parliamentary elections of May 1921, in which the right-wing parties experienced a dramatic defeat. He proclaimed this event as the real end of the oligarchic regime in Chile and declared that the class struggle in Chile was not between the bourgeoisie and the proletariat, but between the oligarchy and the middle class: "The history of our country is the history of two classes. On the one hand, the aristocracy, who built the Republic, possesses the land and has the support of the clergy. On the other hand, we have a democracy which is supported by the middle class, whose vigorous character is now beginning to burgeon" (1921b, 36).[7]

His meritocratic orientation pushed most strongly to the fore when he became minister of education. He was one of the most fervent supporters of the Law on Compulsory Education: this was an explicit attempt to eliminate or reduce the class advantages the upper class enjoyed because they had access to better education. His meritocratic view went hand in hand with his obsession to modernize the country as quickly as possible. From this perspective, Ramírez regarded the introduction of a system of compulsory primary education as an indispensable condition for the achievement of modernization. In a speech to the Senate in June 1919, which opened the debate on the proposed law, he said: "In the new democracy, the priority in the state expenditures— which in the past were decided by the monarch and the privileged castes—is now given to the education of the poor. The very existence of a modern nation is indivisible from compulsory schooling, which constitutes its solid

---

7. A couple of years later, in 1928, Alberto Edwards came to the same conclusion: "The influence of the working classes in the events of the past years has been fairly indirect. . . . The real class struggle broke out between the petit bourgeoisie educated in the *Liceos* and the traditional society. . . . The rebel middle class rejected domination by an oligarchy which they regarded as incapable, de-nationalized, devoid of morality and patriotism. The political aristocracy, for its part, did not pretend to hide its contempt for these newcomers, defeated in the struggles of economic and social life, who attempted to supplant it in the leadership of the country" ([1928] 1952, 234–35).

and lasting basis" (1921a, 2). In a later debate he again defended the adoption of this law by referring to its positive impact on modernization: "If one knows what a modern state is, if one understands the importance which the education of upcoming generations—particularly of the popular sectors—holds for the organization of the state, then one can comprehend the expediency for voting this law in" (21).

His meritocratic weltanschauung is also plainly revealed in his constant criticism of the *mediocrity* of the country's political elite, underlining the need for generational renovation. In a speech to the Parliament in August 1920 he spoke of the need to overhaul the political class in order to enable it to face the challenges posed by modern times. "The present situation not only finds us without the required instrument of governance, but also with a ruling personnel that is incompetent to deal with the circumstances. Everywhere in the world, public service has required the elimination of those persons who, stricken by their advanced age, are no longer able to contribute effectively to the national development." This attack was not addressed only to the aristocratic old guard, but was also aimed at the aged leadership of his own party. In a discussion with an elderly Radical senator, Ramírez exclaimed: "The generation to which I belong is very daring and quite free of prejudices. . . . The honorable senator, a survivor of a glorious past, is no longer sensitive to the palpitation of the new generations of his own party; he no longer comprehends many things and many men" (1921a, 7–8). His intransigent stance and his direct style made him many enemies, particularly within conservative circles, who would waste no opportunity to criticize him in Parliament and the press in the years that followed.

In short, even when serving as an elected official, Ramírez expressed three key elements common in technocratic thinking: a disdain for tradition in and of itself; a faith in the revolutionary power of merit; and a commitment to efficiency as the core principle of government.

The Disenchantment with Democracy

The electoral victory of Arturo Alessandri in 1920 had created great expectations among the middle class and the popular sectors, as the oligarchic forces had finally lost their grip on the government. Alessandri's Liberal Alliance had promised to carry out profound social reforms and to initiate a political regeneration of the country by eliminating the vicious political practices of the old regime.

As Ramírez stated during a Chamber session, the 1920 elections should mark the point of departure for a genuine and sweeping social revolution in Chile (Pike 1963, 174). It did not take long for Ramírez's initial optimism about the new administration to fade. He doubted whether the new authorities had the ability and the political will to implement the needed reforms. The fact that his party was a member of the ruling coalition did not deter him from openly criticizing the government's performance. For instance, he argued with Alessandri's minister of the interior (and later president) Pedro Aguirre Cerda: "I have not yet seen the determination to tackle the important problems that are still afflicting the country. The [conservative] coalition has been defeated, but it seems that its spirit and its methods of government have survived." Prophetically, he warned Parliament and the government that if the promised but still pending legislation was not adopted soon, "sixty thousand men [an allusion to the military] will turn against the Senate and the Chamber of Deputies, forcing them to adopt the reform program of the Liberal Alliance" (1921b, 10). This was exactly what finally happened in September 1924.

Not only did Parliament continue its traditional practice of blocking government initiatives, Alessandri gave no sign that he was planning to break with the old custom of making "deals" with the opposition for each measure he wanted to adopt. Ramírez hated this chicanery: "In Chile people do not argue to convince but to establish the basis for a transaction. . . . Here ministers govern by relinquishing; in other countries, by resisting and fighting" (1921b, 53).

Ramírez praised Alessandri for motivating the Chilean people, but he demanded results: "Alessandri has touched the country with his words, now he has the obligation to touch it with his deeds" (1921b, 43). He demanded from Alessandri the fulfillment of a series of objectives, which also plainly revealed Ramírez's own priorities: "To fight for the renewal of values, in an ordered and evolutionary fashion; to unfold the embryonic natural resources of this still poor country; to introduce a labor legislation according to our traditions, . . . [and] to conclude parliamentary debates by simple majority" (44).

Ramírez had a very clear picture of the serious economic and financial problems the country would be facing in the years to come. In the first place, he linked the crisis in the nitrate industry to the urgent need to increase tax revenues to finance state expenditure. As he pointed out, nitrate has been "heaven-sent riches, helping us to cover all expenditure; but today the nitrate industry is in the throes of a crisis and tomorrow, if it disappears, these resources will have to come from the tax-payers' pockets. In Chile today, as a result of the oligarchic system of indirect taxation, most of the burdens lie almost exclusively on the poorest classes" (12). So he stressed the urgent need to establish a system of direct taxation in which the wealthiest social groups would have to pay the lion's share of the tax contributions.

In his proposals, he realized that the financial problems of the state could not be solved merely by obtaining more tax revenues. He also proposed a fundamental transformation of the country's public administration. On May 13, 1921, he delivered his final address to Parliament calling for the administrative reform of the state: "The Chilean public administration is one of the most annoying and expensive in the world. The technical and organizational methods being used in model countries are totally unknown here, while the selection of personnel is ruled by the clumsy favors of politicking. The public administration requires a complete and radical reform to permit a rapid, technically based, and cheap management of the public services" (48). Although Ramírez became Consejero de Estado (state adviser) in 1921, the gap between him and Alessandri widened, eventually deteriorating into open enmity. In March 1922, during a parliamentary debate, Ramírez even demanded Alessandri's resignation. As Nunn describes the event, "Ramírez's tirade ended in an unveiled demand that Alessandri admit his failure and get out of public office. Ramírez stated: 'O'Higgins . . . handed over the reins of government. Balmaceda put an end to his life with his own hands.' Ramírez did not need to press his point" (1970, 34).[8] This demonstrated the extent of the political crisis, as Chile became ungovernable because of the continuous conflict between Alessandri and Parliament, exacerbated by the social conflict simmering throughout the country. After the military intervention of September 5, 1924, Ramírez temporarily withdrew from active political life.

Ibáñez's Authoritarian Technocratic Project

Ramírez came back onto the political scene in February 1927, when Ibáñez, minister of the interior of President Emiliano Figueroa, appointed him minister of

---

8. Alessandri would later insinuate that Ramírez's attacks against his person and government were retaliation for not being appointed minister of finance in 1920 (1967, 2:30–31).

finance in a historic cabinet reshuffle. Ibáñez had already indisputably become the strong man of Chilean politics and enjoyed widespread support among the population.[9] The "February Cabinet," as it became known, was composed of men of action who were committed to profound reforms in all fields of Chilean society in order to build the foundations of what they called a "New Chile."

The relationship between the civil society and technocracy has generally been approached from a negative perspective, that is to say, by stressing the ways in which public opinion can constitute an *obstacle* to the expansion of the technocrats' influence (see Meynaud 1968, 131–32). Less attention has been paid to situations in which public opinion can *facilitate* the adoption of technocratic solutions. Although the latter situation is less common, in my opinion it was a decisive factor in the emergence of a technocratic cabinet in 1927. The Chilean population was extremely tired of politicking and of incompetent governments. Many supported the establishment of a powerful cabinet of new, capable, well-prepared, nonpolitical figures. It was the perceived general failure of the political class and their organizations that permitted the emergence of the technocratic solution (see P. Silva 1994).[10] The general "antipolitics mood" then pervading the country is palpable in all the publications of that time. For instance, the announcement of the "February Cabinet" was welcomed by *La Nación* in the following terms:

> The new cabinet convenes in the La Moneda Palace in the name of an energetic policy, searching for solutions to the national problems. . . . Ibáñez has formed a cabinet which brings together a group of young personalities enjoying solid prestige, whose public activities have been characterized by their modern ideas about managing the state. . . . They have generally lived apart from the everyday political circles, but not from public matters, as they possess firsthand knowledge of national problems. . . . The idea is to create a strong government. This constitutes an aspiration that is shared by the large majority of the national forces who daily observe the effects of the absence of an efficient, vigorous, and reliable governmental action across the country. (February 10, 1927, 3)

9. Two months later President Figueroa resigned and Ibáñez became vice president of the country until the presidential election of May 22, 1927. The most disparate social and political forces supported Ibáñez's candidacy, including important sectors of the Radical Party.

10. As Nunn points out, "The vast majority of Chileans were apolitical, but unemployment,

In this general mood of renewal, Ramírez personified best the cabinet's firm decision to act fast and without rumination.[11] His remarkable zest for work and his uncommon speed at making decisions and translating these into policy were really striking.[12] A few days after his appointment Ramírez informed the press about his plans for the reorganization of the Chilean economy and public institutions in the following terms:

> My first objective is to solve the nitrate problem. . . . My second purpose is to get rid of . . . useless functionaries and other inconceivable burdens. The third goal is to achieve an effective organization of tax collection. . . . The fourth objective is the organization of the state finances, which it is safe to say, does not exist: because there is neither control nor coordination. . . . After having solved these problems—and in the possession of an administrative instrument which will provide a maximum range of efficient services—the government will launch a vigorous program for the active protection of all national industries. The task is arduous, painful, but necessary, and we are fulfilling it by giving real merit true justice, thereby establishing real democracy. Neither privileged position nor fortune nor political stratagems will be considered in our decisions. (Quoted in Montero 1937, 75–76)

Ramírez maintained that state agencies should function according to the same standards of excellence as those used by modern industry. As he pointed out during those initial days:

> The Ministry of Finance thinks that in order to start with the organization of the public services, the idea of the public administration as being an organization of beneficence—characteristic of decaying nations—has to be totally abandoned. The public services must be ruled by and the

---

nonpayment of the salaries to the employed, inefficiency, corruption in government and inflation made them . . . aware of the failure of their political system" (1976, 133).

11. As Ibáñez commented: "In the government I have surrounded myself with people of good will, open to everything, carrying the ability to achieve victory in the accomplishment of their tasks in their own hands; they are capable young men, with a fresh mentality for the search of solutions" (*La Nación*, March 29, 1927, 3).

12. As the press repeatedly observed, he made almost no distinction between day and night in working at the ministry. As well as this function, he was *ad interim* minister of education, development, and agriculture, using the opportunity to introduce profound reforms in these ministries and new legislation in these fields (Hernández Parker 1945, 9).

same basic principles must be applied to them as those used by private business in achieving success. . . . The organization of the public services corresponds to the government's obligation to ensure that all the services must run efficiently, and, at the same time, to perceive the need to obtain a financial equilibrium, which is the basic constituent of any reliable administration. . . . Good public employees must be remunerated well, while bad and useless functionaries must quit the service. The organization of the state services must be based on the principles which rule commercial business. In order to realize this reform, in each branch of the service a commission will be appointed, preferably with the inclusion of young technicians, because the chiefs of the service have generally not fulfilled these objectives. (*Las Ultimas Noticias*, February 16, 1927, 7)

Many years later, Ibáñez presented a character sketch of his eccentric minister that clearly matched the features of a purebred technocrat. According to Ibáñez, Ramírez developed a very conflictive relationship with the members of the political class, whom he fought both in Parliament and the public arena. Besides, Ramírez was one of the fiercest supporters within the cabinet of reducing the power and the field of action of politicians, even at the cost of political liberties. Moreover, he dared to confront openly people who represented very powerful economic interests, not permitting them to influence his reorganization plans for the public services.[13] Finally, in his Ministry of Finance, he declared war on the traditional bureaucracy, whom he constantly accused of incompetence (Correa Prieto 1962, 144–48).[14]

The Moral Crusade

Ibáñez and his "February Cabinet" soon became a symbol of the national desire to restore integrity and sobriety to Chilean public affairs.[15] The moral

13. "A permanent desire for action is [his] prime justification . . . in a world of general inertia. Clearsightedness, courage and sometime temerity in the face of the powerful [certain pressure groups] are traits of the technocrat's character" (Meynaud 1968, 210).

14. This underlines one of the main distinctions existing between technocracy and traditional bureaucracy. "The mentality of the official is absolutely foreign to technocracy. It implies a maximum of irresponsibility, passivity and subordination. The reign of technocrats . . . may . . . find its beginnings in the bureaucratic machine, but it will never be, either in its conceptions or its repercussions, a bureaucratic institution. Technocracy is establishing itself as a wholesome challenger to bureaucracy" (Alfred Frisch, quoted in Meynaud 1968, 210).

15. Even his adversaries recognized these qualities of the Ibáñez's regime. This was also the impression gained by many foreign observers. For instance, in a letter dated January 1928 to Prime Minister Chamberlain, the British ambassador to Chile characterized Ibáñez in the follow-

regeneration of the country was Ibáñez's main goal: "The purposes of this government can be reduced to a single one: achieving the moral . . . resurgence of the country. . . . We have already begun with the task of purifying the political system. . . . In order to guarantee respect for morality we will pursue our duty unwaveringly. We will eradicate the ills and the rottenness, accumulated after so many years of administrative disorder and political *compadrazgos* [kinship relations]" (*La Nación,* March 13, 1927, 17). This resulted in a veritable moral crusade against corruption at all levels of the state institutions, accompanied by a marked strengthening of the regime's authoritarian nature.

It was Minister Ramírez himself who personally took charge of the struggle against corruption and mismanagement within the public administration. He began with the most sensitive departments: the Oficina de Impuestos Internos (Taxation Department), and the Oficina de Especies Valoradas (Department of Customs and Excise). At Impuestos Internos a major swindle was discovered in which its director was directly involved. When the police attempted to arrest him, he committed suicide. This tragedy shocked public opinion, but it also gave a clear warning to everyone that the government was really combating corruption at all levels within the bureaucracy. The Impuestos Internos affair also showed the population how far corruption had spread within important public institutions.

The following target was the Oficina de Especies Valoradas. Many months before the appointment of the "February Cabinet" it had been discovered that its director had attempted to transfer his own private losses on the stock market to the institutional account. The judge in charge of the case deliberately delayed and obstructed the passing of a sentence because the entrenched judiciary was not prepared to cooperate with the new line of action. Making use of the extensive powers conferred to it by Parliament, the government decided to dismiss the judge in question, together with a dozen other magistrates across the country who had shown notorious negligence or had even been involved in complicity when hearing criminal cases (*El Mercurio,* March 16, 1927, 13). Ismael Edwards Matte later commented that "the entire country applauded this measure" (1937, 12).

---

ing way: "He is a man of few words, very reserved, and a keeper of his own counsel; he is poor . . . his house is a model of Spartan simplicity. He is one of the very few men in public life in Chile against whom I have never heard a charge of corruption or venality. I believe that he himself is inspired merely with his desire to serve his country to the best of his ability and his lights" (quoted in Blackmore 1993, 78).

Ramírez and his men also began a comprehensive reform of the entire public administration. "From his office Ramírez controlled all the public services and for some time came to be a sort of universal minister" (Galdames 1964, 382). Entire institutions and departments were abolished, institutions with overlapping tasks were combined, and interministerial coordinating entities were created. This operation resulted in the loss of four thousand public-service jobs (Haring 1931, 24). The press firmly supported the cleaning-up of the state bureaucracy. As Fredrick B. Pike puts it, "For the first time some degree of scientific efficiency was introduced into the Chilean bureaucracy" (1963, 196). Although public opinion strongly supported these measures to economize and attain efficiency in the public administration, the battalion of dismissed public functionaries was to be among the foremost enemies of Pablo Ramírez, as they identified him as the brain behind this massive purge.

Taxation

With the same self-assurance that characterized his parliamentary career, Ramírez aggressively defended his plans to transform the taxation system in order to put an end to the traditional evasion. He again successfully combined technocratic arguments with anti-oligarchic charges to defend his viewpoints: "The government position is forceful, because it is based on technical knowledge, experience, universal legislation, and the reports presented by the experts of the Kemmerer commission."[16] He accused conservative groups of

16. Ramírez refers here to a team of American financial experts led by Edwin W. Kemmerer, who conducted a far-reaching reform of the country's monetary, banking, and fiscal system in the period 1925–27. One of the many results achieved by the mission was the creation of the National Comptroller (Contraloría General de la República) in 1927. Pablo Ramírez, already in charge of the Ministry of Finance, also took charge of this institution during the first months of its existence. See, for the impact of the Kemmerer mission on Chile's financial and institutional reality, Drake 1989, 76–124. The possible influence of this mission on the technocratic orientation in people like Ramírez and other state top officials has not yet been studied.

As Sergio de Castro did later under the Pinochet government, Ramírez also sought external legitimacy from prestigious foreign scholars. So while de Castro invited Milton Friedman from the University of Chicago to express public support for his neoliberal model in March 1975, Pablo Ramírez invited Edwin W. Kemmerer from Princeton University, who also openly endorsed his administrative reforms in July 1927. In a speech during a dinner in his honor at the La Moneda Palace, Kemmerer stated: "As I have not been in Chile for the past two years, I am in a good position to perceive the great change which the public administration has experienced. Undoubtedly a clear improvement in the quality of its services has been achieved. . . . It seems that the public officials work with more commitment and are proud in their assignments, and that "doing their best to cover up the absurd privileges of the great proprietors to help reduce the already tiny amount of money they pay in tax contributions." Moreover, he depicted the existing tax system in terms of an "aristocratic conquest of Chile's organized capitalism, created for the advantage of the opulent and to the detriment of the entire country, the working class in particular." Finally, he accused the members of Parliament of utilizing stratagems of the old oligarchic regime as they tried to organize their opposition to the new legislation (*El Diario Ilustrado*, June 15, 1927, 5).

Ramírez had in fact carefully prepared the ground before this final confrontation with Parliament on taxation. In the months previous to this he had contacted representatives of several social and economic sectors, asking them for their support in the government's efforts to improve the national tax system. He even directed an unusual letter to the president of the Supreme Court, asking for the law to be applied severely to those attempting to evade taxation. This was tantamount to an indirect criticism of the usual laxity shown by many judges in cases of tax arrears. In that letter Ramírez stated:

> It is not the intention of the government to influence the sentences of the tribunals, for we are the first to recognize their autonomy. However, we find it is our duty to require of those in whose hands lies the supreme inspection of the magistrature, to adopt a firm stand on this. There must be no reason which could allow even the shadow of a doubt that the state—either through weakness or complacence—is not able to obtain the revenues necessary for the maintenance of public services. . . . I earnestly beseech you to require that the functionaries in your institution show a better spirit of cooperation with the government's goal of national reconstruction. (*El Mercurio*, March 12, 1927, 9)

To Ramírez, tax evasion also represented a cultural problem, which accordingly demanded a cultural change in the Chilean population to redress it. For this purpose he even sent a quite peculiar letter to the leader of the Chilean Catholic Church, Archbishop Monsignor Crescente Errázuriz, asking him for

---

consciousness of good public service has been assimilated better than it was two years ago. . . . It is a great pleasure to verify the increase in the number of men fulfilling these conditions in service of the Chilean state. For me this is the best augury for Chile's economic future." Santiago, July 29, 1927. Original text in Spanish. The Kemmerer Collection, Seeley G. Mudd Manuscript Library, Princeton University, box 38.

help in the task of inculcating the value of tax-paying among Chileans. He wrote:

> This Ministry considers that within the national conscience there is neither a propensity for paying taxes nor a convention of either honest income declaration or the payment of dues to the community. On the contrary, the number of contributors who resort to dishonest methods to avoid the observance of their duties toward the state is not a few. This serious situation demands that the government make an appeal to all the moral forces in order to obtain their essential help for the sake of the national reconstruction. . . . We ask you to make use of your high spiritual position to induce the taxpayers to make an honest and correct discharge of their obligations toward the state, and to influence the public to desist from their stubborn resistance against the state's legitimate right to tax.[17]

Team Building and the Colonization of the State

Ibáñez's project for the institutional modernization of the state required the presence of a techno-administrative bureaucracy to take charge of and to give form to the plans for expanding the public sector. Therefore, Ibáñez invited a new generation of technicians and professionals, who committed themselves to the building of an efficient public administration, to conduct these reforms. As Aníbal Pinto indicates, the Ibáñez administration gave center-stage prominence to a public technocracy that emerged from the highest strata of the middle class. This occurred throughout the entire bureaucratic machine, leading to the improvement of both the technocrats' own socioeconomic status and to the strengthening of the state apparatus (Pinto [1958] 1985, 13).[18] As a result of this, an increasing number of state institutions were to gradually achieve a sort of "relative autonomy" by which managers, technicians, and

17. Archivo del Ministerio de Hacienda, letter nr. 208 of March 8, 1927, Biblioteca Nacional (Archivo del Siglo XX).

18. In the late 1950s Ibáñez was to reminisce about his attempt twenty years earlier to renew the country's politico-administrative class in the following terms: "I managed to bring young and independent men to top positions within the public administration, most of them from middle-class backgrounds. It did not matter that they were not well known on the political scene or in Santiago social circles. One had to initiate new customs, something one cannot achieve with people compromised by their political environment" (quoted in Correa Prieto 1962, 151).

professionals in general acquired a large amount of room to maneuver for the formulation and application of developmental policies. In this way, the public technocracy began to exercise a decisive influence in the decision-making process in ministries, state enterprises, and the public administration at large.

Personnel were eliminated from public service not only by the purpose to conserve financial resources and increase administrative efficiency. This measure was also used to replace the old state personnel with a new generation that would be able to implement the ambitious developmental programs of the government. Ramírez was searching for a group of young men who were technically competent, apolitical, honest, and desperate to prove themselves. He sagaciously focused his attention on engineers. They were indeed the most suitable group of professionals to shape and implement his technocratic plans, as they had assimilated the principles of meritocracy, technical excellence, and apoliticism during their technical training. So the group chosen to command the top positions was mainly recruited from a contingent of young *ingenieros*,[19] all of them about thirty years of age, who became known as "the *cabros* [boys] of Pablo Ramírez" (Ibáñez Santa María 1984, 9n).[20]

Minister Ramírez repeatedly stressed the competence and outstanding technical performance of this group of engineers and his desire to expand the level of participation of technicians within the state machinery. In a letter of December 1927 to the president of the Instituto de Ingenieros de Chile, the professional association of university-trained engineers, Ramírez praises the "efficient contribution" of engineers to the administration of state agencies. After mentioning an impressive list of engineers who occupied key positions in state institutions,[21] he implicitly stressed the meritocratic and apolitical nature of their recruitment when he added: "They were called to command

19. They were university-graduated engineers, most of them civil engineers, who studied at the Escuela de Ingeniería of the University of Chile. I am indebted to Adolfo Ibáñez Santa María's historical essay on these *ingenieros* (1984), which provides very valuable archival information about this professional group.

20. It becomes almost irresistible to make a parallel between Pablo Ramírez and Sergio de Castro, leader of the neoliberal team that conducted the economic policies and the administrative reforms under the Pinochet government, which was commonly called "the [Chicago] boys of Sergio de Castro" (P. Silva 1991, 1992).

21. So, for instance, engineers were in posts such as comptroller general of the republic, director of the budget office, superintendent of insurance, superintendent of the customs house, director of inland revenue, superintendent for the nitrate industry, director of administration for state supplies, chief of the department of industry of the ministry for development, chief of the department of commerce of the same ministry, "and many others, who are too numerous to be mentioned here" (quoted in Ibáñez Santa María 1984, 9).

important positions, which in the past were occupied only according to the political pressure exercised by the different political parties" (Ibáñez Santa María 1984, 9).[22]

The fact that the rise of these engineers to top positions within the state administration was mainly determined by a series of political factors beyond their own control does not mean, however, that they were passive instruments in a larger political game. At the beginning of this century Chilean engineers already constituted a well-entrenched pressure group that defended the idea of economic independence and state protectionism and demanded the development of large-scale programs of public works (Crowther 1973). So what they did from 1920 on was simply to take advantage of a favorable political and institutional climate to expand their influence within the state apparatus in order to foster their professional interests and aspirations. With time they would develop a self-assigned "mission" to achieve the overall development of the country (see Ouweneel 1996). The interesting point is that this "mission" to accomplish modernity and progress was presented in a nationalistic guise, which perfectly matched the government's goal of fostering national industrial development by and for Chileans.[23]

The efforts of Pablo Ramírez and his team of engineers were specially directed toward the creation of the foundation for a broad program of state-led industrialization in the country. In his economic program, announced in 1927, Ramírez mentioned the "active protection of industry" by the state and financial and tax reforms as the key elements of the new economic policy. In order to achieve this, that year he created the Department of Industry, assigning it the task of formulating a plan for industrial development. As Fernando Silva has pointed out, this was the first time that the Chilean state explicitly

22. This account is supported by Loveman, who in similar terms expressed that "technicians and middle-class professionals staffed growing ministries and public agencies previously manned overwhelmingly through political patronage by the traditional parties." As an example of the almost autonomous teamwork of these state professionals, Loveman mentions the formulation of the Labor Code of 1931: "Intellectuals and professional administrators in the Labor Department produced the Labor Code which incorporated the 'social laws' of 1924 and created an elaborate framework for a modern industrial relations system" (1979, 249).

23. In an essay published in *Anales*, the leading engineer, Ramón Salas Edwards, stated for instance that "when the best Chilean engineers energetically dedicate themselves to the task of developing trade and industry, it will represent an act of national salvation. It also will bring a higher level of welfare for everyone and help to nationalize both industry and commerce. . . . What must Chilean engineers do to prepare themselves for the full accomplishment of their mission? I think that the prime and most effective preparation is the formation of a conscience about this mission" (quoted in Ibáñez Santa María 1984, 16).

adopted the idea of "global planning" of the country's economic development (F. Silva 1974, 860). A year later the Ministerio de Fomento (Ministry of Development)—the direct predecessor of the Corporación de Fomento de la Producción (Chilean Development Corporation, CORFO)—was founded.

The creation of the Ministry of Development heralded an undisguised conflict between the government and the pressure groups formed by the landed and industrial interests on the question of "participation" in (read "control of") the formulation and implementation of ministerial policies. The conflict about the exercise of influence was in fact a confrontation between two models of state administration. While the supporters of a technocratic model stressed the need to protect the "relative autonomy" of the state from powerful pressure groups, the supporters of a corporatist model strongly urged the active participation of the productive forces in state policymaking.

The Sociedad de Fomento Fabril (Society for Industrial Development, SOFOFA) was among the most active pressure groups. SOFOFA leaders proposed the creation of a national economic council (similar bodies already existed in several European countries), in which all "active forces" (*fuerzas vivas*) of society would participate (in a corporatist fashion) in the decision-making. Although the Ibáñez government publicly expressed its interest in establishing closer links between the entrepreneurs and the state, he did not in fact create any effective institution for this purpose. This, in his view, would politicize and corrupt the mechanisms of decision-making and also alienate the support that his regime obtained from the middle class, who realized they were the main beneficiaries of the expansion of the administrative machinery of the state and of educational facilities. The middle class also appreciated his "firm hand" in dealing with both the oligarchy and the organizations of the popular sector.

As Clarence H. Haring states, the Ibáñez government "made a clean sweep of the ministry of finance and introduced an entirely new personnel. Virtually all of the latter were engineers, as contrasted with the lawyer element which previously monopolized such offices. They were inexperienced, but under the guidance of the minister of finance, Pablo Ramírez, . . . they have proved to be an honest, intelligent, and progressive group of men" (Haring 1931, 23).[24]

---

24. Ramírez's meritocratic orientation inhibited him from following too narrow a nationalistic policy in the recruitment of state personnel; he simply wanted the best. For instance, on several occasions he talked about the need to encourage the immigration of specialized foreign workers and engineers in order to develop the national industry (see *La Nación*, September 29,

The professional association of university-trained engineers, the Instituto de Ingenieros de Chile, did not hide its delight at the new professional opportunities offered to its members. Its institutional journal, *Anales*, repeatedly praised the government and celebrated its own role in the public administration. In the issue of June 1927, on its first page, *Anales* reproduces a letter from Pablo Ramírez to the president of the institute, Rodolfo Jaramillo, in which he reaffirms his intention to encourage the access of Chilean engineers to several new institutions related to the nitrate industry. In December that year, the editor's introduction of *Anales* is dedicated to the theme "the government and the engineers," in which among other things it says:

> The minister of finance, by bringing the national engineers to the highest posts within the public administration, has learnt to value and to employ the cooperation of engineers, who are always ready to participate in every task waiting to be carried out which, without the hindrance of sterile political and social doctrines, is really focused on the economic reconstruction of the country. . . . Mr. Pablo Ramírez, a modern leader, has understood this and has asked engineers to work for it.

Needless to say, Chilean engineers enthusiastically embraced Ramírez's plan to modernize the state. As Ibáñez Santa María (2003, 120) indicates, a large part of the young engineers recruited by Ramírez to command high positions in the government came from Ferrocarriles del Estado, the Chilean state railways. They already possessed a strong sense of public service and were heavily influenced by modern European technocratic ideas, as a result of their close ties with the French National School of Bridges and Roads. Moreover, many of them had visited countries such as the United States, France, and Germany to take a personal look at the latest technological innovations in the field of railway transportation.

These young Chilean engineers became frantically engaged in the formulation of an ambitious plan to carry out huge infrastructural works. The high

---

1927, 16). Indeed, many foreign experts, particularly in the fields of accountancy, health, and education, were contracted during the Ibáñez administration. Ramírez wanted to have the best European advisers at his ministry, no matter what they cost. Cablegrams such as the following were very common. In a note to the Chilean ambassador in Germany, Ramírez wrote: "The government wants the technical organization of a statistical service and asks you to contract the best person you can find. Please make contact with Mr Wagemann, chief of the German Statistical Service, and ask him to search for the appropriate person." Archivo del Ministerio de Hacienda, letter nr. 288 of March 23, 1927, Biblioteca Nacional (Archivo del Siglo XX).

priority given by the government to the modernization of the country's infrastructure was also visible in the growing importance acquired by the Dirección General de Obras Públicas, the governmental agency in charge of the implementation of the plan. Thus, in 1930 this agency was restructured and its director obtained the de facto status of a minister without portfolio.[25]

Just as it can be said that Ramírez was Ibáñez's right hand, Raúl Simón, an engineer, was definitely the man behind Ramírez. This young and very bright engineer (he was thirty-four in 1927) was Ramírez's closest adviser.[26] He was behind all the major economic and financial decisions and the architect of most of the legal decrees and programs dealing with financial matters, public works, and economic development in general. Moreover, Simón was a leading figure within the Instituto de Ingenieros, playing a key role in the recruitment of new engineers for the public administration.

During those years, the services of engineers were thus required not only at managerial levels, as they also became the main professional group in charge of the technical implementation of the huge program of public works deployed by Ibáñez. Under his government, Chilean engineers had the long-awaited historic chance (and the required financial resources) to deploy their professional skills fully in the construction of numerous public buildings, roads, railways and stations, industrial complexes, tunnels, port facilities, irrigation canals, sewage systems, and so forth. This public works program also constituted a key instrument in Ramírez's objective to reduce unemployment and to stimulate the domestic economy in general.

The Ibáñez government could count on a generally good reception abroad,

25. The "absorption" of engineers by the state in the period 1927–31 can easily be verified in many of the entries in the 1939 edition of *Who's Who: Guía Profesional de la Ingeniería en Chile*, published by the Instituto de Ingenieros de Chile.

26. Although Simón rarely vented his political views in public, like many other engineers he was clearly sympathetic to authoritarian rule because he saw it as a requisite condition to accelerate the decision-making process. In *Chile: A Magazine of Information and Service*, he once wrote: "The political changes which, by the middle of 1924, brought about the suspension of Congress and the temporary absorption of legislative power by the Executive, opened the way for the Government not to delay any longer the reform of our monetary system. [One has to] take advantage of the favorable circumstance that the sterile debates in Congress can be avoided—out of which debates in a period of thirty years a complete and final solution had not been found. . . . A government junta of strong and honest men had rolled into the executive and legislative powers. Whatever project the Kemmerer Mission should choose to present, could be made a law without having to wait for a debate by parliament" (Simón 1926). This magazine was published in New York by Simón and some close associates, where he lived for a while as a representative of the Chilean railways. The Kemmerer Collection, Seeley G. Mudd Manuscript Library, Princeton University, box 55.

as people praised his ability to reestablish authority and political order in the country, as well as the standard of administrative efficiency achieved. This allowed Minister Ramírez to obtain large sums in foreign loans to finance the reform of the public administration and the huge program of public works. Ramírez's policy on foreign loans later constituted one of the most discussed and criticized aspects of his ministerial period (see Contreras Guzmán 1942, 161–62). The fact remains that thanks to these loans, Chile was able to reduce substantially the negative effects of the nitrate crisis, which began in the late 1910s, to maintain economic and financial stability, and to keep the people at work until Ibáñez's fall in 1931. This occurred when the world depression had already hit most of the other Latin American countries. In Ramírez's eyes, foreign loans represented a modern and strategic instrument for encouraging national economic growth and development. As Nunn has correctly indicated, "The 'política prestamista' [loan policy] . . . and . . . public works . . . rarely receive objective treatment by Chileans. To some this was the beginning of modern Chile's economic woes (an unjust accusation) or a continuation of unsound government economic policy, heightened by dependence on foreign capital and soundingly punctuated by financial collapse in 1930–31. To others, some of whom criticized Ibáñez in other areas, public works and modernization, however dependent on outside financing, created a new Chile" (1970, 148–49).

The Nitrate Question

As Ramírez declared, following his appointment at the Ministry of Finance, his first priority would be the reactivation of the nitrate industry, which accounted for about 50 percent of Chilean exports. Competition with synthetic nitrate production in Western Europe and the United States, technical problems, and union unrest at the nitrate *oficinas* triggered off a severe depression in this strategic sector of the Chilean economy. This had an immediate impact on the country's finances, since for the previous fifty years the export taxes paid by Chilean and foreign nitrate companies operating in the northern region had represented the main source of income for the national treasury.

The "February Cabinet" had to deal with a difficult situation as the private nitrate companies demanded the elimination of export taxes. They claimed this was the only way to avoid total paralysis in the sector. Directly after his appointment, Ramírez summoned the president of the nitrate producers' association to his office. On that occasion, Ramírez informed him that the government was not going to accept their demand, because he considered it an unpatriotic act contrary to the national interest. Ramírez also asked him to restart production in the *oficinas* where production had been interrupted; otherwise they would be liable to financial penalty in a form of an additional tax (*La Nación,* February 13, 1927, 19).

The importance of the nitrate question was not simply economic. It also had a very sensitive political dimension, since for many Chileans the control of this industry by foreign stakeholders was the symbol of the imperialistic domination of the country's natural resources. Since the end of the War of the Pacific, this industry had become a virtually autonomous domain free of direct state intervention. The Chilean state had only a "delegación fiscal salitrera" (national nitrate office), which had actually been reduced to a mere decorative agency without any practical attributes (Montero 1937, 76–77). The failed attempt by President José Manuel Balmaceda to impose a larger degree of national control on the nitrate industry in the late 1880s still represented a major source of inspiration to many Chileans who saw him as a victim of a joint conspiracy between foreign imperialism and the national oligarchy. As Nunn points out, Ramírez was almost fanatical in his evocation of *Balmacedismo* (1970, 131). For Ramírez and many other countrymen, Balmaceda represented an honest nationalist government that was brought down by the same social and political forces against which he had fought since 1912 as a member of Parliament.[27]

Ramírez also made no bones about the fact that the government was planning to play a more active role in this economic sector. At the same time he used the opportunity to show his contempt for the aristocratic groups controlling this industry:

The time to discuss the nitrate problem in aristocratic circles is long past. Those meetings were only accessible to a few initiated who always claimed that the problem was too complex and delicate, and that the country could trust only in particular gentlemen. They were considered

---

27. Ibáñez's identification with Balmaceda was expressed, among other ways, in the appointment of his son, Enrique Balmaceda, as his minister of the interior. On July 2, 1927, when Ibáñez became president, Enrique Balmaceda draped over him the presidential sash used by his father, as he saw in him the incarnation of the principles of patriotism and republican austerity for which his father had fought (see Nunn 1970, 129–33).

to possess an extraordinary competence to deal with the matter, which they veiled in an impenetrable mystery. The principal political leaders of the country were at the same time the lawyers and representatives of the nitrate producers. Historically, the entire relationship between the state and the nitrate producers has been characterized by the absolute lack of general regulations: on the part of the state, there was a complacent weakness and ignorance; on that of the nitrate producers, a poor business policy which often adversely affected fiscal interest. The fact is that the nitrate industry is a national industry, and that the government, as its protector, must ensure that the national interests are served first, and that the producers' interests should only come in second place. (*La Nación*, September 29, 1927, 17)

Following Ramírez's admonition, the nitrate companies adopted a fairly challenging attitude toward the government as a signal that they were not disposed to accept a larger degree of state intrusion in what they were accustomed to see as their exclusive preserve. However, after a communiqué from the minister of the interior, in which he delivered a final warning to the producers in the strongest terms, the latter backed down and later announced their willingness to collaborate with the government. Within a few days many *oficinas* had resumed production. Ramírez was out for more than a temporary solution for the nitrate industry as shown one month later when he sent to Parliament a legal proposal for the creation of the Superintendencia del Salitre y Yodo, a technical institution whose task would be to study and resolve the existing problems related to the production and marketing of Chilean nitrate.[28]

The nitrate question also shows that Ramírez knew quite well that the solution to the national economic problems should not be sought only within the country. Solving Chile's problems would also require a more active and audacious attitude toward both financial partners and economic competitors from other countries. In mid-March 1929 Ramírez launched an extended mis-

28. Ramírez himself followed the performance of natural and synthetic fertilizers in the international markets very closely. In the Archivo del Siglo XX, there are several copies of cablegrams sent by him to Chilean embassies in Europe and the United States, asking them to keep him personally informed of any single change noticed in the production, distribution, and marketing of synthetic nitrates.

sion to the United States and several European countries.[29] In New York he met bankers and investors; in Washington he met President Herbert C. Hoover at the White House.[30] He then journeyed on to London, where he had talks with nitrate producers and bankers. Abroad Ramírez explicitly stressed the technocratic nature of the Ibáñez government, presenting it as one of its greatest assets. In London he stated: "Our government today is exclusively technical; engineers, bankers, and experts in economic affairs have replaced professional politicians. In this way, the government has been able to restore economic activity, to solve the nitrate crisis, to initiate a huge plan of public works, to obtain an adequate return of tax revenues, to control the money resources, and to organize the credit system" (*La Nación*, May 17, 1929, 10). In Germany he visited the main synthetic nitrate companies, where he signed cooperation agreements. His trip ended in Paris, where the main topic for discussion was financial matters. In each country that he visited he was received by the most important political leaders, which was a demonstration of the country's international prestige and the prevailing interest in Chile's nitrate industry.

A few weeks after his return to Chile, Ramírez left the Ministry of Finance during the cabinet reshuffle of August 23 and was replaced by his friend and close associate, Rodolfo Jaramillo. The reason for his departure is still unclear, as nothing indicates that he had problems with Ibáñez or that his departure took place in a fit of pique. The most plausible explanation is that he decided to dedicate himself fully to the detailed development of the nitrate policy, both in Chile and abroad. In any case, after his return to Chile he began to work on the creation of the Chilean Nitrate Corporation (COSACH), which was intended to regulate the production and marketing of Chilean nitrate. This constitutes an early case of a joint venture between the Chilean state and

29. See Bernedo 1989, 101–4. According to Contreras Guzmán, his foreign trip was related to the strong opposition met by Ramírez from those former officials harmed by his austerity programs in the public administration, who had instigated a sordid campaign against him. "An official foreign trip was planned in order to dissipate the bad atmosphere around him" (1942, 173).

30. Hoover, an engineer, had a special relationship with Chile and the Instituto de Ingenieros de Chile. He had visited Chile in December 1928 as president elect. He was enthusiastically received by the Instituto de Ingenieros de Chile, who made him an honorary member (see *Anales*, January 1–5, 1929). In 1927, when he still was secretary of commerce, the Chilean press had already lauded Hoover's technical capacity and apoliticism. "Hoover . . . has became famous because of his aversion to politics, and simply because of this, he is one of the Republican candidates with the highest chance of succeeding President Coolidge" (*La Nación*, September 10, 1927).

the local and foreign companies exploiting Chilean nitrate, with the corporation's shares divided into equal parts. The COSACH initiative was criticized for several reasons. The conservatives perceived this as an unacceptable intrusion by the state in private business affairs; the communists denounced it as a victory for American imperialism, arguing that the Guggenheim interests (the American company that controlled the largest part of the nitrate production) had been strengthened by this deal (Pike 1963, 198; Ramírez Necochea 1958, 231).

COSACH and other, similar initiatives eventually failed when the worldwide depression struck Chile in 1931. The economic crisis triggered increasing social and political unrest in the country, which led to the fall of the Ibáñez regime in July 1931, followed by a period of political anarchy. Ramírez did not personally experience the end of the Ibáñez government. In 1931 he was in Paris representing Chilean financial and economic interests in Europe.

The End of a Technocratic Experiment

With the fall of the Ibáñez government a period of profound political and administrative transformation came to an end. In just four years, the Chilean state had been radically restructured and modernized under the banner of austerity and efficiency. Pablo Ramírez had indeed been the brain behind these structural changes, which constituted an unequivocal reaction to the weak, slow, and inefficient oligarchic structures. During his parliamentary career, Ramírez personally witnessed the structural inability of the old aristocratic political system to solve the national problems and to prepare the country for the new challenges of the twentieth century. Being extremely conscious and proud of his middle-class background, he fought against the very restrictive nature of Chile's political class, which in the 1910s was still dominated by a traditional Basque-Castilian aristocracy. Against the dominating principles of social ancestry and wealth, he defended the principles of personal capacity, effort, and merit. In this manner, his meritocratic weltanschauung was only reinforced by the social barriers built by the ruling oligarchy.

Initially Ramírez found in radicalism an evolutionistic and advanced doctrine that supported social change and human progress in general. Its anticlerical attitude and anticonservatism fit well with his own stance against social and religious prejudice and in favor of modernity. Nonetheless, he seems to have always been more convinced of radical*ism* (as a set of ideas and objectives) than of the Radical *Party* as such, for he remained a solitary and independent man within its structures. The breakdown of the oligarchic order not only demonstrated the weakness of the conservative forces; it also showed the inability of the opposition parties to form a strong and stable alternative to rule the country. In the end, not only Ramírez but large sections of the Chilean population found themselves increasingly disenchanted with politics in general and politicians in particular. The lack of political order and stability in the country during the mid-1920s facilitated the rise to power of Ibáñez, and with him, of a group of young men with the will to effect profound changes in the administration of the state in order to break with a very disappointing past.

Ibáñez showed full confidence in Ramírez, who enthusiastically shared his objective of modernizing the country and eliminating political corruption. In line with this, Ibáñez allowed him extensive freedom of action, which he utilized fully for the building of a modern public administration and the improvement of the national infrastructure. He was the prototype of a modern man in the 1920s, as he truly believed in the advantages of the newest technological and administrative methods, in industrialization and in the inevitability of what we today call "globalization." He possessed an internationalist and universalistic vision of development, as he was conscious of the opportunities but also the limitations of a peripheral economy like Chile's.

The presence in the country of a very well-prepared engineer corps, and their disposition to join Ramírez's efforts to modernize the country, proved to be a decisive factor in the formulation and application of the economic and administrative reforms undertaken under the Ibáñez government. The fact that many engineers joined the public administration not only allowed a better technical performance in the various services but also strengthened the technocratic orientation of the state apparatus as a whole. Meritocracy, faith in scientific knowledge, and contempt for politics brought these engineers and Ramírez together.

Ramírez was an idealist and a realist at the same time, for he clearly understood that in order to construct the utopia of a "New Chile," free of corruption and politicking, he would have to fight against powerful vested interests and strong political ambitions. The world depression, the conscious absence of an organized political base for the government, combined with a mounting opposition from conservative and radical forces, put an end to this early technocratic experiment on South American soil.

3

Technocrats and the Entrepreneurial State

When scholars look at the political role played by technocrats, two main interpretations come frequently to the fore. Sometimes, the ascendancy of technocracy is regarded as being mainly the result of the technocrats' own efforts to obtain a larger share of power and influence to the detriment of politicians and other contenders for power. For this purpose, technocrats may make use of their technical credentials, expertise, and professional prestige to obtain their final political objective. In contrast to this, technocratic ascendancy is sometimes presented as being mainly the work of political groups in governmental positions who resort to technocrats for their own political and ideological purposes. In other words, technocrats are rather seen as passive tools employed by others. Technocratic experiences worldwide can undoubtedly provide numerous examples supporting either of these interpretations.

What these distinct readings have in common is the fact that in both cases the technocratic ascendancy is presented as a result of the supremacy achieved by a particular group (technocrats or politicians in power) who eventually impose their will on the rest of society in a kind of "winner-take-all" situation. I suggest that there is another path to technocratic ascendancy, one that in my view corresponds to what has been taking place in Chile since the late 1930s; namely, technocratic ascendancy as a result of a political stalemate.

In this manner, the consolidation of the state technocracy in Chile since the late 1930s can be seen as the result of a very fragile equilibrium of forces.

On the one hand, we find center-leftist reformist forces that control the government but are not strong enough to impose their agenda on the rest of the country and on the other, right-wing conservative forces, which since the mid-1920s have lost direct control of the executive but are still able to block most governmental initiatives. I suggest that the strong presence of technocrats in state agencies since the 1930s must be regarded as a kind of "demilitarized zone" established between these contending sociopolitical forces to make the functioning of the Chilean democracy possible. As a matter of fact, these technocrats constituted the sole actor that was acceptable to powerful groups in society (agrarian and industrial entrepreneurs, bankers, and conservative political parties) to be the main administrator of the nation's financial resources. The alternative was that public policies should be designed and implemented by radical, socialist, and even communist politicians, which in the eyes of conservative Chile was totally unacceptable. On the other hand, Chile's progressive forces had in general great confidence in the professional expertise of the engineers in charge of the most important state agencies related to production and infrastructure. They generally regarded these technocrats as honest and competent public servants who did not represent any political current and who were mainly motivated by the goal of expanding and modernizing the Chilean industry and the state apparatus. The evidence of the tacit acceptance by the Left of this pivotal role assigned to technocrats since the late 1930s is the fact that in those years technocrats never became the focus of criticism within the socialist movement and labor organizations.

For these reasons, the consolidation of the state technocracy since the late 1930s cannot be regarded as disconnected from the establishment of the Estado de Compromiso—as the old Chilean democracy became known—because it was a vital expression of that compromise. From this perspective it can be argued that as a result of a particular balance of forces and the necessity of the political system to subsist, the Chilean state technocracy became a key facilitator of democracy in the country. It is for this reason that later attempts to perturb this equilibrium in favor of one of the contending sociopolitical forces weakened not only the foundations of the Estado de Compromiso but also the buffer function played by the state technocracy. As the final section of this chapter shows, this is exactly what occurred when in the late 1950s the conservative sectors attempted to reshape the foundations of the Estado de Compromiso. In their effort to break with the pattern of state-led industrialization and to impose free market policies, the Right in power launched an open attack on the technocrats who had administered important state agencies for decades, and replaced them with technocrats coming from private enterprises that supported a free market agenda. As I show in Chapter 4, the same was to happen during the governments of Frei Montalva and Allende, who opted for the colonization of the state apparatus with technical personnel who were fully in line with their political projects. Thus as the Estado de Compromiso entered into its terminal phase, the technocrats' buffer function disappeared.

Following the Popular Front victory in 1938 and the creation a year later of the National Development Corporation (CORFO) the state's entrepreneurial role became definitively consolidated. This also meant the consolidation of the state "technostructure,"[1] which with the passing of time was to play a strategic role not only in managing the state apparatus but also in balancing conflicting socioeconomic demands on the state coming from civil society. Within the technostructure a specific strategic group of engineers can be identified who, from the late 1920s to the mid-1950s, played a key role in the formulation and implementation of the state industrial policies. From their CORFO headquarters they were able to formulate a veritable "ideology of industrialization," in which the aims of economic independence, industrial growth, and social justice became successfully integrated in a coherent discourse.

As I show in the third section, this state-based technostructure came under severe attack during the liberal government of Arturo Alessandri's son, Jorge Alessandri Rodríguez (1958–64). He saw this technostructure as the very heart of state capitalism, which he aimed to replace by a more market-oriented system under the leadership of private entrepreneurs. Paradoxically, for this purpose he also made use of a technocratic discourse, in which the state technostructure was pictured as being the product of incompetent party politics that impeded the adoption of rational and efficient decision-making. In the end, Alessandri succeeded in removing the leading figures of the technostructure from the ministries, state enterprises, and the public administration. They were replaced by industrial managers, technicians, and professionals associated to the private sector. Although Alessandri's liberal technocratic experi-

---

1. Galbraith's (1967, 71) term for a group of technocrats with considerable influence in the internal process of decision-making within an enterprise or an administrative body.

ment finally failed, it represented the first attempt to elevate the private entrepreneurial sector to the position of key actor of development in the country. The second attempt would occur a decade later—under military rule.

Crisis and the Quest for Order

The collapse of the Ibáñez regime was followed by a short period of political chaos and instability. Several short and weak governments attempted one after another to contain the economic crisis and the social unrest in the country. But even during this turbulent period, all the governments in power in 1932, from the Carlos Dávila administration to the "Socialist Republic" of Marmaduque Grove, offered arguments in favor of "technicity." As Góngora indicates, Dávila invited a group of "new men, who were totally independent to participate in his cabinet" ([1981] 1988, 219). Even the goal of socialism, which acquired strength in the early 1930s, was presented as being a mere technical matter. For instance, an editorial article of the government newspaper *La Nación* concludes that "in short, the realization of socialism is nothing more than a problem of technical organization" (Góngora [1981] 1988, 217).

Despite the great political instability of the early 1930s, a clear continuity can still be observed in the expansion of state activities. In fact, the short government of Dávila represented a bridge between the administrative reforms initiated by Ibáñez and the later increase in state intervention with the Popular Front in 1938. Adolfo Ibáñez Santa María is right when he indicates that "despite the ideological and personal differences of the governments of the period 1927–39, there is continuity in relation to their administrative efforts" (Ibáñez Santa María 1984, 3). In his analysis of the Dávila government, Góngora says that "the accentuation of the idea of 'technicity,' of planning, makes of the brief Dávila government a forerunner of the 'planning rage' [*planificacionalismo*] of the 1960s" ([1981] 1988, 217). The same can be said of Carlos Ibáñez and Arturo Alessandri, who, in Góngora's words, "left a decisive track in the state structure, i.e. the idea that new state and semi-state institutions must be created for the quantitative incrementation of public administration" (187).

Following his return to power in 1932, Arturo Alessandri took up the task of consolidating the administrative and institutional transformations of 1920–

31. He also decisively supported the idea of industrializing the country. One of the lessons learnt from the Great Depression was that Chile urgently needed to enter the stage of industrialization; to accomplish this the state would have to play a leading role. As Pinto points out, after the 1930 crisis Chile was compelled to move forward because there was no way back to the past: "The collapse of the economic sustenance left the social organization, and the economic expectations arising from it 'hanging in the air.' Neither the political scene nor the traditional patterns of expenditures fitted in that scenario. However, the already established sociopolitical structure prevented 'going back' or accepting the consequences of the contraction of the foreign trade, as had happened in less developed countries in the region" (1973b, 308). This does not mean, however, that the Chilean process of industrialization in the post-crisis period took place without any general guide. Two phases can be observed in the evolution of this process. The first stage covers the period 1931–38, the second begins in 1938 and ends in the late 1950s. The first period is characterized by the pragmatic nature of the economic measures adopted by the government. These measures were directed to confront only the most urgent problems of the moment in order to find a way out from the suffocating depression affecting the country. During the second period a global developmental strategy emerged that was intended to guide the economic development of the country in the middle and long term (see Mamalakis 1965, 15–16).

The economic measures adopted during Alessandri's second administration (1932–38) were intended to achieve three main objectives. First, these measures sought to give a new impulse to economic activity as a whole, for the entire national economy had been extremely weakened by the crisis. Second, they were directed to meeting the local demand, especially from the middle class, for consumer goods, which before the crisis had been satisfied through imports. And finally, they pursued the creation of new jobs for the thousands of unemployed. All these measures also strengthened the role of the state in the economic organization of the country, constituting a decisive step toward the import-substituting industrialization that would be consolidated with the coming of the Popular Front government in 1938 (CORFO 1965, 447).

In an attempt to gain the ability to influence governmental decision-making processes directly, the entrepreneurial organizations, as they had done before under Ibáñez, tried to convince Alessandri of the need to create corporatist mechanisms of consultation and participation. In 1934 they started a campaign to achieve the creation of an active economic council, a demand that they presented to the government in that year (Ibáñez Santa María 1984, 39–40). This and other attempts to bend the state administrative apparatus to their personal advantage eventually ended in failure. The entrepreneurs found instead a technocratic official discourse that became even more uncompromising than what was the case under Ibañez.

The group of engineers who had been integrated into the state institutions during the Ibáñez regime were about to propose an industrialization program that would require the electrification of the country. They presented their ideas, which were soon to become state policies, in two key documents. The first contains seven lectures given by a group of leading engineers at the end of 1935 under the title "Chilean Electric Policy." The second document, "The Concept of National Industry and State Protection," was presented by a group of engineers at the First South American Congress of Engineers.[2] The latter document dealt with the question of state intervention as a mechanism to foster industrialization. Although there was no general agreement among the authors on the type and degree of state intervention, none questioned the principle itself. They stressed the need to establish a national energy enterprise to generate and guarantee the energy required for the state-led industrialization program. However, behind this technical project a clear political program had begun to emerge assembling all the social and political forces supporting this strategy of industrialization.

In chapter 9 of "Chilean Electric Policy," these engineers stressed once again the need to keep the technical management of the energy enterprise free from political pressures. They demanded "the establishment of a complete independence of the enterprise from political influences, and from particular interests and pressure groups. . . . This enterprise needs to have a broad technical and . . . economic autonomy" (Ibáñez Santa María 1984, 24). In their argument they combined their own professional interests with nationalistic aspirations, when they indicated that the top managers of this enterprise had to be engineers, and all the personnel had to be Chilean.

---

2. The first document appeared in two installments in *Anales* (December 1935 and January 1936) and was later published in book form under the same title (Santiago: Nascimento, 1936). The second document was published in SOFOFA's journal *Industria* (December 1938) and later in *Anales* (June 1939). Ibáñez Santa María (1984, 17–34) reproduces some key parts of both documents, to which I refer here.

The attitude adopted by the entrepreneurial sectors toward the engineers who filled top positions in the state apparatus was markedly ambiguous. As we shall see later, the private entrepreneurs recognized the high professional standards of this group of public technocrats.[3] However, their main goal was to intervene directly in the state policies, and not through the "intermediation" of these technicians. Even when the technocrats implemented policies that entirely coincided with the wishes of the entrepreneurs, the latter could not overcome a certain distrust of the former because of their unpredictability and independence. On the other hand, however, the entrepreneurial organizations were well aware of the fact that the presence of this group of technicians in the state decision-making machinery constituted a guarantee to prevent key state institutions from coming under the command of "thirsty politicians" who could use them for electoral and clientelistic purposes. Especially after the anarchic years 1931–32, most of the private entrepreneurs were disposed to accept this "technocratic buffer."

In order to prevent the "infiltration" of political *caciques* into state institutions, entrepreneurial organizations such as SOFOFA and SNA closely monitored the appointment policies followed by the government, stressing time and again the need to appoint people with technical expertise in top positions. Guillermo Subercaseaux, for example, in an article in September 1932 issue of *Boletín* (the official publication of SOFOFA at the time), reminded the government that the persons in leadership positions in state and semi-state organizations had to be chosen according to meritocratic principles, not partisan criteria. In this way, Subercaseaux demanded that the government appoint people "in executive functions according to efficiency . . . , knowledge and working ethos, without any distinction of political orientation" (quoted in Ibáñez Santa María 1984, 39).

In retrospect, it can be concluded that during Alessandri's second administration, the efforts initiated during the 1920s toward the modernization of the

---

3. Public technocrats are those technocrats who work in state enterprises and governmental agencies. From the late 1920s on, Chilean public technocrats gradually adopted a quite distinctive vision of their own role in society and how to achieve economic growth and development in the country. In contrast with technocrats operating in the private sector, public technocrats firmly believed in state planning and state interventionism. They also defended nationalist positions about control of national resources and maintained a safe distance from private entrepreneurial groups and their organizations. See, for instance, *Anales,* the official journal of the Instituto de Ingenieros de Chile, in which many contributions by public technocrats since the late 1920s express this pro-state, nationalistic vision.

public administration and the expansion of the state role in the economic and social development of the country became markedly strengthened. Besides, the technical and professional strata continued to expand their power and influence within the state institutions. As a form of legitimation, they developed a technocratic discourse in which the state's relative autonomy (and hence their own) was strongly defended.

The Popular Front and the Entrepreneurial State

Following the electoral victory of Pedro Aguirre Cerda and his Popular Front coalition in 1938, the industrialization process received a systematic and decisive impulse from the state. The objective to industrialize the country was unanimously supported by the center and left-wing forces that formed the government coalition. They also agreed that as a result of the relative weakness of the local industrial class, the industrialization process had to be led by the state, which had to acquire a clear entrepreneurial function.

The CORFO Project

Beginning with the Popular Front, state efforts to enlarge the industrial base of the country were channeled through the Chilean Development Corporation (CORFO). From its creation in 1939 until the military coup in 1973, CORFO constituted the organizing pivot of the industrialization process and the main planning agency for the country's economic development. As Oscar Muñoz and Ana María Arriagada point out,

> [CORFO] acquired functions that no other state agency had before, such as the formulation of a national production plan and the consequent allocation of investments. Through this institution the state came to play a coordinating role in the interests of the various productive sectors and an openly entrepreneurial function through being allowed to make direct public investments in activities other than the traditional infrastructure works. (1977, 27)

It has to be stressed that both the CORFO project and the general economic policy of the Popular Front did not stem from the social and political forces

that brought Aguirre Cerda to power. Although the coalition parties supported the idea of state industrialization, they did not have it perfectly clear
in their collective mind what kind of economic policy they should apply after
the possible victory of the Popular Front coalition. As Pinto has indicated,
"The true history of the pro-developmental initiatives and the creation of
CORFO indicates that its origin came not from the Popular Front political
leadership, but from a group of state officials and technocrats, most of them
engineers, who formulated and put it into motion. For this purpose, they
utilized the personal support they obtained from some key politicians, among
them, President Aguirre Cerda himself" (1973b, 315).[4] However, it would be
mistaken to conclude from Pinto's words that CORFO was simply the result
of resolute action by a technocratic group, determined to attain a larger share
of decision-making power within the state apparatus. The creation of CORFO
is rather the culmination of the growing process of state intervention in the
Chilean economy that, as mentioned before, was initiated in the early 1920s.[5]
Together with this, the CORFO project, as well as the rest of the Popular
Front's initiatives to foster industrialization, was strengthened by several
international factors. For instance, the outbreak of World War II favored the
initiatives directed toward the achievement of a larger degree of autonomy
for the Chilean economy. Besides, the Soviet experience in state planning
became a clear example to follow for the left-wing parties in the Popular
Front coalition (a political strategy that, in turn, was proposed by the Third
International).[6] One also has to mention the example of Roosevelt's economic

4. In a later work Pinto describes the role of these engineers in the following terms: "A
decisive element in the creation of CORFO was the rationalizing and catalyzing influence of a
group of technicians. . . . It should have been very difficult to materialize and to consolidate the
CORFO project without that human, and in a certain sense historical, ingredient" ([1958] 1985,
24).

5. It is interesting to see that the *continuity* we already observed from the Ibáñez regime
until the Popular Front government (in relation to their state policies) was also valid for the
technicians who filled key positions at the Aguirre Cerda administration. As Cavarozzi indicates,
"The majority of the engineers who filled CORFO's higher positions were neither owners of, nor
had been permanently employed by private (industrial or otherwise) business firms. CORFO's
founders were a handful of professionals—five or six engineers with a background of service in
public organizations during the late 1920s and 1930s. . . . Many of the top officials and founding
fathers of CORFO were members of the so-called 'Ramírez clique,' a kind of informal group of
technically oriented young public functionaries that pushed for administrative reform during the
1920s. Ramírez, a former Minister during Ibáñez' administration (and a Radical), was the main
supporter and implementer of the important structural changes which most of Chile's governmental agencies underwent between 1925 and 1930" (1975, 128–29).

6. With respect to the Socialist Party, Drake indicates that it played a key role in the consolidation of CORFO. As he points out, "The Socialists were among the major architects and boosters

policies in the United States and, in particular, his huge energy project in the Tennessee Valley (Pinto [1958] 1985, 23).[7] All these factors were compounded by a totally unexpected event that rapidly accelerated the decision to create this corporation: the devastating earthquake of January 1939, which hit the southern region of the country a few months after Aguirre Cerda took power. The huge wave of destruction caused by this natural disaster demanded a rapid response from the state to provide aid for the population and to begin the reconstruction of the affected areas. The idea defended by the government was in fact to combine the reconstruction efforts with the attempt to transform the productive structure of the country.

The Politics of Compromise

The passing by Congress of the bill creating CORFO was preceded by a short but intensive period of debates and negotiations between the parties involved. The discussions of the bill showed not only the different interests and fears of the main participating actors (government, parliamentary opposition, and entrepreneurial sectors) but also the very nature of the "politics of compromise" that characterized the Chilean political system in 1938–64. It is not my intention here to analyze the details of this discussion.[8] I shall only mention some elements that may facilitate the understanding of the way public technocrats did finally strengthen their positions within CORFO.

During the discussion of this bill in the Chamber of Deputies, the opposi-

---

of CORFO. . . . At least in the early years, however, the PS was deeply involved in giving the agency its developmentalist orientation. . . . The Socialists and their allies did not make CORFO a vehicle for their earlier economic programs. . . . They were soon engrossed in pragmatic, day-to-day government administration. Consequently, the PS leadership became more enamoured of technocratic projects and problem solving than of ideological conquests. In somewhat populist fashion, they concentrated on immediate solutions rather than on long-run strides toward socialism" (1978, 19–20).

7. Another important factor that at least indirectly reflects foreign influences is the creation in 1937 of the Faculty of Economics of the Universidad de Chile, which immediately became the main source of diffusion of the new economic vision as posited by John M. Keynes and his *General Theory*, which had been published just a year before. The academic staff of this new faculty did especially propagate his ideas about the need for a more active role of the state in the economy (F. Silva 1974, 838). It was also expected that the Faculty of Economics had to function as a kind of "training camp" for future state technocrats. As Muñoz indicated, "One of Pedro Aguirre Cerda's major preoccupations—before he became presidential candidate—was the creation of the Faculty of Economics of the Universidad de Chile in order to promote the formation of specialists who could contribute to the running of the state" (1986, 230).

8. For an in-depth analysis of the discussion around the creation of CORFO, including the parliamentary debate, see Muñoz and Arriagada 1977, 24–39.

tion initially managed to introduce some amendments to prevent CORFO from being used by the executive to promote political activism within this public agency. CORFO should be overseen by the General Comptroller of the Republic, and it had to keep Parliament permanently informed about its activities. Moreover, the technical nature of the different departments of CORFO was stressed, while the influence of the president was reduced. During the discussion in the Senate, the right-wing parties attempted to put CORFO completely under the authority of Congress. The opposition proposed that CORFO should present each development project to Congress for approval, with the intention of making it difficult for the government to get control of huge financial resources through CORFO.[9] In the end, however, the opposition parties were not able to reduce the autonomy of CORFO, partly because Aguirre Cerda made use of his presidential veto to reject many of the amendments they proposed. In this manner, the autonomy of CORFO from the government as well as from Parliament and the entrepreneurial groups was officially approved (Ibáñez Santa María 1984, 52).

There is sufficient evidence indicating that the final readiness of the opposition to accept the CORFO project had been the result of a back-door agreement between both parties on the question of peasant unionization. The Popular Front victory had led to a wave of social agitation in the countryside, in which left-wing parties actively participated. So during the discussion of the CORFO project in the Parliament the right-wing parties stressed the theme of confidence, arguing that without achieving this they could not support the government. They indicated that the entrepreneurial sectors could not have confidence in the government when it with one hand it fostered industrialization and, with the other, radicalized the peasantry. In this manner, both the right-wing political parties and the entrepreneurial organizations urged the government to reestablish "social calm" in the countryside.[10] With this, the negotiation between the government and the opposition about the CORFO project took concrete shape: the right-wing and the entrepreneurs associations would accept the state plans (through CORFO) of huge intervention at

9. This is why the question of CORFO's autonomy from Parliament was so important; autonomy meant obtaining total freedom to use financial resources provided by the state for the implementation of development projects.

10. Loveman (1996 and 1992) has thoroughly studied this period of political agitation in the countryside. See also Kay and Silva 1992.

the industrial field, if the government prohibited rural unionization and the penetration of urban-based left-wing parties in the countryside.[11]

By creating CORFO and expanding other state agencies dealing with industrial activities, the Popular Front government also aimed to attain some political gains. As Loveman puts it,

> The new state institutions . . . create new employment opportunities for a growing group of salaried professionals and white-collar workers. The political implications of thousands of attractive government jobs were not lost on the political parties in their efforts to capture legislative majorities or to form government coalitions. . . . These developments provided the basis for the consolidation of a bureaucratic "middle class" associated with an interventionist state. It would mean that a large proportion of the middle groups in Chilean society would support a further expansion of public activity in welfare, health care, education, and government-owned enterprises. (1979, 259–60)

Corporatism and Technicity

Both their fears about the possible political use of CORFO by the government and their desire to have a direct say in its administration led the entrepreneurial organizations to demand representation on CORFO's board of directors. SOFOFA and the Corporation of Production and Commerce (COPROCO) attempted to expand their direct influence even beyond CORFO by reviving the old proposal to establish an effective national economic council. This council would be expected to have a consultative status at the highest level, and its membership would include individuals from both the public and the private sectors (Muñoz and Arriagada 1977, 16–17). In the end, CORFO did get a decision-making structure that possessed a clear corporatist style. Thus, the board of directors comprised representatives from the government and entrepreneurial organizations, as well as one single representative of the Chilean Workers Confederation (Loveman 1979, 277). In practice, however, it soon became clear that it was the technocratic group that had in fact the final say

---

11. This thesis about the existence of a modus vivendi between the Radical government and the Right (which lasted until the early 1960s) is supported by several scholars (see, for example, Mamalakis 1965, 17; Kaufman 1972, 26; and Loveman 1979, 280).

in CORFO's internal decision-making. Marcelo Cavarozzi, who in the late 1960s carried out a survey among a large group of entrepreneurs, indicates that most of the businessmen who received any form of support from CORFO "coincided in asserting that the central factor in deciding the fate of every project was the opinion of the technical functionaries at the department and section levels. They did not know of any case of a project supported by the technicians that had been rejected by the board of directors" (1975, 124). Cavarozzi correctly identifies the technical expertise possessed by these technocrats (who controlled the most valuable resource, namely, technical information) as one of the main factors accounting for their predominance over CORFO's board of directors and its executive vice president during the Radical years. Even the government representatives "were seldom able to challenge the choices made, or for that matter, the criteria used, by the technicians" (124). The same was true of entrepreneurs, who by that time had little access to technical information and general statistics not directly related to the productive processes of their own enterprises. Because of this, they were often technically unable to verify the technocrats' opinions.

The power of the CORFO technocrats, however, was primarily the result of the more or less explicit decision of the different Radical administrations not to impose policy criteria on CORFO top officials. As Cavarozzi points out, "The directives of the executive, which were usually transmitted via CORFO's executive vice president, were always quite general and imprecise. . . . Aguirre Cerda and Roberto Wachholtz, his minister of finance, agreed to leave CORFO functionaries to decide on policies, and to free them from 'political' pressures (their own at least)" (125). This seems to be confirmed by the fact that SOFOFA never denounced any possible political pressure on the Development Corporation by the government. This has led Cavarozzi to a categorical conclusion: "CORFO decisions on individual projects and sectorial plans were not strongly influenced by Parliament, by cabinet members, or even by the president of the Republic" (407).

The government defended and justified CORFO's broad autonomy and the need to keep its independence from Parliament, by using technical arguments. As Muñoz and Arriagada put it,

> The elaboration and realization of developmental plans by technicians and experts—on the basis of exclusively scientific considerations, with full autonomy and without any political interference—constituted

for the government one of the main guarantees that CORFO would operate successfully and the government would achieve its general developmental goals. For this reason, special attention was paid to the professional credentials of those who had to lead the planning activities. (1977, 28)

Technocrats and the "Ideology of Industrialization"

The technocratic group within CORFO elaborated a true *ideology of industrialization,* and became in fact the organic intellectuals of the state-led industrialization project. The ideological cohesion of this group was strengthened by a common professional training and by the assimilation of a sort of "culture of development" by which they reserved for themselves the role of formulating and implementing the industrialization policies (Muñoz and Arriagada 1977, 52). This technocratic group possessed a strong esprit de corps. As Cavarozzi indicates, "The founders [of CORFO] were able to build a small but cohesive cadre of capable young technicians who were highly committed to the organization's goals, filled the middle levels of CORFO's executive hierarchy, and later provided the replacements for the top positions" (1975, 129). This full identification by these technocrats with CORFO as an institution was accompanied by a pervasive and coherent organizational ideology.

The CORFO ideology grew around the conviction that industrial development was the only way Chile could overcome the crisis and stagnation that had affected its economy since 1930. This ideology was not developed only for "internal use," but especially to channel external support from several social sectors to this institution.[12] The CORFO ideology also provided the needed "linkage" between "the individual objectives of the members of CORFO's technical elite—such as an adequate remuneration, possibilities of upward mobility, or a successful professional career—with their 'service vocation'"

---

12. Particularly important was the consolidation of the support coming from the bureaucratic sector. As Drake indicates, "The most significant segment of the middle strata for the Front parties was the bureaucracy. Mainly as a result of state expansion in response to the Depression, the percentage of the active population in public administration doubled from 1930 to 1940, with the most rapid increase under the Front. . . . Bureaucrats often identified with middle class 'socialism,' with the Radicals and Socialists, because of a belief in incremental reforms through state expansion. . . . Bureaucratization of the Popular Front was an integral part of institutionalization. Bureaucrats poured into the Front parties after the 1938 victory. In turn, members of those parties inundated the bureaucracy" (1978, 226).

(Cavarozzi 1975, 132). Cavarozzi found from his interviews with former CORFO technocrats that the majority of those working at CORFO in the 1940s until the mid-1950s stressed their "sense of mission." This sense of mission made them feel different from (other) public employees: "They felt that, contrary to the vast majority of public functionaries, they were serving the country" (132n). Their commitment to CORFO was also the result of their pragmatic and rational analysis of CORFO's great potential, through which they could channel their professional "need to achieve" (McClelland 1961). They had the conviction that CORFO "was the only public agency *through which* they could contribute to 'the production of a *worthwhile result*'" (Cavarozzi 1975, 132; emphasis mine).

The elaboration of an ideology of industrialization and the technocrats' great capacity to implement their initiatives went beyond the entrepreneurs' own expectations (Muñoz and Arriagada 1977, 43). The CORFO technocrats filled a remarkable vanguard position, setting the pattern and pace of industrialization with more imagination and audacity than the private industrialists. Cavarozzi has stressed their strategic importance in the following terms:

> The "catalyzing" function performed by a small group of *técnicos,* professionals with technical background and orientation, who filled strategic positions in different public agencies, particularly in CORFO. . . . These *técnicos,* and particularly the CORFO engineers . . . were actually more strongly convinced of the necessity and convenience of industrial development than Chile's industrialists themselves. They not only had the last say about the use to which a large proportion of the resources that were poured into the industrial sector were put to, but they also seem to have provided the "industrializing ethos" that the industrial bourgeoisie was clearly unable to articulate by itself. (1975, 114–15)

The ideology of industrialization was structured around a national energy plan, based on the "plan for the country's electrification," which was approved in 1939 and became the basis for CORFO's initial activities. This was the same electrification plan of 1935 mentioned before, which had not been implemented yet, mainly because of the strong opposition of the Compañía Chilena de Electricidad, which in the mid-1930s was still in foreign hands (Pinto [1958] 1985, 24).

CORFO became not only the main instrument by which the public technocrats did operate but also their main "training center" and reproduction site. As Muñoz stated, "Through this elite—and there is no denying they were that—of technicians, [CORFO] was able to formulate and materialize the specific tasks to achieve the industrialization of the country. The implementation of these tasks became a practical school for the training and the achievement of expertise for many generations of highly qualified professionals, becoming a model for other countries" (1982, 207).

Technocrats as Political Brokers

Public technocracy also played a key role in the mediation between the political class in control of the state apparatus and the entrepreneurial interests by providing guarantees and confidence to both sectors. The public technocrats, for instance, succeeded in resolving the initial differences over several aspects of the CORFO project that emerged between the government, the right-wing opposition, and the business interests.

The Popular Front parties as well as public technocrats and entrepreneurs agreed on the need to protect the national industry by building up tariff walls. However, when the discussion addressed the question of state intervention in other fields, differences rapidly arose. The entrepreneurs' attitude toward state intervention remained quite ambivalent and contradictory. They constantly complained about a lack of state support for Chilean industry, while at the same time they warned about the dangers of an inappropriate degree of state intervention (Cavarozzi 1975, 133–34). This ambiguity was the result of the twofold nature of the entrepreneurs' expectations from the state: a strong state presence in some fields, and its total absence in others. What they actually wanted was the building up of external protectionism on the one hand and a free internal market on the other. This idea was particularly unpopular among the left-wing parties in the Popular Front coalition. They only saw in this formula an increase in the profits of the private entrepreneurs, at the cost of the working population who would have to pay higher prices for industrial products.

As far as scope of CORFO was concerned, the entrepreneurial organizations permanently argued that this state corporation should only be a credit agency providing support for private initiative. From the very onset they rejected the idea of state-owned enterprises, and even that of joint ventures between the state and the private sector. They argued that these new entrepreneurial activities of the state and the creation of enterprises with a mixed state-private structure would lead to "unfair competition," for the state was in a much better position than the private sector to get loans and new technologies from abroad.[13]

In the end, this and other latent conflicts between the executive and the business organizations were defused by the state technocrats. Their strategic position to mediate between both actors was partly made possible because of their important positions within the state decision-making bodies, but also as a consequence of their social connections with the entrepreneurs with whom they shared similar ideological orientations. So Pinto is right when he states that "the majority of the key figures who decided on development policies, and who managed the institutions created by the state, had right-wing backgrounds" (1973b, 315). Cavarozzi also stresses the relevance of the ideological factor when he points out that "the technicians and professionals who filled the top echelons of public autonomous organizations largely shared the ideological and political orientations of the dominant bourgeoisie, and of its different fractions" (1975, 352–53).

Despite their similar social origins, however, it would be erroneous to conclude that the public technocrats were totally subordinated to the entrepreneurial sector. To begin with, these public technocrats were moved by a professional project of their own, namely, to conciliate the objective of expanding the tasks and institutions of the state with the improvement of their own working conditions and the enlargement of their professional influence.[14] Moreover, the relation between state technocrats and private entrepreneurs was not free of tensions, which were mainly originated by the industrialists' interest in short-term profits, and the technocrats' goal to secure a solid overall industrial development in the long term. The existence of these tensions did not produce an open conflict because eventually COR-

13. This criticism persisted after the creation of CORFO. Múñoz and Arriagada (1977, 41–42) reproduce an extract of an article of 1942 in *Industria,* the SOFOFA journal, in which Jorge Alessandri strongly criticized the formation of mixed enterprises because, in his view, this would be to the detriment of private capital.

14. For instance, the president of the Institute of Engineers of the Universidad de Chile, Raúl Simón, expressed in a letter in 1939 with great joy that the electrification of the country "should open new working fields for engineers, technicians, and electricians" (quoted in Ibáñez Santa María 1984, 31).

FO's objectives coincided with those of the industrialist class (Cavarozzi 1975, 133). This has led Cavarozzi to conclude that the CORFO technocracy "represented the interests of the industrial bourgeoisie without becoming the party of the industrial bourgeoisie. This relative autonomy of the technopolitical specialists was . . . one of the factors that most decisively contributed to the success of Chile's industrialization" (1975, 402). The technocrats' nationalism and their ideas on economic independence and industrial protection were in this way functional to the interests of the private entrepreneurs (Pinto [1958] 1985, 13).

In the end, the CORFO technocrats succeeded in consolidating the establishment of a mixed economy in the country in which both state and private initiatives obtained the CORFO's active support. Moreover, planning was presented as a leading method to organize the further industrial development of the country. The existence of state enterprises was presented as a complement to the private industrial initiative, which required a decisive support from the state.

The Technocrats' Prestige

The entrepreneurial interests adopted the same tactic toward Aguirre Cerda as they had used before with Alessandri and Ibáñez. At first, they attempted to directly influence the industrial policies of the state by trying to place their own representatives in the executive bodies of key public institutions. When this failed, they concentrated their attention on monitoring the selection of public officials appointed to technico-administrative positions. As already mentioned, the Aguirre Cerda government also supported the idea of making CORFO a fully technical agency, in which the executive positions had to be filled by technical personnel with outstanding professional records.

When one looks at the list of CORFO executives during its initial period, one can confirm the conscious decision of the government to leave the managing of these institutions to technocrats. For instance, the executive vice presidency[15] and the post of general manager were in hands of Guillermo del Pedregal and Desiderio García respectively, both engineers who were brought into the public administration by Pablo Ramírez in 1927. Moreover, four of

15. This was the leading figure of CORFO. The minister of economic affairs became automatically the corporation's executive president, but he left the actual managing of the institution to the executive vice president.

the seven CORFO's departments were run by engineers with long administrative careers (Ibáñez Santa María 1984, 54–55).

The CORFO technocrats were widely respected: on several occasions SOFOFA expressed its full satisfaction with the technical team in charge of CORFO.[16] Both the public officials and industrialists interviewed by Cavarozzi were unanimous in their praise of the high quality of CORFO's technical personnel during the 1940s and early 1950s. As he puts it: "They agreed in pointing out that the institution had been able to attract technicians that largely surpassed the levels of professional expertise and performance of their colleagues in other public, and even in business, organizations" (1975, 129). Unlike other public departments, where political patronage and the spoils system were the main mechanisms of recruitment, CORFO executives enjoyed total autonomy to freely contract their personnel, succeeding in attracting the best technicians because of the high salaries paid by CORFO, which were substantially higher than in the rest of the public administration. As Cavarozzi indicates, CORFO was often even able "to outbid the private corporations in competing for the most capable (and scarce) professionals available in the market" (1975, 130). Moreover, the recruitment of new technicians was facilitated by the fact that most of CORFO top technocrats also taught at the Institute of Engineers of the Universidad de Chile, and thus had the chance and the time to choose the future CORFO technicians from among their brightest students.

Changing Economic and Political Scenarios

The industrialization strategy followed by CORFO led to a clear improvement in the country's industrial activity. From 1940 until the mid-1950s, industrial production increased at an annual average rate of 7.5 percent. Besides, the industrial sector's share of the Gross Domestic Product (GDP) grew from 13.4 percent in 1940 to almost 23 percent in 1955, which made it become the most important productive sector of Chilean economy. Although the growth rate of the industrial sector dropped in the following years to an annual average of 4.7 percent, its GDP share reached the 25 percent mark in 1970 (Vergara 1982, 39). This notwithstanding, the industrialization process confronted serious

16. Cavarozzi reproduces several passages from articles in the journal *Industria* in which SOFOFA officials praise CORFO technicians (1975, 127–29).

difficulties. The levels of consumer goods imports were reduced, and local demand was satisfactorily met by the national industry. However, the industrializing efforts led to a growing increase in the import of fuel and capital goods. This affected negatively the balance of payments, which, with the exception of the years of World War II and the Korean War, had shown a structural deficit (CORFO 1965, 448–50).

At the political level, profound disagreement arose within the Popular Front as a result of tactical and ideological differences among the coalition parties. These disagreements became more pronounced as the Radical Party, the central force in the alliance, began to adopt clearly right-wing positions. Because of this, the left-wing parties and the labor organizations became increasingly alienated from this political alliance. On the other hand, the right-wing parties had no confidence in the Radical government's ability to contain the pressures and demands of the leftist political parties and the workers' organizations. Thus, the Popular Front period (1938–52) was characterized by a continuous zigzagging between reformist and conservative positions (and even repressive positions, as was the case during the period 1948–52), leading eventually to the discredit of not only the Radical Party, but the party system as a whole.

This general disillusionment with party politics made possible the successful political comeback of the aged Carlos Ibáñez, who won the presidential elections of 1952 without the electoral support of any major political party. As Timothy R. Scully put it, "Ibáñez and his antiparty political style emerged at a moment when the Chilean party system was characterized by an entrenched and defensive right, a discredited and isolated center, and an increasingly radicalized left. . . . The 1952 candidacy of Ibáñez . . . was the expression of an open and generalized sense of disenchantment with party politics. Ibáñez contrasted his managerial style with the inefficiency and corruption of traditional parties" (1992, 125–26). He adopted the broom as the symbol of his campaign, promising to sweep away inefficiency, corruption, and narrow party interests from government. However, the economic situation abruptly deteriorated after 1952 as result of a severe contraction in foreign trade and a strong increase in the rate of inflation in the years 1954–55. This situation forced Ibáñez to concentrate his efforts on the solution of the economic difficulties instead of his ambitious plan of institutional and administrative reforms.

Following the recommendations of the American Klein-Saks Mission, in

1956 Ibáñez adopted a monetarist anti-inflationary program, which did not produce the expected results. Moreover, these measures were extremely unpopular among the population. The program was also criticized by the entrepreneurs, who saw their short-term interests threatened as a result of several measures adopted such as the introduction of a progressive tax reform.[17] The program's lack of success and its strong rejection by the population, forced Ibáñez to abandon this stabilization scheme (see Sunkel 1963 and Sierra 1970). At the end of his administration, Ibáñez, having aliented those who had brought him to power, was opposed by almost everyone.

Alessandri and the Managerial Revolution

The traditional political parties did not capitalize on the fast political erosion affecting Ibáñez at the end of his government because they were still recovering from the "*Ibáñista* earthquake," as his influential antipolitical discourse was called. In this manner, his administration succeeded in strengthening an antiparty climate within the Chilean electorate. In this scenario, Jorge Alessandri Rodríguez, an engineer, an industrialist, and a son of Arturo Alessandri, the "Lion of Tarapacá," ran as an independent and was elected president of the Republic in 1958. The Alessandrista project constituted the first attempt based on the entrepreneurial state to change the pattern of development followed by the country since 1938.[18] Alessandri's main goal was to place private entrepreneurs center-stage of the development process.

The support given by CORFO for more than two decades to private entrepreneurs had markedly increased their relative strength within the Chilean economy and society, resulting in the constitution of powerful industrial and financial conglomerates, the so-called *grupos económicos* (see Lagos 1961). This strengthening of the private sector had important repercussions in the relationship between the state, private entrepreneurs, and political parties. As Pinto points out, these new industrial interests began more and more to com-

17. One has to add to this the entrepreneurial sector's marked distrust of Ibáñez's associates with technocratic backgrounds. As Cavarozzi indicates, "Ibáñez's entourage, composed of a group of politicians who did not come from 'responsible' parties, and a heterogeneous combination of technocrats, aroused nothing but a strong suspicion among the bourgeoisie" (1975, 332).

18. The second and definitive attempt would be carried out by the neoliberal technocracy under Pinochet (see E. Silva, 1991).

municate directly with the state and public opinion, thus ignoring the traditional intermediary role played by the political Right ([1958] 1985, 30).

Alessandri adopted a marked technocratic discourse as his government philosophy, which was organized around the binary opposition of *técnica* and *política*, in which "*política* was seen as the dark world of corporatistic interests, whereas *técnica* was presented as the world of rational decision-making" (T. Moulian 1982, 24). His government stimulated the expansion of free enterprise and reduced state interference in the economy. For this purpose a series of measures was adopted to create a favorable investment climate for both local entrepreneurs, and foreign capital. Together with this, the government attempted to reduce spending and the growth of the public sector. As Angell points out, "Alessandri's stance as an independent also represented his genuine belief in the virtues of technocracy over party politics. He hoped in government to avoid the political compromises and concessions of previous administrations" (1993, 142). Talking about his cabinet, Alessandri described it in the following way: "The cabinet possesses no political character and does not represent any interest group whatsoever. Its administrative and technical physiognomy makes it particularly suitable to provide the support I need to organize a national government. The cabinet's members are independent men who have achieved their positions due to their particular personal qualities by which they can efficiently exercise the tasks ahead" (quoted in Cardemil 1997, 29). Despite the technocratic orientation of his government, however, he had to confront the state technocracy in an attempt to reduce the role of the state in the economy and to expand the role of the business community and the market.

The Technostructure Under Attack

Alessandri was aware of the fact that his plans to reduce state interference in the Chilean economy and society would meet with strong opposition from the public technostructure and the state bureaucracy, in defense of their interests and influence within the state apparatus. Already during Ibáñez's second administration the state elite had been attacked by the government. However, during his campaign against corruption and inefficiency in the public sector, Ibáñez had been mainly interested in eliminating those officials with clearly political credentials. The career professionals and technicians, on the other hand, were not touched by Ibáñez's broom.

The Alessandri government, in turn, attempted not only to put an end to corruption and inefficiency in the state apparatus but also to eliminate the technocracy entrenched in CORFO, the Banco Central, and other public agencies. Alessandri chose this target because he saw in it, as Cavarozzi put it, "the most important gear of the interventionist machinery mounted during the 1940s" (1975, 357). Indeed, most of the figures who in the previous decades had helped to establish the entrepreneurial state, and who still commanded strategic positions in the state apparatus, could be found in those agencies. Alessandri finally managed to eliminate the top figures of the public technocracy by replacing them with well-known representatives of the new entrepreneurial generation, who had emerged in the 1940s, and with technocrats associated with the private sector (Stallings 1978, 86). Because of its marked entrepreneurial nature[19] Alessandri's administration become known as "the managerial revolution" (*la revolución de los gerentes*).[20]

However, despite his attempt to reduce state intervention, Alessandri did not privatize the enterprises that were already under CORFO control. But from that moment on, CORFO restricted itself to providing credit for private enterprises, which had always been one of the entrepreneurs' main demands.[21] Alessandri's attack on the state technocracy started at the Banco Central by replacing the president of this key monetary institution with an associate of the minister of economic affairs, Pablo Vergara. With this move Alessandri succeeded in subordinating the Banco Central to his minister and his economic policies. The same occurred with CORFO, where Alessandri appointed businessman Pierre Lehmann as its new executive vice president. In contrast with all the functionaries who had occupied that position in the past, Lehmann made it very clear that he, and not the technocracy, was in charge of CORFO. He also dismissed the general manager, Luis Adduard, the heads of departments, and the group of engineers reporting to Adduard (Cavarozzi 1975, 358).

19. One needs only to mention that at the moment of his presidential victory, Alessandri was the acting president of the Confederation of Production and Commerce (COPROCO), one of Chile's main entrepreneurial organizations.

20. Alessandri's government obtained this nickname after James Burnham's book *The Managerial Revolution* (1941). In this popular scientific book Burnham analyzed technocratic ascendancy in the world. His ideas became known in Latin America following the translation of this book into Spanish in 1943 (Burnham 1943).

21. It must to be said that although Alessandri attempted to put an end to the entrepreneurial and planning role of the state, he did not break (as Pinochet later did) away from the state's traditional economic responsibilities in order to care for public investments.

The same changeover of personnel took place in all the state agencies, with the object of eliminating the influence of political parties, especially the Radical Party, within the public administration. Minister Vergara, the brain behind this "cleaning operation," repeatedly identified the "excessive influence" of party political interests within the public administration as one of the roots of Chile's evils. This wave of massive replacements in the state institutions put an end to the traditional relative autonomy that the mesocratic sectors had possessed within the state apparatus since the 1920s. It was also for the first time since the 1920s that members of the dominant social sectors took *direct* control of strategic positions within the state apparatus.

> What had constituted an exception during the previous twenty years of the country's political history—namely, the occupation of key governmental positions at the level of ministries, undersecretariats, and departments, by members of the large propertied classes—became a rule since Alessandri's assumption. The large cohorts of party politicians, who, albeit of different party origins, had almost monopolized the top echelons of the state apparatus since the 1920s, were partially replaced by entrepreneurs, and by former officials of the entrepreneurial associations. (Cavarozzi 1975, 361)

This penetration of the state apparatus by members of the dominant social sectors and their corporative representatives led toward what Cavarozzi called the "relative de-autonomization of the state" (1975, 395). This radical change in the social nature of the group in charge of the state apparatus contributed to the further polarization of the political process. In fact, it eliminated the moderating role played *de facto* by the middle-class technocratic strata by now equalizing the social nature of the leading figures of the administrative sector with that of the economically dominant class.

One of the most interesting aspects about the elimination of the public technocracy from the state apparatus was the attitude adopted by entrepreneurial organizations in general, and SOFOFA in particular. One has to recall that in the past, SOFOFA had always made public its desire to keep the decision-making bodies of state and para-state agencies under the management of technicians and professionals, as a means to avoid the politicization of these institutions. For this purpose, SOFOFA and the other business organizations praised the high professional standards of state technocracy in general and CORFO engineers in particular. After 1958, however, not a single business organization criticized the massive dismissal of those state technocrats. They indeed tacitly approved Alessandri's decision to get them out of the state apparatus and to replace them with a new group of liberal technocrats coming from the private sector. As Cavarozzi concludes, since Alessandri's electoral victory, "not one more candle would be burned in the altar of '*técnicos* are better than *políticos*'" (1975, 360).

While Alessandri seemed to have been successful at removing the traditional political class and the traditional public technocracy from the centers of power, his austere economic policy was strongly rejected by the unions, left-wing political parties, and in the end, even the industrialists themselves. Like his predecessor, in 1961 Alessandri was finally forced to abandon his technocratic strategy halfway through his presidential term and to readopt a traditional type of government (Scully 1992, 139). So in the economic field, the efforts to free the market from state controls and regulations were interrupted, while he reintroduced the price control system that he had eliminated before. At the political level, Alessandri was forced to search for support among Radicals, Liberals, and Conservatives, in order to strengthen the government's weak political base. This move led to a rapid "politicization" of the government and its economic policies, which in turn, produced a growing alienation of the entrepreneurs from the government. By 1962 almost all of the entrepreneurs who had closely collaborated with Alessandri abandoned their positions in the government and state institutions, and were mainly replaced by elements of Radical affiliation. This entrepreneurial disengagement, however, never became a complete formal rupture with the government. In that year, Liberals, Conservatives, and Radicals formed the Democratic Front, a parliamentary alliance, which in a tripartite fashion ran many strategic positions within the state institutions. From that moment until the 1973 military coup, the state technocracy never again recovered the privileged position within the state apparatus that it had held prior to "the managerial revolution."

The Schumpeterian Appeal

In return for changing policies that they objected to, Alessandri demanded in return that the entrepreneurs become more efficient and competitive so that in the near future he would be able to eliminate the protectionistic tariffs.

However, this appeal to the "Schumpeterian spirit" of Chilean entrepreneurs did not encounter the expected reception. In fact, those sectors had been born under the protection of the state and developed in a way that did not fit well with the technocratic and rationalist assumptions behind the Alessandrista project. Moulian refers to the attitude of Chilean entrepreneurs in the following terms: "State protection (import restrictions, high tariffs, tax exemptions, and credit advantages) made any attempt of modernization unnecessary because it artificially preserved the national industry. Because of this, the modernization as proposed by Alesssandri did not represent for the entrepreneurs an immediate class interest, being rather a project which could affect their position in the short term" (1983, 128).[22] The failure of Alessandri's technocratic experiment made it clear that the dominant groups in general and the industrialists in particular were unable or unwilling to become the leading force of Chile's economic and social development. The entrepreneurs' attitude toward Alessandri's challenge had also cultural undertones. Among industrialists the *latifundista* mentality, more centered on family lineage than on the achievement of personal commercial success, was still dominant, preventing the rise of the meritocratic, individualistic, and competitive attitude needed in industrial activities (T. Moulian 1983; Muñoz 1986). So although the landed oligarchy was not the dominant economic class any more, its cultural influence still marked the attitudes of the industrialists, who by origin and family ties were intimately related to the traditional rural elites (see Zeitlin 1988).

The lack of aggressiveness and clarity in the positions defended by conservative sectors during the period 1938–58 was also determined by the balance of power existing in the country, which was definitively against the right-wing parties. Because of this, they were forced to adopt a defensive position, and often had only the possibility to choose between the worst and the "lesser evil" for their interests, as they called the proposals presented by the dominant mesocratic coalition. However, until the late 1950s the right-wing sectors were still able to keep a significant capacity for political negotiation in Parliament, which permitted them to limit or at least to delay the policies defended by the center-leftist governmental coalitions (Petras 1969, 100).

What can be observed in Chile during the Alessandri government is the existence of a marked maladjustment between the existence of a moderniza-

---

22. As Petras put it, "The Chilean industrialists are not the free-wheeling, risk-taking adventurers of Schumpeterian fame: they prefer to take subsidies from the state and seek its protection exploiting a limited internal market" (1969, 66).

tion project that was explicitly intended to benefit Chilean industrialists and the scant support it received from the industrialists themselves. Alessandri's technocratic vanguardism did not take into consideration the historical background of the behavior of Chilean entrepreneurs. So this maladjustment occurred twice within a decade; first under Ibáñez's second administration—when he attempted to implement the corrective policies as recommended by the Klein-Saks mission—and then under Alessandri with his policies on market liberalization and economic rationalization. As Tomás Moulian has pointed out, one can find in this a clear cleavage between a governmental technocracy that supported a strategy of capitalist modernization, and the entrepreneurs' conduct, in which the general capitalist interest clashed with this group's immediate interests (1982, 27).

Following Alessandri's abandonment of his technocratic approach in 1961, the entrepreneurs finally recognized they had failed to develop a political alternative that would not require making concessions to the popular sectors and mediation by the technocratic group (Cavarozzi 1975, 390). From now on, the dominant social and economic sectors redeployed their traditional defensive positions. Cavarozzi sees SOFOFA's withdrawal of its support from the government in 1961 as a historical turning point in Chile's dominant groups, which began to look at democracy and popular participation as major threats to their strategic interests (1975, 398). In the end, the Alessandrista strategy of modernization not only failed to meet the expectations of the Chilean entrepreneurial class. It also failed to incorporate the demands of the middle and lower classes for more access to health care, education, and housing—demands that the Alessandri government was not willing or able to satisfy.

4

The Age of Global Planning

From the mid-1960s on, the Estado de Compromiso entered into its final phase, which was characterized by growing political and ideological polarization and the adoption by most political forces of an increasingly confrontational stance. The failed attempt of Alessandri Rodríguez to restructure the state along free market principles had left the state administration in a sort of disarray. The dismissal of leading senior engineers—who for decades had provided continuity and relative stability in the state administration—was a serious blow to the running of many state agencies. In addition, the liberal technocrats who occupied their positions had neither the experience nor the conviction to administer institutions aimed first and foremost at serving the entire nation not at generating private profit. As these technocrats became totally identified with the liberal agenda, they were not spared by the center and left-wing forces that strongly criticized the economic team and frustrated the full application of Alessandri's economic liberalization program. Already in the early 1960s the balance of power had definitively shifted in favor of the center-left forces. This announced the conclusion of the fragile equilibrium of power between the Center-Left and the Right, which had generated the Estado de Compromiso in the late 1930s. In other words, the very *raison d'etre* of this particular type of democratic arrangement had actually come to an end.

This chapter also shows that technocrats were often profoundly divided along paradigmatic lines. This has been the case in Chile since the late 1950s. The replacement of engineers by professional economists in top state functions has visibly reflected these divisions. Unlike engineers, who mostly operated on the basis of generally accepted technical and scientific tenets related to their professional training, the Chilean economists were instead markedly divided into two distinct and almost antagonistic schools of thought: structuralism and monetarism. While the structuralist economists defended an active role of the state in formulating developmental policies in order to transform Chilean society, the monetarist economists rejected state interventionism and praised the alleged benefits of a market economy to foster economic growth and prosperity. In the period 1964–73 the structuralist economists had a historic opportunity during the Frei Montalva and Allende governments to put their ideas into practice. The monetarist economists would have their turn, which arrived after the military coup of 1973.

In the Chilean case, the structuralist economists not only constituted the technical cadres for the formulation and application of the several reforms envisioned by Frei Montalva. As we will see, they also became the main ideologues of this reformist project, by providing a critical and convincing diagnosis about the most fundamental problems affecting Chilean society and by suggesting a course of action to face them.

In this chapter I also underline the president's attempts to insulate his economic team from external demands coming from their own political parties and from pressure groups in society. So for instance, the creation in the mid-1960s of a planning agency directly linked to the president represented a clear attempt by Frei Montalva to exert some control in the formulation of the reform program. He hoped by this to reduce to a minimum the interference of the Christian Democratic Party and to keep at a safe distance those *socialcristianos* who disagreed with the strong technocratic orientation adopted by his government. Allende, on his part, tried for a short time to insulate his economic team from pressures coming from the radical groups supporting his government, but he clearly failed in that attempt. Amid a situation characterized by a deep economic crisis and a virulent struggle for power between the government and the center-right opposition, almost no room was finally left for people with technocratic profiles. In contrast, intellectuals were appointed to powerful positions in governmental circles because it was they who provided guidelines about how to pave the way to socialism. I will return to this point in the final chapter.

In his analysis of the role of the state in the political history of Chile, historian Mario Góngora refers to the period 1964–73 as the "age of global planning" ([1981] 1988, 246). And indeed, one of the main characteristics of that decade was the strong globalizing nature of the projects for change in the socioeconomic, political, and institutional spheres promoted by the governments of Eduardo Frei (1964–70) and Salvador Allende (1970–73). While Frei promised no less than a "revolution in liberty," Allende announced the start of the so-called Chilean Road to Socialism. Both projects intended to bring about these profound changes within the framework of the existing democratic system.

Also characteristic of both projects for change how greatly both governments would emphasize economic and social planning. To a large extent, this was the result of the strong influence exerted by the Economic Commission for Latin America and the Caribbean (ECLA/CEPAL) on these governments and their sectorial policies. Ever since the late 1940s this great think tank had gathered together a select group of Latin American economists concerned with diagnosing the reasons for underdevelopment and possible solutions. Although Frei was influenced by the more moderate version of "Cepalian" structuralism, in the years of the Unidad Popular administration it was the more radical streams of "Cepalism" and "dependencia," that were to have the greater impact on the policies of the government. In both cases, it was economists with a strong technocratic orientation that offered the core ideas to articulate a discourse of "structural" reforms and change.

In the decade of global planning, we also witnessed the changing of the technocratic guard within the state apparatus. In fact, the technocratic hegemony within the different specialized state agencies (CORFO, Ministry of Finance, and so on), that senior engineers had exerted from the late 1920s until the late 1950s was about to come to an end. Beginning in the mid-1960s technocratic hegemony was taken over by a young generation of Christian Democratic and independent economists, who began to take up positions within the state agencies. It was they who were responsible for the planning of the new economic policies and the supervision of the implementation of a series of transformations, such as the application of the Agrarian Reform, the nationalization of large-scale copper mining, public housing policies, social organization of the urban poor, and so on.

The Oficina Nacional de Planificación (ODEPLAN) was created during the Frei administration and became the nerve center of governmental technocracy. Also within the cabinet an economic council (Consejo Económico) was formed, to which Frei allowed an ample margin for action in carrying out the economic and social plans of his government. Ultimately, the technical cadres became the new actors in the government of Frei, who provided a new incentive for the consolidation of technocratic action at government level. However, from 1967 on, economic trouble mounted, as did political and social unrest. Under these new circumstances, the technocratic policies became inconsistent and were soon being questioned by even the Christian Democrats. This originated a struggle between those in favor of a firm fiscal hand (the more traditional technocratic sectors) and those in favor of satisfying the immediate needs of the population, paying less attention to the financial and budgetary consequences thereof. In a way this was a foretaste of things to come with even more dramatic force under the government of Salvador Allende.

The victory of the Unidad Popular in 1970 marks the beginning of another cycle in Chilean political history, with the formulation of a project for the transition to socialism. The need to plan economic development, this time from a socialist perspective, was given top priority. For this purpose economists and financial experts were placed in important positions in the economy and in the administration of companies that were transferred to the public sector after having been nationalized or whose management had been taken over by the state. At CODELCO, the Copper Corporation, civil servant engineers and economists were to become the managers of the main national industry following the departure of the foreign managers and technical cadres after the nationalization in 1971.

As Verónica Montecinos points out, during his first months in office Allende did in fact seek technical support from the same source as Frei, namely, CEPAL. He also initially attempted without much success to protect his economic team from the party political pressures of that wide-ranging and heterogeneous government coalition that was the Unidad Popular (Montecinos 1998b). As we shall see in this chapter, the process of rapid political radicalization in the country was to lead to over-ideologization within the Allende government, which translated into, among other things, the clear hegemony of sociologists over economists. The former became the true ideologues of the regime, in charge of defining the different road maps to reach the desired socialist society. In open contrast, the economists were often branded as "technocrats," which in those years was almost synonymous with "bourgeois" and "counterrevolutionary." The glorification of workers or *obrerismo* prevailing within the Chilean Left made the government technocracy and its actions not only problematic but downright invisible.

The Economists' Ascendancy

The economists' increased presence and power under Frei was the culmination of a process that started in the early 1950s and had different political and ideological aspects.

At the beginning of the decade, a generalized reaction about things not working well pervaded the country. The economy was growing at a very low rate, and inflation was about to reach alarming levels. Thus, from all the points of the political compass, including the Left and the traditional Right, there was a feeling of urgency about the need to do something radical to attack the problems of the country. It was during the second government of Ibáñez (1952–58) that for the first time professional economists exerted a visible influence on the government in the formulation of sectorial policies oriented to tackle the main economic problems. As already mentioned, Ibáñez resorted to the professional services of a group of economists from the United States, who became known as the Klein-Saks Mission, to evaluate the economic problems of the country and, above all, to formulate a proposal for solving the problem of inflation, which was increasing strongly in the early 1950s. The Klein-Saks Mission recommended the adoption of strong orthodox measures, including the reduction of demand and of the fiscal budget, the elimination of subsidies to basic consumer goods and services, and a tax reform that would have a negative effect on the more affluent sectors (Zahler 1977, 46). As Barbara Stallings has pointed out, these proposals were rejected not only by the workers' organizations but also by the industrial sectors, which saw the possible application of such policies as a harsh blow to their interests (1978, 33). Although eventually Ibáñez would find himself politically unable to apply these orthodox prescriptions because of lack of support, the Klein-Saks Mission set the precedent of intervention by orthodox economists to attack the main economic problems of the country.[1]

However, even more important for the growing importance of the role of

1. It is worth noting that many of these and other measures proposed by the Klein-Saks Mission resurfaced in 1975 in the economic program of the Chicago Boys.

economists in the debate of the 1950s was the presence in Chile of the United Nations Economic Commission for Latin America and the Caribbean (ECLA, or CEPAL, its acronym in Spanish). CEPAL, created in 1947, assembled an outstanding group of Latin American economists under the direction of Raúl Prebisch, a prestigious Argentine economist. Through rigorous technical studies written in a technocratic and apolitical language, CEPAL alerted the Latin American countries about the need to protect the national industry, carry out agrarian reforms, and modernize the administrative structures of the state.

Under the CEPAL wing, 1962 saw the creation of the Instituto Latinoamericano de Planificación Económica y Social (ILPES), which was to become one of the main disseminators of the idea of global planning of development in Latin America. Top-level economists and sociologists like Osvaldo Sunkel, Fernando H. Cardoso, and José Medina Echaverría worked there. ILPES organized numerous courses addressed to administrators, public officials, and professionals engaged in industrial and agricultural activities both in Chile and the rest of Latin America (C. Kay 1989, 135). An ILPES document of 1966 refers to the general acceptance in Latin America of the concept of planning, which, unlike in previous years, was no longer objected to on account of political and ideological prejudice. The report concluded as follows: "Everywhere [in Latin America] it is possible to see social forces imbued with the ideas of development and planning, as a result of the influence of economists, engineers, technicians, and modern entrepreneurs in the dissemination of these ideas, combined with the importance of industrial diversification and action by the state" (quoted in Devés Valdés 2004, 345). At CEPAL there were many Chilean economists who had a direct line of communication to the economic authorities of the country and to different political and party political factions. I am referring especially to Aníbal Pinto Santa Cruz and Jorge Ahumada, who exerted great influence on future generations of economists and within the political class. Interestingly enough, they each wrote a book describing the national problems from a global perspective, and urging the implementation of profound economic and social transformations in the country. Both books were written for a wide readership, and both authors show their versatility by dealing not only with economic issues but also carrying out deep historical and psychological analyses of the evolution of Chilean society.

Aníbal Pinto's *Chile, un caso de desarrollo frustrado* (1973a) is an exhaustive historical analysis of the development of the country from 1830 to the 1950s (the book was originally published in 1958). In the first part of the book, Pinto describes the boom of the Chilean economy in the 1840s, based on agricultural exports, and the economic bonanza resulting from the nitrate industry that began in the 1880s. However, from a Cepalian perspective he exposes the serious risks that Chile ran with this outwardly oriented developmental pattern, in which the prices of the raw materials exported declined steadily and the country was left unprotected from the ups and downs of the international economy. All this was dramatically illustrated by the harsh effects of the crisis of 1929, in which "the collapse of the economic support left the social organization hanging on air, and a strong feeling of frustration in the country" (1973a, 308).

In his analysis of the evolution of the economy from 1930 on, his thesis is that the strong expansion of democratic ideas and practices that the country had experienced was not consistent with the meager growth of the economy and the generation of resources. There was a tension, and not only on the economic system. As he points out, "Economic *underdevelopment* and relative political *overdevelopment* pose a sharp contradiction, which is the source of friction, frustration, and imbalance" (1973a, 128). Together with this imbalance between political and economic development, Pinto criticizes the absence of modernization in the agricultural sector (where unproductive latifundia prevail) and the lack of integration of agriculture to the needs of the industrialization process. This book made many Chileans aware of how the national tradition of laissez-faire policies had thwarted progress and development.[2]

En vez de la miseria ([1958] 1973), by Jorge Ahumada, a colleague of Pinto's at ECLA, was also published in 1958. Ahumada's book presents a systematic discussion of the problems that affected the country in the 1950s from a vision more in tune with Social-Christian tenets. This book projects a more technocratic vision of development, yet at the same time has clear views on how to attack the problems affecting the country. In fact, the book was later to become a sort of action platform for the so-called *cuadros técnicos*[3] of the Christian Democrats after the victory of Eduardo Frei in the 1964 elections.

2. This work provided the foundations for the future formulation of the theory of dependence formulated by, among others, André Gunder Frank (1969) and Cardoso and Faletto (1969).

3. Sergio Molina's term for the Christian Democrat *técnicos* who cooperated with Eduardo Frei during his adminstration (Molina 1972, 159 and passim).

Like Pinto, Ahumada criticizes the liberal policies adopted in the country in the past and their meager results. In addition, he criticizes the naïveté of left-wing sectors for believing that replacing the the capitalist regime with a socialist regime would solve most of the country's problems. Ahumada's argument is that Chile is in the midst of an "integral crisis":

> The defects of our social machinery do not reside in just one of the many components that constitute its delicate mechanism. Because it is not only education that is in crisis, or only the administrative organization, or the economic system or the mechanisms pertaining to legal or juridical processes in general, or the moral foundations of the nation. This is in fact an integral crisis, the total disruption of the different components whose correction demands an enormous effort of imagination and resolve, but which under no point of view can be considered insoluble. ([1958] 1973, 17)

Ahumada devotes an important part of his book to the deficiencies of public administration and the need to adapt it to the requirements of modern times to confront the alleged integral crisis.[4] Thus, he criticizes the growth of a state bureaucracy lacking the technical capability to undertake the new tasks. Above all, he criticizes the absence of a presidential technical council to advise the executive on complex issues:

> For the president to be able to perform his functions in an effective way, it is necessary to create an administrative machinery capable of providing the information that will enable him to form an opinion about the course the country is following, and that can offer the indispensable technical advice. Regardless of how cultured or well informed the presidential incumbent may be, he will always be in need of specialized advice, since he must make decisions on so many and varied matters. ([1958] 1973, 41)

As we shall see in the following section, Frei paid heed to this advice, and after being sworn in he created an economic council to solve the shortcomings

---

4. The thesis that Chile had fallen into a deep crisis was later called into question by such respected scholars as Albert Hirschman ([1963] 1965, 304) and Alan Angell (1988, 100–101), who suggest that such a dramatic diagnosis was more motivated by the desire to undertake profound change in the country than grounded in fact.

identified by Ahumada, thus strengthening the position of a technocratic elite around him.

Finally, Ahumada analyzed what in his view constituted the four great barriers to development in Chile, namely, agricultural stagnation as a result of retrograde production forms; endemic inflation; a very unequal income distribution; and centralism, which inhibits the economic development of the different regions of the country. Later, the government of Frei was to pay much attention to each of these problems, with mixed results.

In the mid-1950s some economists in Chile had begun to look at the problems of the Chilean economy from an entirely different perspective. Trained in Chicago, these economists rejected structuralism and the Cepalian hegemony that had so far monopolized views on development in Chile in favor of a monetarist approach (cf. Calcagno 1989). Monetarists consider state intervention as one of the main sources of the problems existing in the country. They support the adoption of free market policies in which private initiative has to lead the process of development according to principles of economic profit, without any state interference. During the 1950s and 1960s, monetarist views in Latin America were sustained by only a small group of economists who had to operate within a very hostile climate, dominated by political sectors that favored social reform.

In 1955 the Department of Economics of the University of Chicago signed an agreement with the Faculty of Economics of the Universidad Católica de Chile. Through this agreement a select group of students from this Chilean university had the chance to take postgraduate courses in economics in Chicago. Another aspect of this agreement was the creation of the Centro de Investigaciones Económicas, which was directed by visiting professors from Chicago such as Arnold Harberger, Simon Rottenberg, Tom Davis, and Martin Bailey. Finally, this agreement contemplated undertaking long-term research on the Chilean economy and its problems, to be carried out at Chicago. Eventually, the group of visiting American scholars succeeded in introducing and consolidating the Chicago School paradigms in the academic curriculum of their Chilean counterpart. At the same time, the "Chile Project" became a major research experiment in development economics at the Department of Economics of the University of Chicago. Between 1955 and 1963 dozens of young economists from the Universidad Católica made use of the Chicago grants. Many of them would later become well-known academicians, industrialists, executives of financial conglomerates, and especially, leading figures in the post-1975 implementation of the neoliberal model under the military government (Valdés 1995).

All this notwithstanding, in the early 1980s both the status of economists and the paradigm of economic and social planning in Chile received a strong boost from Washington, where the Alliance for Progress project demanded that if a Latin American country was a prospective candidate to receive assistance, its authorities should plan medium- and long-term development using complex econometric tools for the formulation of sectorial policies. Thus, Alessandri, who was initially against economic planning, made use of the first Ten-year Development Plan published by CORFO in 1961 to apply for the technical and financial assistance offered by the Alliance for Progress.

In retrospect, there is evidence that by the 1958 elections the PDC had the backing of an ample core of economists and specialists in development-related issues. The members of this expert group gave shape to "equipos técnicos," technical teams, which produced a diagnosis of several fields of action (economy, health, housing, agriculture, and so on) that would later serve as the PDC political platform during the presidential campaign of 1964 (Molina 1972, 40). Thus the platform for both the elections of 1958 and 1964 was the product of a systematic effort to give a coherent response to the global stagnation of the country.[5] What is more, two years before the 1964 election, a 108-page-long document was prepared to guide the discussions of the first congress of the PDC and independent professionals and technical experts. This four-day congress convened representatives from forty-three different professional fields to discuss a series of possible reforms, such as administrative decentralization, agrarian and tax reforms, educational policies and social policies, economic planning, and so on (Montecinos 1998a, 22). After the 1964 victory, these technical teams became part of the state administrative machinery and rapidly, with the full support of President Eduardo Frei, set in motion the implementation of their plans for economic and social change.

Frei and the "Cuadros Técnicos"

Frei won the 1964 elections by an overwhelming majority (55 percent of the vote, an unprecedented result in Chile), and the following year was to obtain

5. Boeninger later referred to the creation of the Christian Democrat technocratic cadres in the following terms: "The PDC had attracted the best technical cadres available in the country as party members or supporters, particularly, a group of young economists who formed the main

a clear victory in the parliamentary elections.[6] Although the Right *en masse* voted for him to prevent Salvador Allende from getting in, it was unable to translate this support into influence.[7] Besides, Frei had the staunch backing of the United States, which saw in him and his reformist and developmental project an example for Latin America of how to prevent the emergence of revolutionary movements inspired by the Cuban example. This means that from 1964 on, Frei's political credit was high enough to give him ample freedom of action to implement his reformist policies. This fact also reinforced within the government the idea that it would be possible for the technocrats to follow a "camino propio," that is to say, their own road, without paying much attention to political games, since the PDC had a majority in Parliament. This resulted in a "single party" government that, for many years, was able to ignore the opposition. According to William Ascher, "Frei's package of reformist initiatives had a notable characteristic. Although it was much farther to the left than any postwar economic program in Chile, the workers' representatives and leftist political groups (besides elements within the Christian Democratic Party) had little to do with its formulation. The technocrats of the party and the administration, themselves satisfied with the progressive merits of the program, attempted to impose it without permitting input from—or political credit to—others" (1984, 125).

The Christian Democratic leader placed much trust in the capability of economists to design and implement his plans for reform, particularly if they were professionals from CEPAL. Montecinos quotes a minister of Frei's, a lawyer, who referred to Frei as being "very Cepalino. He helped the establishment of CEPAL headquarters in Santiago. Most of Frei's close advisers were economists for he had a lot of respect for the profession. He lived surrounded by economists" (1998a, 46).

Frei had expressed his economic views in his book *Pensamiento y Acción* (1958), in which he fully adheres to the different principles formulated by CEPAL, and uses them to legitimize his own program of economic and social changes (L. Moulian and Guerra 2000, 79). He refers to the documents pre-

---

core of the first modern technocracy in the country with political vocation and concern for social issues" (1997, 124).

6. The PDC was to get 43 percent of votes and elect 82 out of 147 deputies.

7. His will not to give in to pressure from the Right was graphically reflected in his famous statement: "Not even for one million votes would I change one single comma of my program" (quoted in Boeninger 1997, 12).

pared by CEPAL as possessing "a true spirit of research and scientific precision," and uses many of these reports as the frame of reference for his arguments (Hira 1999, 45). Frei was also convinced of the need to plan development and persevere in the implementation of the programs already agreed on. He stated this in the following terms in his State of the Nation Speech of 1970:

> Democracy requires the existence of efficient and responsible political leadership which has to make use of planning to reach its goals. Once a plan or program has been approved by general consensus, it can neither be terminated nor distorted in spirit and basic guidelines. It is up to us and to our capability to give ourselves the right institutions to be faithfully respected that this fundamental instrument of modern politics may or may not be applied in democracy. (Quoted in Cardemil 1997, 160)

As was to be expected, Frei had his eye on Jorge Ahumada as minister of finance, not only because of his great professional prestige and not only because he was central to the formulation of the program, but also because he had great charisma and exerted an innate leadership on the young PDC technocracy. However, Ahumada turned down the offer on personal grounds and recommended young Sergio Molina in his stead.[8] Frei appointed Molina although the latter was not a member of the PDC on the strength of his excellent technico-professional credentials and his experience, for despite his youth, he had acted as economic adviser to the two previous governments.

However, not everybody within the PDC shared Frei's enthusiasm for the advice coming from CEPAL and the preference he gave to the advice of the "cuadros técnicos." Traditional politicians, most of them lawyers, resented the young professional cadres being center-stage, and this resentment was to generate an enormous tension within the government. Verónica Montecinos (1998a) has collected a series of statements from the political leaders and from the technocrats who were part of Frei's government containing allegations of mistakes and weaknesses that each attributes to the other. For example, when referring to his experience in Frei's cabinet, a former minister thus com-

---

8. Ahumada's sudden demise in 1966 deprived the Christian Democrats of one of their main intellectuals and inspirers of their economic policy.

plained about the economists in the government: "Ministers need to know things that are not taught in the School of Economics, like how to deal with public opinion and the mass media. It is important to measure the political cost of a given policy, and that cannot be done by economists. People think this is something very technical . . . but it has been an error to appoint economists as ministers. That never occurred to Frei!" (quoted in Montecinos 1998a, 47). Possibly Frei may have felt inclined to favor technocracy over politicians because he did not want his government to be dominated by the leaders of the PDC. In practice, however, Frei acted as a sort of liaison between the technocratic and the politico-doctrinal sectors, in an attempt to strike, as far as possible, some kind of balance between them.

Planning and Economic Decision-Making

Shortly after taking office, Frei expressed the need to create a national planning agency that would report directly to him. An organization with these characteristics was already operating within CORFO, and the idea was to expand its staff and areas of responsibility and place it under the presidential eye. This marked the birth of the Oficina de Planificación Nacional (ODE-PLAN). Although ODEPLAN was not officially inaugurated until 1967 (because of time-consuming legalities), it was in *de facto* operation early in 1965. ODE-PLAN was responsible for gathering and updating statistical data on the different sectors of the economy and for quantifying the current situation and existing deficits in such areas as housing, employment, education, and so on. In addition, ODEPLAN prepared an annual government work plan, which was the result of the coordinated efforts of several working groups in the different ministries and agencies responsible for the economic and social areas. Equally important was the design of regional policies. For this purpose, ODEPLAN opened offices in the main provinces of the country. The bill creating this planning office stated that by doing so "true planning of the economic and social policy would be made possible, reserving for the executive the initiative to legislate on matters that might interfere with the fulfillment of the plans" (quoted in Cardemil 1997, 196).

Together with the creation of ODEPLAN came the formation of what was known as the "Economic Committee," chaired by the president or his deputy, the finance minister.[9] The weekly sessions of this committee were regularly

9. This coordinating body was also to play an important role in discussing economic policies during the Allende government.

attended by the ministers of economy, labor, and agriculture, the director of ODEPLAN, the chairman of the Banco Central, the vice president of CORFO, the chairman of the Banco del Estado, the president's economic adviser, and the director of the Budget Office. This committee was responsible for short-term economic decisions to be implemented or communicated by ODEPLAN, which acted as the executive secretariat of the committee. Thus, the executive brought about politico-technical integration in its sphere of action (Molina 1972, 161–62).

According to Peter Cleaves, the Economic Committee turned into a self-contained decision-making group that kept itself relatively protected from the larger social and ideological forces around it. As he points out:

> The Christian Democrats believed that their regime was a technocratic aristarchy; it was true that all the permanent members of the Committee were highly qualified professionals in their respective spheres. Their common party affiliation, their allegiance to the president, and their high regard for rationality should have eliminated almost all points of contention. In addition, they were riding the wave of the government's extraordinary large popular vote in the 1964 elections, which promised to pave the way for the easy application of the Committee's decision-rules in the society-at-large. (1974, 83)

However, as time went by, it was clear that within the committee two large informal coalitions had been formed. At one end there was a restrictive pole led by the finance minister, with the support of the presidents of the Banco Central and the Banco del Estado. These officials formed the technocratic hard core and their main concern was to preserve fiscal equilibriums. At the other end was the developmentalist-oriented coalition, represented by ODE-PLAN, CORFO, and the ministers of economy and agriculture. This coalition placed a stronger emphasis on stimulating the growth of the economy, pro-ductivity, and promoting social development. However, according to Cleaves, this latter coalition was weaker than the former because it lacked internal coordination and failed to adopt a common position prior to the discussions within the Economic Committee. In addition, this coalition was further weak-ened by institutional rivalry between CORFO and ODEPLAN and between the Ministry of Economy and the Ministry of Agriculture (Cleaves 1974, 94–95).

During the 1964–67 period, the leadership of the PDC did approve, at least

tacitly, most of the decisions made by the heavily insulated Economic Committee. However, from 1967 on, because of a worsening economy and mounting social tension, the PDC was no longer willing to give its support to the
"optimal solutions" proposed by this committee if these policies generated
strong public discontent. As Stallings has noted, "The Frei regime sought a
much greater measure of relative autonomy than was the norm in class-domi-
nated Chilean politics. During the 1965–66 period, this approach achieved
substantial success. . . . But at the end of the biennium, however, opposition
to the 'neutral state' was beginning to build up on all sides" (1978, 100). There
was growing dissent among the Christian Democratss in Parliament about
governmental technocratism in general, since the proposals coming from the
Economic Committee were becoming increasingly difficult to defend (Cleaves
1974, 118).

Sergio Molina, who was finance minister and later vice president of CORFO
during the Frei administration refers to, among other things, the great influence of the Ministry of Finance on the decision-making process within the
Economic Committee. The reason for this was that the Budget Office reported
to the finance minister and that, traditionally, finance ministers have exerted
much influence on decisions related to monetary credit and foreign trade
policies because of their close relationship with the Banco Central and the
Banco del Estado. Molina acknowledges that ODEPLAN had a significant
influence within the committee, as reflected in the importance assigned to its
reports in the allocation of investment resources in the annual budget and the
fact that it acted as technical secretariat for the Economic Committee. However, at the same time, he notes that, at the end of the day ODEPLAN only
played an advisory role in decision-making, and its relative power depended
on the leeway that the minister of finance and transitory political influences
left for its operation (1972, 163).

In the first years of his term, Frei was able to capitalize on the presence of
young technical cadres in his administration, since they gave it an air of
renewal, progress, and purpose. However, the presence of technocrats also
produced communication problems with the public administration, entrepreneurs, and eventually, public opinion. Thus, for example, Constantine C.
Menges (1966) refers to the strained relations existing during Frei's government between the state administrative agencies (such as CORFO and CORA)
and the country's main business associations (SNA, SOFOFA, and so on). As
he indicates, many of the mechanisms used by the business organizations to

influence policymaking possessed an informal character. According to
Menges, the recruitment of the technocratic personnel during the Frei government threatened the continuation of these informal mechanisms. As he
points out: "The Frei government . . . demonstrated the fragility of these
informal and non-institutionalized means of access to policy-making. The
Christian Democratic government brought its own complement of economists and technicians to government service, and there has hardly been any
prior collaboration between government ministries and the business groups
in the drafting of economic policy legislation" (1966, 353–54). He concluded
that the technocrats' attitude of avoiding consultation with the entrepreneurial organizations forced the latter to strengthen their relations with the members of Parliament. There are even authors like Arturo Valenzuela and
Alexander Wilde (1979, 211) who relate the later collapse of democracy to the
ascent of technocrats and planning ideologies in the 1960s. In their view, these
rigid and rationalistic schemes of technocrats had collided with the national
political culture of accommodation and compromise characteristic of the previous decades. In a similar vein, John Sheahan refers to Frei's economic program in the following terms: "The coherence of the program was a result of
technocratic design, without drawing on input from the labor and business
leadership; leaving them out of the design made things easier in the first
instance but made it difficult to get their cooperation later" (1987, 207).

Another element that has been much criticized *a posteriori* was the over-
confidence of the state technocracy. It tended to project the results of its
initiatives using exact figures. Thus, for example, in the implementation of
the agrarian reform the publicized target figure was 100,000 peasant families
to be benefited by these changes, but in fact the final result was 28,000.
According to Ascher, what Frei's government achieved with his agricultural
policy was most impressive; yet the announced target of 100,000 families
made it seem to the public like a failure (1984, 122).

This error was recognized by one of Frei's ministers with a strong technocratic background. As he put it: "We induced Frei to make grave political
errors. He announced goals in quantitative terms: 100,000 new landowners,
600,000 houses . . . the Frei government did more than any other, but it
accomplished less than it had promised. People evaluate on the basis of prom-
ises, not accomplishments" (quoted in Montecinos 1998a, 49). Many Christian Democratic officials knew that in relative terms their administration had
been quite successful. Because of this, it was very hard for them to understand

why the government of Eduardo Frei was not followed by another Christian Democratic government (Boeninger 1997, 132).[10]

A very special case that demonstrates the inability of the Christian Democratic technocrats to anticipate an extreme public reaction was the announcement in November 1967 by Minister Molina of the so-called Fondo de Capitalización de los Trabajadores (Workers' Capitalization Fund) in his annual report to Congress on the state of the economy. Through this compulsory savings program (applicable to both workers and employers), the economic authorities were attempting to put a brake on inflation and increase the savings rate of the country, which was below 12 percent of GDP. Molina explained the technical rationale of the project and its advantages in a retrospective analysis (1972, 144–47); however, the truth is that, regardless of eventual advantages and disadvantages of the proposal itself, Molina lacked the political skill to choose the right moment and suitable tone to introduce such a proposal. In addition, this example shows the arrogance of the technocrats, for they did not bother to do the necessary political groundwork to gain support among the organizations of workers and employers and right-wing and center parties before announcing the plan. The plan was not fully understood by ample sectors of the population while the Left and the unions under its control undertook a successful mobilization effort against it. In addition, the Right and the organizations of employers also rejected this plan. This resulted in a resounding defeat for the government, which was forced to withdraw the bill from Parliament (Angell 1972, 168), and led to the resignation of Minister Molina, who had announced beforehand that he would resign if Parliament did not approve the bill. Molina was replaced by Raúl Sáenz, one of the most explicit advocates of technocracy in those days. However, after a few months Sáenz resigned when he saw that the technical plans were completely "mutilated" in the Senate. He was replaced by a politician and lawyer, Andrés Zaldívar, who got on well with Parliament and the entrepreneurial sectors. When Molina resigned, Frei reshuffled the cabinet to strengthen the politicians and weaken the technocrats in an attempt to tackle the growing dissatisfaction of the population and to put a brake on social mobilization. What is interesting is that, despite the president's decision to abandon the Workers' Capitalization Plan, the Economic Committee continued to support

10. We should remember that in their initial enthusiasm many of Frei's followers had predicted that now that the PDC had attained the presidency, it would rule the country for the next thirty years.

it. The committee even sent Frei a letter reminding him of the precise effects that nonimplementation of this plan would have on inflation (see Cleaves 1974, 124–27). In other words, and in a classic technocratic attitude, the generalized lack of political support did not make the members of the Economic Committee change their collective mind about Molina's plan, which for them still represented the "technical optimum" to attain the objective of lowering inflation.

Scheming for the Popular Sectors

The Christian Democrats' technocratic project was not restricted to the traditional economic and productive areas, but also daringly ventured into the social sphere. According to the diagnosis of the technical cadres, there was an urgent need to solve the problems of the urban and rural poor. Whereas efforts in cities focused mainly on solving the housing problem and on communal organization, in the country the efforts of the government concentrated on the application of the agrarian reform. From a Cepalian point of view, it was argued that the improvement of the living conditions of the popular urban and rural sectors would contribute to the growth of the domestic market for industrial production. In addition, the modernization of the agricultural sector would contribute to increased agricultural production and thus reduce the country's degree of dependence on food imports. This concern for the weakest also originated in doctrinal considerations that highlighted the need to promote solidarity among Chileans in order to rein in the individualistic values upheld by liberalism. In a way, this meant spreading "communitarianism," which was meant to constitute a new form of social order based on solidarity and social cooperation and an alternative to capitalism and communism. The ideological and doctrinarian basis of communitarianism can be found in the writings of the French philosopher Jacques Maritain, whom Eduardo Frei admired profoundly. In 1951 two young social-cristianos, Jacques Chonchol and Julio Silva Solar, published Hacia un Mundo Comunitario, in which they proposed a new approach to organizing and mobilizing the population to achieve (from above) their social, economic and political emancipation (see Cardemil 1997, 133–37; Van der Ree 2007, 92–98). Under the name of promoción popular, the Frei government supported the creation of hundreds of women's centers, neighbors' associations, cooperatives, community centers, trade unions, sports clubs, training workshops, and so on. The idea was to integrate the community into the big debate on the political, social, and economic changes that the government was striving to bring about. From the very beginning, *promoción popular* formed part of the program of government. During his election campaign Frei referred to it in the following terms: "Family, neighborhood, municipality, labor union, region, enterprise are all values that should attain their full expression; they should assume responsibility for, and participate in a suitable way in the whole of the economic, sociocultural, and political process" (quoted in Cardemil 1997, 251).

The practical translation of communitarian goals into the formula of *promoción popular* was mainly the contribution of Roger Veckemans, a Belgian sociologist and priest, and founder, in the late 1950s, of the School of Sociology of the Catholic University. Veckemans introduced a curriculum oriented to sociopolitical problems and, particularly, to the phenomenon of social exclusion, which was just becoming a popular theme in of Latin American sociology. He founded the Centro para el Desarrollo Económico y Social de América Latina (Center for Latin American Economic and Social Development, or DESAL), in which he spread the social doctrine of the Catholic Church and translated it into targets of economic and social development. The first cohort of sociologists that graduated from this school joined Frei's campaign in 1964 and contributed to the formulation of the social program (Brunner 1988a, 246–47).[11]

The stimulus given to the organization of the urban poor into neighborhood associations, movements formed by modest settlers, women's centers, and so on was quite successful. After a few years, a strong movement of popular urban sectors emerged, going beyond the limited objectives of the government and attaining a growing degree of autonomy from the PDC and the government (L. Moulian and Guerra 2000, 181).

Even more marked was the process of social organization and mobilization that went on in rural areas. Through the Corporación de la Reforma Agraria (Land Reform Agency, or CORA) and the Instituto de Desarrollo Agropecu-

---

11. During the Frei administration, the nonacademic labor market for sociologists expanded, particularly in the public sector, which grew rapidly as a result of the Christian Democratic government's reformist policies. In particular, after the university reforms in 1967, there was a rapid increase in registration for social science degrees, which caused a dramatic increase in the supply of social analysts. The different universities increased their teaching staff and created new institutes.

ario (Agrarian Development Institute, or INDAP), the Frei government expropriated large latifundia and at a later stage organized agricultural production
through peasant settlements. Important resources and technical staff were
allocated for the implementation of this project, which was considered the
central undertaking of the government in the social sphere. Thus, hundreds
of young engineers, agronomists, teachers, sociologists, architects, economists, and anthropologists offered their services and joined the different state
agencies. Many of them were later employed by specialized bodies during the
government of the Unidad Popular. The government also passed a bill allowing agricultural workers to form and join labor unions, which made it possible
for an important part of peasant workers to become unionized for the first
time. Both the course of expropriations and peasant unionizing were to lead
to a process of radicalization in the countryside. On the one hand, the owners
of latifundia opposed the reforms and, on the other, the peasant unions with
the support of the left-wing parties put pressure on the government to speed
up the pace of expropriations (see P. Silva 1987).

The growing frustration over the slowness of the changes and the consequent radicalization also included some Christian Democratic functionaries
and experts working in the different areas of *promoción popular*. One of them
was Frei's minister of agriculture, Jacques Chonchol, who was initially technocratic in profile, but little by little in the course of the process of reforms was
later to adopt attitudes that were more political and doctrine-inspired and
alienate himself from the Christian Democrats. He was one of several Christian Democratic leaders[12] who resigned from the party in 1969 to form the
Movimiento de Acción Popular Unitaria (United People's Action Movement,
or MAPU), which later gave its support to Salvador Allende when he was
running for president.

In the last phase of his government, Frei had to confront a strong opposition coming both from within the party and from the other political forces of
the country. The economic and political Right grew even more opposed to
the economic and social policies of the government as with growing concern
they witnessed the process of radicalization of the popular sectors and the
deepening of the process of agrarian reform. In turn, the Left capitalized on
the popular discontent and promised the masses that it would intensify and

12. Among them were also figures such as Rodrigo Ambrosio, Agustín Gumucio, Alberto
Jerez, Julio Silva Solar, Enrique Correa, and Jaime Gazmuri, who were to play an important part
during the Unidad Popular government and subsequent period.

accelerate the process of change in a future government that it would head. The PDC finally got involved in an internecine fight between conservative and progressive sectors, which ultimately eliminated all possibility of constituting a cohesive electoral proposal for the elections of 1970.

With hindsight, we can detect that the changes encouraged by Frei's government were affected by a fundamental contradiction: it simultaneously promoted, on the one hand, an economic policy that was formulated and implemented in a top-down and technocratic manner and, on the other, a social policy that privileged civil society activation and popular participation. The technocratic aspects of the government produced a growing distancing of the elite taking part in the decision-making process from important social and political actors such as entrepreneurial organizations, the great trade unions federations, and the opposition parties. In addition, the social mobilization of the deprived sectors contributed to the articulation of their demands to the government and to their full integration into the ongoing political process. This in turn resulted in their growing radicalization and consequent alienation from the Christian Democratic government.

Intellectuals, Technocrats, and Socialism in Chile

The left-wing forces grouped in the coalition known as the Unidad Popular were victorious at the polls in 1970. Their platform was quite radical. Its main objective was "to put an end to the domination of the imperialists, monopolists, and the land-owning oligarchy, and to initiate the construction of socialism in Chile" (UP 1969). Thus, from the very beginning, the government of Salvador Allende was engaged in an unbridled fight against the U.S. interests in the Chilean economy (particularly in mining) and the land-owning, entrepreneurial, and banking sectors. In addition, the Unidad Popular had to confront the coalition of the Right and the Christian Democrats, which had a majority in Parliament (see O'Brien 1976; Roxborough, O'Brien, and Roddick 1977).

Although the economic transformations were center-stage in the agenda of the Unidad Popular, the accent was stronger on the change of ownership of companies, banks, and the land, and to a lesser degree on attaining productive efficiency. Thus, the political agenda focused on divesting the traditional elites of their power and tabled issues such as the administration of the state or an efficient economic policy. Both the planning of the policies of the state and the search for administrative and productive efficiency were initially one of the concerns of Allende and his main economic advisers; however, the rapid and dramatic deepening of the political conflict and the generation of a catastrophic economic and social crisis was to divert the government's attention and energy to managing the day-to-day, away from the planning of an increasingly uncertain future. As for the public administration, the intense politicization and radicalization of those years was to lead to strong sectarianism within the public agencies that brought about the confrontation of the different forces of the Unidad Popular and the Christian Democratic and conservative civil servants. While many Christian Democratic technocrats managed to remain in the public agencies despite this hostile climate, others were forced to resign and were replaced by individuals who saw social polarization and total confrontation between the government forces and the opposition as an inevitable reality on the way to the consolidation of socialism in Chile.

As a result of this radicalization of the political process, government technocrats were rapidly replaced by politicians and left-wing intellectuals as the main designers of the project for change and of the guidelines for the ideological and political struggle against the forces of the opposition.

From Planning to the Struggle for Survival

At first glance, the policies of the Unidad Popular differed from the project for change implemented by the Christian Democrats more in degree than in kind. Like Frei, Allende placed a strong emphasis on agrarian reform, operating with the same institutions created in the early 1960s and with the same agrarian reform law inherited from the previous administration. The difference resided more in the speed of expropriations and the final number of latifundia affected. With respect to the copper policy, the Unidad Popular ended up by nationalizing the copper mines still owned by U.S. companies, which only completed what the Christian Democrats had already begun. The Unidad Popular also continued with the efforts to organize the more deprived rural and urban sectors, a process that had been initially launched by the Christian Democrats, but this time under the name of *poder popular* (popular power) instead of *promoción popular* (see Cancino 1988). If we take a look at the initial positioning of the Unidad Popular with respect to economic planning, we can also observe similarities with the previous administration. However, the big difference between both global planning projects resides in the fact that Frei's project sought to modernize the productive and social structures of capitalism in Chile, whereas the Unidad Popular attempted to put an end to it and replace it with a socialist system.

The government program put it as follows: "In the new economy, planning shall play a most important role. . . . The economic policy of the state shall be carried out through the national system for economic planning and such mechanisms as control, guidance, credit to production, technical, political, tax and foreign trade assistance, as well as the management of the state sector of the economy" (UP 1970). The program also gives a broad description of the different objectives for different areas such as education, housing, health, and so on, stressing over and over again that each and every one of these policies will be put into practice "within the general framework of national planning."

After Allende's installation, ODEPLAN was assigned responsibility for the national planning system, under the direction of prestigious economist Gonzalo Martner. Martner was responsible for the design of a pyramidal structure for national planning, which, at the presidential level, operated through the National Development Council, whose members were government officials, the ministers of economic and social affairs, and six representatives of the workers and six representatives of the industrialists, who had the status of consultants. ODEPLAN operated as the technical secretariat and was the entity where the medium- and short-term development plans were discussed. Above ODEPLAN was the Executive Economic Policy Committee, whose members were the president of the Republic, a coordinating vice president, the minister of finance, and the minister of economy together with the minister of planning, who acted as technical adviser. ODEPLAN also produced an annual economic report, which was presented to the president and the Parliament. As Martner pointed out, ODEPLAN sought to create a system for popular participation in planning by integrating workers' organizations into the different levels of planning.

> An important aim is that planning should cease to be a superstructure and becomes the basis of the system, and to this end an agreement is being drawn up with the Central Trade Union Confederation (CUT) to establish a joint ODEPLAN-CUT Commission. . . . This commission will

propose operational models for planning mechanisms with full worker participation for each enterprise. The Popular Unity government believes that planning is a way of enhancing participation, enabling discussion on and participation in the substantive issues of development issues. (Martner 1973, 71–72)

In 1971 ODEPLAN published an extensive "Six Year Plan, 1971–1976," which included sixteen large volumes of national and regional plans for economic and social development for the entirety of Allende's term of office. In this document, ODEPLAN specified the main goals that the government wanted to achieve in the different productive areas, as well as the main social targets expected to be achieved by the end of the six-year period. The prognoses were overwhelmingly optimistic, anticipating, for instance, an overall growth of about 50 percent in the GDP in that period, that is to say, an annual average cumulative rate of growth of 7 percent. The plan also contemplated a huge expansion of the state services and coverage in areas such as public health, housing, and social security (Zammit 1973, 287–316).

However, the hard facts of the daily management of the mounting economic problems show a rather hectic situation caused by a lack of efficient coordination between the political and economic leaders and their objectives. As Sergio Bitar, former deputy minister of economic affairs under Allende, put it,

> Anyone who observed the activity of the government from within can affirm the evident weakness of the leadership in confronting the complexity of the situation. The coordination among the Ministers of Economy and Finance, the Banco Central and CORFO was weak; no structured central command existed at all in the first phase. The Economic Committee, the group effecting liaison between the economic offices and the President, functioned precariously, and it was not until the middle of 1972 that technical support staff for the Committee was organized. . . . Since powers were shared and each group acted autonomously there existed no single focus of authority, no body or person responsible for the direction or economic policy as a whole. This was a major failure in the conduct of the economy. (Bitar 1986, 220–21)

This evident lack of coordination led, among other initiatives, to the formulation of a peculiar and almost unknown initiative ("Project Cybersyn") by which some technocratically oriented UP officials hoped to efficiently manage the productive process in the nationalized enterprises run by the state. It consisted in the installation of a computerized center in Santiago to process "real time" economic data (inputs, outputs, and so on) coming via telex from several industries from all over the country. This initiative was based on the ideas of British cybernetician Stafford Beer, who visit the country several times to personally supervise the implementation of the project. The idea to apply cybernetics to the management of the Chilean economy during the Allende government and to contact Beer for this purpose came from the young engineer Fernando Flores, who at that time was the general technical manager of CORFO. He controlled a wealth of resources that permitted him to finance the very high costs of the project. Flores and Beer also presented this project as a great opportunity to improve communication between workers and managers. But as Eden Medina points out, "Instead of promoting social transformation and augmenting worker participation at every level of government, a principle upheld on paper by Beer and CORFO, these interactions between Cybersyn engineers and workers in the nationalized sector reflected the Chilean social and cultural hierarchies generally and reinforced the project's technocratic image" (Medina 2006, 602).

The Allende government placed a large body of managers (the so-called *interventores*) in charge of the requisitioned factories. While many of them were political activists without any specific technical or professional training, others possessed clearly technocratic profiles, eager to increase production and efficiency levels in the plants they administered. The relations between this new class of managers and the workers were dominated by tensions and animosities. As Mark Falcoff indicates, "Workers who seized a plant were often loath to subordinate it to ODEPLAN, CORFO, or other government agencies. . . . Members of the economic team frankly admitted frequent 'management difficulties' arising out of government attempts to impose technocrats as opposed to labor militants as interventors of requisitioned enterprises" (Falcoff 1989, 138, 139).

Like Frei, Allende had great confidence in the technical competence of economists and brought a large number of them into his government. He also shared with Frei a deep respect for CEPAL and this agency's professional support of the deep economic and social reforms he had committed himself to bringing about during his administration. Verónica Montecinos quotes an economist who worked with Allende and who admits, *a posteriori*, that they did not live up to the president's expectations: "Allende thought economists knew how to solve the country's problems. In many speeches he said the left had the best economists of the country. He was convinced of that. I think he was not quite right . . . economists had a partial training . . . and some of us were relatively inexperienced. The economists are prisoners of an artificially built partial science; they are unable to understand the deeper nature of political problems" (1998a, 53). Allende also pursued the idea, at least at the very beginning of his government, of protecting and sheltering his technical teams from direct pressure by the political parties that formed part of the heterogeneous Unidad Popular. Thus, it was his personal decision to appoint Pedro Vuskovic—a former CEPAL economist for twenty years—as his minister of economy, despite his not being a member of any of the parties of the government coalition and having a markedly technical profile. From the very beginning, Vuskovic acquired a prominent position within the cabinet. Allende granted him a strong degree of autonomy in his doings as a minister, which was resented by the political parties that had hoped to place one of their own in such an influential position. Allende also selected the director of ODEPLAN and the chief executive officers of the Compañía de Aceros del Pacífico (CAP) and the National Copper Corporation (CODELCO) from a group of close personal economic advisers.

Despite Allende's intentions, the process of radicalization led very rapidly to the politicization of the different structures of the state, which were placed at the service of the consolidation of socialism in Chile (see Sigmund 1980). Such was the case, for example, of CORFO, which was assigned a leading role in the administration of the dozens of industries, banks, and financial and services companies expropriated by the government of the Unidad Popular and forming part of the so-called social ownership area. Thus, from 1970 on, CORFO lost a large part of its relative autonomy and its purely technical nature. A technical study of the fifty years of CORFO draws the following conclusion with respect to the period of the Unidad Popular: "From November 1970 on, [CORFO] was made to play an entirely different role: that of the instrument for the application of a program of revolutionary transformation in the country. For the first time in its history, the political function became central, with its classical activities of research and development being subordinated to it" (Ortega et al. 1989, 224). This was combined with the practice of "political quotas" affecting the public sector, with each political party demanding control of a particular ministry or state agency. Consequently,

President Allende was not always able to shelter the economic policy from direct interference by the political parties. Such was the case of the appointment of Américo Zorrilla, a member of the political commission of the Communist Party as minister of finance. In addition, the quota system was to weaken the technical nature of several public agencies in a serious way. As Sergio Bitar points out, this system

> led to the removal or shunting aside of functionaries who did not share the coalition's ideas, or of those who were sympathizers but lacked the political support of one party or another. As a result technical personnel were underutilized precisely at a moment when more professional skill was required to manage the ever-growing intervention of the state into the economy. Once ranks of politically trustworthy technicians had been exhausted, there was increasing resort to unsuitable persons of questionable competence to fill important positions. This practice provoked anti-UP sentiments among a growing number of public officials, men who had not originally opposed the goals of the coalition. (Bitar 1986, 59)

In general, and unlike Frei's government, the Unidad Popular did not have a wide spectrum of technical support.[13] However, Allende's government gained an important group of trained professionals with the breaking away from the PDC of two splinter groups, first the MAPU and later that of the Izquierda Cristiana. Many economists, agricultural engineers, and managers in general who joined the government ranks already had extensive experience in the state apparatus, given that they had worked there during the Frei administration. However, they were often the object of distrust by the parties of the Unidad Popular, as they were seen as opportunistic groups wishing only to keep their public administration jobs after the end of the PDC government.

The deepening of the economic problems in 1972 led the government in June of that year to a reformulation of the economic strategy, which weakened the influence of the technocrats even further and strengthened the political

13. Referring to the problems faced by the expropriated industries, De Vylder indicated that many problems were "the result of scarcity of experienced personnel. It was, of course, necessary to fill almost all high managerial posts in the state enterprises with people to be trusted, but political dedication and responsibility did not always compensate for lack of economic and technical training among the new industrial leaders. Adaptation problems necessarily arose" (De Vylder 1976, 154–55).

parties' control of the economy. Thus, Vuskovic became the head of CORFO, and Minister Zorilla was later replaced by Orlando Millas, another member of the Communist Party. From then on, until the coup d'état in September 1973, the main stress would shift to the political efforts to increase the number of Unidad Popular members of Parliament and the political organization of the masses to resist the onslaught of an opposition demanding the end of Allende's government. As Stefan de Vylder concluded in his classic work on the Chilean economy under Allende,

> Through planning the "anarchy of the market" was to be at least par-
> tially overcome, and by means of planning the UP's medium and long-
> term development objectives . . . were to be achieved. Within the social
> area imperative planning was to rule, and well defined investment crite-
> ria were to be established. . . . This was, in very few words, the Allende
> government's blueprint. But things did not work that way. The anarchy
> of the market was replaced by the anarchy of neither plan nor market.
> (1976, 152–53)

So what we see is that in the end planning was in fact abandoned because the general crisis did not allow any planning at all, while political struggle domi-nated the minds and actions of all the actors involved.

Radicalization and the Rise of Left-Wing Intellectuals

Any satisfactory attempt to explain the marked strengthening of the techno-crats' position within Chilean society following the coup of September 1973 until the present must begin with a critical account of the intellectuals' role in the process of sociopolitical change during the Unidad Popular government. I consider the rapid changes in the country's social structures and the expan-sion of educational opportunities that began in the 1960s to be important factors in any explanation of this phenomenon. It is evident that there cannot be technocratic hegemony without a significant number of technocrats. This, in turn, is only possible if there is a relatively developed, complex system of higher education. However, although the education factor is a necessary condition for the rise of a technocracy, it is not sufficient in itself. There must also be appropriate political, economic, and ideological conditions for technocracy to grow in strength.

It is clear that in Chile the process of social modernization and the expansion of the state apparatus between 1964 and 1973 facilitated the rise of a reformist technocracy, which took charge of the technical aspects of the social programs to be applied. As already said, these experts were subordinated to the intellectuals who outlined the road ahead, based largely on political and ideological considerations.[14] Although they professed left-wing ideas and expressed varying degrees of loyalty to the socialist experiment, they were not necessarily members of any political party. Their influence on political leaders and UP partisans in general was primarily based on their academic expertise and knowledge of broad political, philosophical, and ideological discussions within the Left in both Chile and abroad. In this manner, during the Allende years, sociologists were at the forefront in counseling the highest levels of the government circles, while economists were of little help in the discussions about the transition to socialism and the like (see P. Silva 1993a).

The military coup, and the destruction of democracy, dramatically displaced the intellectuals from their hegemonic position within the political class, for they were largely identified with the overthrown regime. At the same time, the change in the political system facilitated (although not immediately) the rise, and undisputed hegemony, of the neoliberal technocrats, as represented by the Chicago Boys.

I believe that the so-called ideological inflation that arose between 1967 and 1973 also made a definite contribution to the shift in the balance of power from intellectuals to technocrats. In retrospect, we can see that not only the military but also important sectors of the population came to identify the intellectuals (whether correctly or incorrectly is not the issue here) as the key protagonists in promoting class struggle and exacerbating social conflict during the "reformist decade." The military regime's propaganda machine took on the task of promoting the association, "intellectuals = political unrest = chaos."

What is beyond doubt is that during the Allende government the issues raised by the intellectuals—anti-imperialism, national liberation, the struggle

---

14. During the Allende years, most intellectuals possessed academic degrees in the social sciences, particularly sociology or political science, and were professionally linked to the University of Chile or other academic institutions. The universities themselves became highly polarized along ideological lines. This polarization was clearly reflected in the running battle between the country's two main centers of higher education. The University of Chile held the progressive banner, while the Universidad Católica symbolized reactionary values.

against the oligarchy, mass political and social incorporation, and so on—dominated the political arena. In the economic program there were no major breaks with the past—in fact, what occurred was more a deepening of the state's role in the economy and in the industrialization process. During this time, authorities who wanted to stress their popular orientation played down the intrinsic nature of the intelligentsia and their importance in outlining the political and ideological course to follow. This is a common phenomenon during periods of radical social change. As Alvin W. Gouldner has put it, "In a revolutionary process based on mass mobilization, the prominence of the intellectuals' leadership is out of keeping with the populist, egalitarian, and communitarian emphasis of the political movement. As a result, there is considerable pressure to disguise, ignore, deny or distort the importance of this elite in revolutionary movements. In revolutionary processes, the intellectual strata has been an invisible class" (Gouldner 1979, 11). This invisibility was acted out in front of the majority of the population, who held them in relatively low esteem. On the other hand, intellectuals had greater standing with the left-wing parties particularly because of their rhetorical skills, their in-depth knowledge of definitive Marxist-Leninist texts, and their general familiarity with national and international history.

José Joaquín Brunner and Alicia Barrios (1987) are categorical about the intellectuals' role in the process of "ideological inflation" during the Unidad Popular years. I will take the liberty of quoting them at length because their analysis is autobiographical and, in my view, makes an important contribution to the collective attempt at self-criticism and demystification regarding the part played by the intelligentsia in general, and sociologists in particular, during the Allende government.

As they indicate, the sociologists' role became redefined, in particular, after the Unidad Popular triumph. In a climate of great political excitement and vigor, this new role was defined in terms of political and theoretical militancy in favor of the revolution:

> The prototype of the militant sociologist [was put forward] whose weapons were critical analysis, and the assessment of sociological debate in terms of commitment, the party, and popular organization. . . . The influence of those revolutionary intellectuals could be felt in the mass media, and in the central revolutionary committees. There is a popular government, a program of transition of the intellectuals and social ana-

lysts. Their words are listened to and taken into account; in short, they are valued in the political and ideological market as never before. It is the Golden Age of the progressive intellectuals. (Brunner and Barrios 1987, 80)

Both sociologists also point out the marked interdependence that existed between the intellectuals and the political sectors that controlled the state's resources; the university played a bridging role in this situation.

> Sociology acquired a revolutionary character, and with it came legiti-
> macy as it demonstrated its progressive tendency. What the sociologists
> lost in professional terms, they made up for in party political audience.
> The state generously financed the rapid transformation of the discipline
> through university budgets and, under this organizational hegemony of
> resources, any social science which did not ascribe to revolutionary
> Marxist and "dependency theory" interpretations, effectively
> disappeared. . . . Marxism . . . provided a conceptual blueprint for this
> veritable transformation of sociology in Chile, by closely linking it to
> politics and offering the intellectuals an audience (the political parties),
> which demanded that they be aware of their "false consciousness," in
> contrast to the true bearers of revolutionary practice and theory (the
> parties). The reformist university, for its part, molded and took in the
> children of the revolution, provided them with employment, an ade-
> quate source of finance, a captive audience (the students), and a sound-
> ing board for their theories, interpretations, and proposals. (Brunner
> and Barrios 1987, 81)

It is ironic that the same criticism that intellectuals subsequently made of the neoliberal technocrats during the military regime—namely, their arrogant belief that they held a monopoly on truth—in fact, could have applied equally to themselves between 1970 and 1973. At least, this is the case if we follow this evaluation by Brunner and Barrios.

> To be a sociologist was, for some years, synonymous with being parti-
> san. Above all, the sociologist was called upon to be an intellectual, in
> the tradition of the "great intellectual" ideologue who was universally
> knowledgeable, who knew society's secret codes, its laws of develop-

ment, and its levels of true and false consciousness. In contrast, the specialist seemed like a cut-out intellectual, in some way fractional and constantly open to contamination from dominant ideologies— effectively, a narrow empiricist. The intellectuals loved by the revolution were like hedgehogs, not foxes. (Brunner and Barrios 1987, 82)

José Antonio Viera-Gallo, a leading figure in the attempt to change Chilean society, recalled, "We claimed that it was necessary and possible to overcome the formal nature of democracy. . . . This criticism of so-called formal democracy did not aim to destroy it, but to advance it further. . . . In fact, by emphasizing only the objectives, and making them out to be absolutes, we helped weaken the democratic practice. . . . We had not yet lived through the experience of authoritarianism" (1986, 46–47).

The attack on La Moneda Palace by the military, the death of Allende, and the dramatic end to the Unidad Popular experiment signified a bitter awakening from the dream that had seemed possible. Both the coup and its aftermath clearly had a traumatic effect on the intellectuals' consciousness.

The fall of the Unidad Popular in 1973 marked the start of a deep process of self-criticism and revisionism within an important part of the political forces that had supported it. This process originated the so-called renovation stream, which strongly criticized the mistakes made in the economic sphere and the political exacerbation encouraged by the ideologues. All this was to create a new political scenario that not only led to the subsequent alliance with the Christian Democrats, but also to the awareness of the need to ensure good economic management in a future democratic government. This was the *de facto* acceptance of the technocratic management of economic issues.

5

Pinochet and the Chicago Boys

The debate on the nature of the bureaucratic-authoritarian regimes established in the mid-1960s and early 1970s sheds much light on the close alliance crafted in those years between civilian technocrats and the military. Indeed, in countries like Argentina, Brazil, Chile, and Uruguay, technocrats played a key role in administering the economy under the military governments. But what is exceptional in the Chilean case is the fact that the economic team did not restrain their actions to the strictly economic and financial domains. As this chapter shows, as time went by the so-called Chicago Boys expanded their influence and authority to all fields in society, including education, health, the pensions system, culture, and so forth. Even more important has been the fact that these neoliberal technocrats eventually evolved to be among the main ideologues of the military regime, as they tried to justify the coexistence of political authoritarianism with economic liberalism. In other words, they finally became all-round "techno-politicians." So for instance, the Chicago Boys actively participated in the efforts to enhance people's support for the military regime and the neoliberal model by constantly stressing the success achieved in expanding the consumption of foreign products among the entire population. In this manner, mass consumerism became one of the main instruments of legitimacy used by the Chicago Boys to obtain at least tacit acceptance by large sectors of society for their free market policies. The creation of a "consumer society," however, generated a new scenario in which the Chicago Boys were expected to satisfy the continuously rising demands of the population for consumer goods. Thus, when their neoliberal economic model came into crisis in the early 1980s, the regime's legitimacy received a severe blow when those demands could not be met.

A second important point for the discussion on technocracy is the impact of foreign ideas and academic experiences abroad on the constitution of technocratic groups. As this chapter illustrates, the University of Chicago played a decisive role in providing the Chilean technocrats with a solid foundation in economics, while their common experience in the United States firmly enhanced their strong cohesion and identity as a group. However, just as Lastarria and Letelier followed French positivism in a very "selective" manner, the Chicago Boys ingeniously adapted the economic postulates learned in Chicago to the specific problems they confronted in Chile. So in fact they became true pioneers in many of the neoliberal reforms applied during the Pinochet regime, for there was no blueprint in the Chicago manuals for many of the problems they faced.[1]

A third factor I want to stress here is the broad receptivity existing among the population for technocratic solutions to economic and social problems, following the collapse of Allende's socialist experiment. An important part of the population had lost all patience with the climate of economic crisis and political conflict that had characterized the final phase of the Unidad Popular, blaming in fact all parties and the entire political class for the final breakdown of democracy. As we have already seen in Chapter 2, a similar generalized antipolitical mood existed in the late 1920s when another military man launched for the first time in the country a genuinely technocratic project. Paradoxically, Pinochet was to put to an end with his technocratic model the long-standing developmental pattern based on state-led industrialization and state interventionism initiated by his comrade-at-arms forty-six years before.

And finally, the case of the Chicago Boys shows how a technocratic vision can transcend the original group and obtain a hegemonic status in society, persuading not only the military and other right-wing sectors but, at the end of the day, also influencing important sectors of professionals and intellectuals

1. As I shall show in the next chapter, the great impact of foreign ideas and academic formation in classical economics in American universities will also become evident in the constitution of the technocratic elite surrounding President Michelle Bachelet.

who opposed the military regime. This partly explains why clear technocratic styles were also adopted by the Concertación governments after the end of the authoritarian era.

Following the military coup in September 1973, the Pinochet government gave great public visibility to technocrats, placing them in strategic positions in the institutions that formulated and implemented government policies. As we have seen in the previous chapter, technocrats also participated actively in the Allende government, but they carefully avoided emphasizing too much their professional-cultural backgrounds. In a period of strong political radicalization and *obrerismo*, the holding of a university degree revealed petit-bourgeois origins, making the holders seem less reliable to the revolutionary process. So while before the military takeover technocrats cautiously kept their diplomas out of sight, after it, they proudly displayed them for all to see.

The junta leaders presented the technocratization of decision-making as the only guarantee for "rational and coherent" policies. The new government also stressed the need to "technify" the entire society, in an attempt to convince the population of the inability of "politics" (that is to say, democracy) to solve the problems of the country.

This chapter starts with a brief historical account of the rise of the so-called Chicago Boys, the neoliberal technocrats in charge of Pinochet's economic policies. I will also attempt to identify the main political and economic factors that allowed this group of young neoliberal technocrats to play a central strategic role during the military government. They not only became the designers and executors of the economic policy applied during the Pinochet period but also contributed decisively to the formulation of the official ideological discourse.

The Chicago Boys played a central role in this technocratization of decision-making. Imbued with a strong *esprit de corps*, this group of young economists conducted a kind of revolution "from above," transforming the social, economic, political, and even cultural bases of Chilean society. Because in the end they achieved economic success, the neoliberal technocracy finally became legitimized among important sectors of the population. The alliance between the military and the civil technocracy represented for years a workable formula, permitting the military government to count on considerable political support from the population, including an important part of the middle class, until the beginning of the 1980s.[2]

Paradoxically, the opposition to authoritarian rule during the 1980s also adopted an increasingly technocratic character. Several private research institutes were established, from which experts in different fields of the social sciences and economics undertook critical studies of governmental policies and formulated alternative programs to be implemented after the restoration of democracy. This dissident technocracy played a key role in the creation of a broad opposition to the military government and in the achievement of the subsequent victory in the presidential elections of December 1989. For years, scholarly criticisms made by these experts were the only voices tolerated against the military dictatorship. Furthermore, during exile abroad many opposition political leaders became connected to the academic world, acquiring expertise in specific subjects.

The severe economic crisis in the years 1981–82 produced a true *resurrection* of the old political parties, which mobilized the population around the demand for the restoration of democratic rule. Beginning in May 1983, several "days of national protest" demanding the restoration of democracy were organized on a monthly basis in Chile's largest cities (see Oxhorn 1995 and C. Schneider 1995). However, as the "days of national protest" began to gain an unexpected radical and insurrectionary character, many democratic political forces decided to withdraw their support of them (see P. Silva 1993a).

The democratic opposition took an important lesson from the "days of protest" that proved decisive for the later adoption of a workable political strategy to put an end to military rule in the country. The protests had shown that mass political actions would not bring down this dictatorship, which still enjoyed considerable support from the population. After this experience, the democratic opposition parties opted for a top-down approach, addressed rather to the achievement of agreements at the leadership levels of political organizations than the political activation of the masses. In this manner, the united political forces of the opposition formulated common goals through

---

2. As C. Huneeus correctly indicates, "Pinochet's enormous power did not rest solely on the backing of the armed forces and his use of coercion, for he was also a skillful politician who drew support from a broad spectrum of civilian groups who were firmly loyal to him. . . . He was supported by a substantial sector of the population; it was not by chance he won 43 percent of the vote in the 1988 referendum. . . . After the handover of power, Pinochet maintained this support, enjoying the admiration and respect of a significant proportion of the public" (C. Huneeus 2007, 72–73).

the establishment of *equipos técnicos,* constituted by technocrats from different political parties, who were experts in specific fields such as education, health, economics, and the like.

The Building-up of the Chicago Project

The origins of the Chicago Boys are directly related to the debate that took place in the late 1950s and 1960s between structuralists and monetarists on the causes of and possible solutions to the main developmental problems of Latin America (see C. Kay 1989).

According to the structuralist approach, Latin American governments needed to play a pivotal role in encouraging economic development by planning and implementing policies directed at promoting import-substitution industrialization. These policies had to be accompanied by protectionist measures to defend domestic industry, such as high tariffs on imported consumer goods, the manipulation of exchange rates, and the adoption of a series of fiscal measures intended to expand the internal market. To back this up, the structuralist recipe stressed the need for land reforms and the redistribution of income to stimulate consumer demand.

The United Nations Economic Commission for Latin America (ECLA/CEPAL), led by Argentine economist Raúl Prebisch, was the most important bastion of structuralist thought in the region.[3] From its headquarters in Santiago de Chile, ECLA successfully propagated its theories on economic development throughout the continent and enjoyed a clear intellectual hegemony in the early 1960s among economists and technocrats, many of whom occupied key governmental positions.

The monetarists, on the contrary, considered state intervention one of the main sources of the existing problems. They stressed the need to adopt free market policies in which private initiative should lead the process of development according to principles of economic profit, without any state interference (see Calcagno 1989). During the 1950s and 1960s, there were very few monetarists in Latin America, and they had to operate within a highly adverse climate, dominated by political sectors who favored social reformism. In the mid-1950s the Department of Economics of the University of Chicago initi-

---

3. See Prebisch 1981 for a synthesis of Prebisch's criticism of the monetarist (neoliberal) school.

ated a strong counterattack against the spread of Keynesianism (and the ECLA approach, which was seen as its Latin American version) in the new field of development economics.

In 1955 Theodore W. Shultz, president of the Department of Economics at the University of Chicago, visited the Faculty of Economics of the Universidad Católica de Chile at Santiago in order to sign an agreement for academic cooperation. Under this agreement a select group of Chilean students were offered the opportunity to pursue postgraduate studies in economics in Chicago.[4] Between 1955 and 1963 a total of thirty young economists from the Universidad Católica made use of the Chicago grants. Many of them later became well-known academicians, industrialists, and executives of financial conglomerates, and in particular, leading figures in the implementation after 1975 of the neoliberal economic model under the military government.

Another result of this agreement was the creation of the Centro de Investigaciones Económicas (Center for Economic Research), which would host visiting professors from Chicago such as Arnold Harberger, Simon Rottenberg, Tom Davis, and Martin Bailey. Finally, this agreement contemplated undertaking long-term research on the Chilean economy and its problems, to be conducted at Chicago. In the end, the group of visiting American scholars succeeded in introducing and consolidating the Chicago school's paradigms in the academic curriculum of their Chilean counterpart. At the same time, the "Chile Project" became a major research experiment in development economics at the Department of Economics of the University of Chicago (Valdés 1995).

During their Chicago training most of these Chilean economists became unconditional disciples of Milton Friedman.[5] They were convinced that the full introduction of a totally competitive free market economy was the only solution to Chile's developmental problems. After their postgraduate studies at Chicago most of them returned to the Department of Economics of the Universidad Católica, where they disseminated monetarist prescriptions to a new generation of students.

In 1968 these neoliberal economists established their own think tank, Centro de Estudios Socio-Económicos (Center of Socioeconomic Studies, or

---

4. For a detailed study of the University of Chicago's activities in Chile, see Valdés 1995.

5. Friedman is considered one of the most influential exponents of the Chicago school. His book *Capitalism and Freedom* (1962) became a leading handbook among his Chilean followers. Friedman was awarded the Nobel Prize for Economics in 1976.

CESEC). This center drew up the economic program of the right-wing candidate Jorge Alessandri in the 1970 presidential elections. However, it was clear that the political climate in Chile at that time was not favorable to their radical neoliberal recipes. They proposed the liberalization of markets, the encouragement of private initiative, the withdrawal of the state from the economy by reducing the bureaucracy and selling off public enterprises, and the opening of the economy to international competition (Délano and Translaviña 1989; Soto 2003).

However, they did not manage to generate sufficient support, even in right-wing circles. As Philip O'Brien has pointed out, "The Chicago model was opposed by many of Alessandri's business supporters and had to be put into cold storage 'as it was a programme difficult to implement within a democracy' as one leading businessman put it. Nevertheless the campaign was useful in winning important adherents to the Chicago plan among key businessmen" (O'Brien 1981, 39; see also O'Brien and Roddick 1983).

Following the Unidad Popular victory in the 1970 presidential elections, the neoliberal technocrats continued their efforts to formulate a general economic program. They expected that sooner or later the Allende government would be overthrown by the army (M. Vial 1981, 26; Fontaine 1989). This resulted in the formulation of a secret alternative economic program, nicknamed "el ladrillo" (the brick), because of its heaviness (Castro 1992b). After the military takeover, however, the new authorities chose to apply more moderate economic policies. The first economic team appointed by General Pinochet consisted mainly of uniformed men and civil technocrats associated with the National Party and the Christian Democrats. The Chicago Boys initially obtained only secondary positions as advisers in several ministries and state agencies. However, after a period of time they obtained control of the State Planning Agency (ODEPLAN), which became their operational base within the government. ODEPLAN was later used as a springboard to secure control of the rest of the state apparatus.

The relatively moderate economic policies adopted after the coup did not yield the expected results, while the international crisis (involving a strong increase in oil prices and a dramatic fall in Chile's export revenues) made the situation even worse. In this critical scenario, the harsh recipes proposed by the Chicago Boys began to gain a broader audience and some support among the military leaders. By the end of 1974, the Chicago Boys controlled most of the strategic centers of economic planning. In order to achieve full control of the formulation and implementation of economic policies, in March 1975 the neoliberal think tank, the Fundación de Estudios Económicos, organized a seminar on economic policy, which received massive media coverage. The Chicago Boys invited well-known foreign economic experts (among them, their old teachers Milton Friedman and Arnold Harberger), who expressed their total support of the application of a severe austerity program to the Chilean economy, the so-called shock-treatment.[6] A month later, the leader of the Chicago Boys, Sergio de Castro, was appointed minister of economic affairs. Immediately afterward he announced the application of the neoliberal prescription, marking the initiation of what later became known as the neoliberal revolution. As noted above, ODEPLAN was crucial for the implementation of the neoliberal program. In Carlos Huneeus's succint account,

> ODEPLAN fulfilled three important political purposes. The first was to recruit professional personnel destined for government posts. It provided them with political and administrative experience so that they could then take on the political commitments of the authoritarian regime. Second, ODEPLAN became the place where some of the principal economic reforms were prepared, such as the privatization of the pension and health care systems, as well as the privatizations of state-owned companies and the dismantling of the entrepreneur state. . . . Third, ODEPLAN helped to act as the "social conscience" of the neoliberal model, by formulating policies to combat extreme poverty. (C. Huneeus 2000, 465)

In all these three functions Miguel Kast, a young and charismatic Chicago Boy, played a pivotal role. Kast, who was ODEPLAN director in the years 1978–80, used his great persuasive flair to convince a large group of young and talented economists who had just graduated from the Universidad Católica to come to work for ODEPLAN and other state agencies, despite the relatively low salaries paid by the public administration. He drew up a "map of extreme poverty," identifying the most deprived segments of the population for whom special antipoverty policies were designed (including labor and empowerment programs) in an attempt to compensate for the high social costs produced by

---

6. Friedman's address to the seminar was simultaneously published and distributed in the form of a small book by the Fundación de Estudios Económicos (see Friedman 1975).

the application of the neoliberal economic model. With his sudden death in 1983 the Chicago Boys lost one of their most influential members (see Lavín 1986).

The Chicago Boys as Organic Intellectuals

The new neoliberal economic team presented the technocratization of decision-making as a guarantee that the government would pursue a rational economic model. From that moment on, government decisions were to be inspired by "technical and scientific" principles and not by political and ideological postulates as in the past (T. Moulian and Vergara 1980).[7]

In the blunt words of Pablo Baraona, a key Chicago Boy, the pattern of development introduced by the neoliberal technocracy was aimed at constructing what he called a "technified society," "meaning by this a society in which the most capable make the technical decisions they have been trained for. . . . Historically, in our country professional capacity has been overshadowed by political factors. The new democracy must be technified, so that the political system does not decide technical questions, but the technocracy has responsibility for utilizing logical procedures to solve problems and to offer alternative solutions" (DIPRE 1978, 305).[8] This technocratization of decision-making was strengthened by the process of selective capitalist modernization put into motion by the neoliberals. This led to the acquisition by the middle and upper classes of very sophisticated patterns of consumption and the mod-

7. It must be said, however, that the leaders of the *gremialista* movement (an ultraconservative political current of Catholic origin) also played an important role in the political system promoted by the military regime (and were the main authors of the junta's *Declaración de Principios* of 1974 and the 1980 constitution). *Gremialistas* such as Jaime Guzmán and Sergio Fernández were as much the architects of the new order as Chicago Boy Sergio de Castro. The fact that neoliberals and *gremialistas* initially defended different economic projects (and held opposing positions on many other issues) was no impediment to their cooperation with the military regime, or to their joint activities in the formation of the right-wing party Unión Demócrata Independiente (UDI). As Vergara has clearly shown, the convergence achieved between the Chicago Boys and the *gremialistas* was primarily the result of the gradual "neoliberalization" of the latter (1985, 168–75). C. Huneeus (2000) is certainly right in stressing the close historical and personal links existing between neoliberals and *gremialistas* within the Universidad Católica. Nevertheless, the point remains that until early 1975, the sector represented by Jaime Guzmán and the group headed by Sergio de Castro maintained different ideas about the orientation that economic policies should have to follow. So for instance, the *gremialistas'* attack on "consumer society" expressed at the 1974 *Declaración de Principios* represents a view that is totally antagonistic to the vision of massive consumption defended by the Chicago Boys.

8. Baraona was one of the leading figures of the Chicago Boys and was twice minister of economic affairs during the military government.

ernization of the banking system and the management of enterprises.[9] At the same time, the entrepreneurial sectors became more integrated into the world economy and its technological standards. The service sector was also modernized but remained accessible only to privileged social groups. The majority of the Chilean population, however, did not participate in the benefits of this process of modernization because of the inegalitarian nature of the economic model and the unwillingness of the economic team to implement redistributive policies (Meller 1984; Tironi 1982).

The Chicago Boys presented themselves as the bearers of an absolute knowledge of modern economic science, thereby dismissing the existence of economic alternatives. All possible criticism of the economic model was rejected by portraying it as either the product of ignorance or the covert promotion of particular interests (Arias et al. 1981, 174).

For many years the dismissal of criticism coming from individuals who were not qualified in economic science, together with the repression exercised by the military against traditional *políticos* and their organizations, left little room for opposition to the Pinochet government and its economic policies.

The increasing influence of the Chicago Boys within the government and among rightist political organizations and entrepreneurial circles was directly related to their ability to manage the crisis and to produce economic growth. The supporters of the military government also realized that the neoliberals could count on the support of the international financial system. As Robert R. Kaufman has pointed out, these technocrats

> were more than simply the principal architects of economic policy: they were the intellectual brokers between their governments and international capital, and symbols of the government's determination to rationalize its rule primarily in terms of economic objectives. . . . Cooperation with international business, a fuller integration into the world economy, and a strictly secular willingness to adopt the prevailing tenets of international economic orthodoxy, all formed a . . . set of intellectual parameters within which the technocrats could then "pragmatically" pursue the requirements of stabilization and expansion. (Kaufman 1979, 189, 190)

9. For instance, between 1975 and 1981 the number of cars in Chile doubled. By 1984, 42 percent of families in Santiago were repaying one or more consumer loans (Martínez and Tironi 1985).

After a severe economic recession in 1975–76 (produced by the application of the shock treatment), there followed years of macroeconomic improvement. The rate of inflation, for example, which was 343 percent in 1975, was reduced to 37 percent in 1979, and 9 percent in 1981. The annual rate of economic growth (which was –13 percent in 1975) reached an average level of 7.5 percent in the years 1977–81. In the same period Chilean exports boomed with an annual average of 10.7 percent. The fiscal deficit (8 percent in 1974) totally disappeared by 1979 (with a surplus of 1.7 percent). In addition, the net inflow of foreign capital reached the impressive figure of more than US$1,600 million per year in 1978–1980 (San Francisco and Soto 2004, 110). In those years, many economists in Chile and abroad began to talk about "the Chilean *wirtschafts-wunder.*" The strongest supporter of the neoliberal plans inside the military junta was General Pinochet himself. He was well aware that he needed the continuous achievement of successes on the "economic front" to consolidate his personal rule.

In a climate of total euphoria, the Chicago Boys developed and implemented what they called "the seven modernizations" in order to establish the rule of neoliberalism in all spheres of society. These "modernizations" involved the introduction of new labor legislation, the privatization of the social security system, the municipalization of education, the privatization of health care, the reorientation of the agricultural sector toward the foreign market, the transformation of the judiciary, and the decentralization and regionalization of government administration (Baño 1982).

The Chicago Boys also played a key role in the attempt to institutionalize the dictatorship. Acting as true organic intellectuals,[10] they devised a sophisticated answer to the latent contradiction in the coexistence of economic liberalism and political authoritarianism. On the basis of the theoretical framework elaborated by Friedrich von Hayek[11] they argued that the political

---

10. Defined by Gramsci (1971, 3) as the thinking and organizing members of a particular fundamental social sector who have the task of directing the ideas and aspirations of the group to which they organically belong.

11. Von Hayek (Nobel Prize for Economics, 1974) taught at the Department of Philosophy of the University of Chicago. His book *The Road to Serfdom* (London, 1944) gave the Chicago Boys the required theoretical and doctrinal foundations to expand their neoliberal thought from economics to the social and political spheres. Von Hayek became intimately involved in the application of neoliberal precepts in Chilean society. He accepted the position of honorary president of the Centro de Estudios Públicos, established by the Chilean neoliberal intelligentsia in 1980. He also visited the country several times, expressing his total confidence in the policies implemented by his ex-pupils (see, for example, his interview in *El Mercurio,* April 16, 1981).

Table 1   Chicago Boys who occupied key positions during the military government

Name	Governmental Post
Sergio de Castro	Adviser to Ministry of Economic Affairs, minister of economic affairs, minister of finance
Pablo Baraona	Adviser to Ministry of Agriculture, president of Central Bank, minister of economic affairs, minister of mining
Alvaro Bardón	CORFO official, president of Central Bank, deputy minister of economic affairs, president of Banco del Estado
Rolf Lüders	Minister of economic affairs and of finance
Sergio de la Cuadra	President of Central Bank, minister of finance
Carlos Cáceres*	President of Central Bank, minister of finance, minister of the interior
Jorge Cauas*	Vice president of Central Bank, minister of finance
Cristián Larroulet	Adviser to ODEPLAN, chef de cabinet at Ministry of Finance
Martín Costabal	Budget director
Jorge Selume	Budget director
Andrés Sanfuentes	Adviser to Central Bank, adviser to Budget Agency
José Luis Zabala	Chief of study department, Central Bank
Juan Carlos Méndez	Budget director
Alvaro Donoso	Minister director of ODEPLAN
Alvaro Vial	Director of national institute of statistics (INE)
José Piñera	Minister of labor, minister of mining
Felipe Lamarca	Director of tax agency (SII)
Hernán Büchi*	Banking supervisor, deputy minister of health, minister director of ODEPLAN, minister of finance
Alvaro Saieh	Adviser to Central Bank
Juan Villarzú**	Budget director
Joaquín Lavin	Adviser to ODEPLAN
Ricardo Silva	Chief of national account, Central Bank
Juan Andrés Fontaine	Chief of study department, Central Bank
Julio Dittborn	Deputy director of ODEPLAN
María Teresa Infante	Adviser to ODEPLAN, deputy minister of social security, minister of labor
Miguel Kast	Minister director of ODEPLAN, minister of labor, vice president of Central Bank

* These people did not study at Chicago, but are considered Chicago Boys because they fully supported the Chicago approach and were active members of the neoliberal economic team.

** He was originally a Chicago Boy and a member of the initial economic team; however, he was forced out for dissenting early on by the inner Chicago Boy circle.

SOURCE: Délano and Traslaviña 1989, 32–36.

system that Chile had experienced in the past was a mere pseudodemocracy because only organized groups such as the political parties and the unions were able to push through their demands, to the detriment of the interests of the majority of the population. The laws passed by Parliament and the policies implemented by the government were, in their view, the result of unacceptable pressure from these organized groups. They stressed the need for a strong government, able to impose a system of general and impartial rules upon the entire society, without permitting the pressure of sectorial interests. Only the supposedly impersonal and nonarbitrary laws of the market would guarantee equality of opportunity for all citizens. They stated that the achievement of (total) economic liberty constituted a key precondition for the very existence of genuine political liberty. The corollary is that only under the supervision of an authoritarian government was the establishment of the basis for liberty (namely, the installation of a free market economy) possible. The very existence of the military government was also presented as a temporary phenomenon that would become unnecessary after the full consolidation of the new economic system (Vergara 1985, 89–106). However, the Chicago Boys pointed out that the future democracy would be "authoritarian" (following again the constitutional recipe of von Hayek), in order to defend it from its enemies. This meant that in the plans for the future political system there was no room contemplated for leftist ideas and political parties.

A landmark in the attempt of the military-technocratic alliance to institutionalize the "new order" was the adoption in September 1980 of a new constitution. This was officially named the "Constitution of Liberty" in a clear act of acknowledgment of von Hayek's philosophical thought.[12]

The Heritage of a Technocratic Style

The supremacy of the Chicago Boys reached its highest point the moment the 1980 constitution was adopted, and almost no one could imagine then that within a year the economic neoliberal model would confront a severe crisis. One of the major weaknesses of this model was the fact that most of the economic development obtained during those years was financed by expensive short-term foreign loans, leading to a rapid increase in Chile's indebtedness. Underlying this was the policy of state withdrawal from economic life, which produced a lack of official control over how the private conglomerates (the so-called *grupos económicos*) utilized those foreign resources, making financial speculation an easy and very profitable business (Ffrench-Davis 1982; Foxley 1983).

The collapse in March 1981 of a leading financial group resulted in a specu-

---

12. Named after von Hayek's book *Constitution of Liberty* (Chicago, 1960).

lative wave that in turn provoked a general panic among the entrepreneurial circles. Many financial institutions (the so-called *financieras*) and enterprises went into bankruptcy, overall production decreased dramatically, and under-employment jumped to critical levels. By the end of that year the GDP had declined by 14 percent (Ffrench-Davis 2003, 35).

Despite the intensity of the crisis, the Chicago Boys continued to argue with dogmatic confidence that the economic difficulties were only temporary, and that the "market mechanisms" would produce an "automatic adjust-ment" to restore economic equilibrium. However, the economic situation became even worse as a result of the international banks' decision to cut down the flow of loans to Chile. The confidence of the population in the govern-ment and its economic policies began rapidly to dissolve, and in April 1982 Pinochet found himself forced to reshuffle his cabinet. Sergio de Castro lost his post as minister of finance and his position as leader of the economic team, and the Ministry of Economic Affairs was placed under the command of an army general. The dismissal of de Castro, however, represented only a cosmetic move aimed to deflect the increasing unpopularity of the govern-ment. He was replaced by Sergio de la Cuadra, another Chicago Boy who decided to continue the policies of his predecessor.

The economic crisis encouraged the rise of an active political opposition to the government, which now had to deal with major political challenges from both the Center and the Left. The outlawed political parties began to operate openly, while the military government, showing clear signs of weak-ness, searched for some formula to tackle the new situation in the country. Pinochet appointed Sergio Onofre Jarpa as minister of the interior, and he initiated a "dialogue" with the opposition. This was intended to gain time and create divisions among its different political currents. Jarpa, a leading representative of the traditional right wing, had never sympathized with the "new right," symbolized by the Chicago Boys. He convinced Pinochet of the need to expel the remaining Chicago Boys from leading positions within the government. In his view, they had to be replaced by an economic team that could implement a more pragmatic policy to tackle the economic crisis. This led to a new cabinet reshuffle in April 1984 in which Pinochet appointed two of Jarpa's associates, Modesto Collados and Luis Escobar, minister of finance and minister of economic affairs (see E. Silva 1996).

After a series of unorthodox measures was adopted, the economy began to show clear signs of recovery. However, the expansionist nature of the new economic approach clashed with the financial restrictions imposed by the IMF, which pressured the Chilean government to return to a stricter financial policy.

On the political level, the government regained control of the situation. The opposition recognized the limitations of staging "days of national protest" that did not lead to the fall of the military government. The political momentum of mid-1983 gradually declined. At that point, the military government estimated that the political situation was sufficiently safe to revert to a neoliberal economic position. Accordingly, in February 1985 Pinochet appointed Hernán Büchi as minister of finance. Although he was not a Chicago Boy in the strict sense (in fact he had studied at Columbia University), he had collaborated with the neoliberals since 1975 and performed several minor functions within the neoliberal economic team. He had the advantage of being relatively unknown to the general public, and of the Chileans who had heard of him, few were aware of his connection with the Chicago Boys.

Büchi implemented a series of heterodox measures, inaugurating by this a period what Eduardo Silva has called "pragmatic neoliberalism" (E. Silva 1996, 173ff.). In a short period of time he was able to restore the international financial agencies' confidence in the Chilean economy. By the end of 1985 the last signs of the economic crisis had disappeared and the country's overall economic performance had returned to very satisfactory levels. The strong recovery experienced by the Chilean economy ever since made Büchi very popular (Rojas 1989). Even economists from the opposition recognized his ability as a manager. The prestige he obtained contributed to the restoration of the technocrats' popular image, which had become seriously damaged as a result of the economic crisis of 1981.

In clear contrast to the other countries in the region, where ministers of finance have very short-lived careers and are often the most unpopular members of the government, owing to the bad shape of most Latin American economies (Ames 1987), the nomination of Hernán Büchi in Chile as the government's candidate for the presidential elections of December 1989 took no one by surprise. During his campaign, he proudly stressed the alleged advantages of his technocratic approach to developmental issues and repeatedly insisted he was not a *político*. Although he came in second after the opposition's candidate, Patricio Aylwin, he obtained, together with the other right-wing candidate, Francisco Javier Errázuriz, a respectable 42 percent of the vote (against 56 percent for Aylwin). Most political commentators agree that Büchi's major handicap was not his technocratic background, but his connection with the Pinochet regime. Hence, he became indirectly linked to the human rights abuses committed by the military government, which constituted a major issue during the elections.

Despite Büchi's electoral defeat, most of the structural reforms introduced by the neoliberal technocracy in the period 1975–90 remained almost unaltered under the new democratic government of Patricio Aylwin. Even if the Aylwin government had wished to do so at the time, it would have been almost impossible to reverse the new pattern of capitalist development established by the Chicago Boys. But what is more important to emphasize here is that within the democratic political forces this desire was absent (Délano and Translaviña 1989, 179–83).

After all, the Chicago Boys had succeeded in their efforts to expand public support for their free market ideas. Even among moderate leftist circles, in the late 1980s one could observe a growing acceptance of many economic postulates defended by the Chicago Boys under the military government such as (1) the need to relegate the state to a subsidiary role in economic matters; (2) a revaluation of the role played by both foreign investment and the local private sector in achieving economic development; (3) the acknowledgment of the importance of using market mechanisms and efficiency criteria to allocate and support certain economic activities; and (4) the need to keep public finances healthy and to consolidate macroeconomic stability.[13]

This radical shift in the traditional economic thinking of the moderate Left was, in my view, the result of three major factors. First, the Chilean Left had already had the experience (during the government of the Unidad Popular) of implementing socialist-oriented economic policies, which were clearly unsuccessful. With that experience in mind, by 1990 there was almost no one in Chile who dared recommend the application of such an approach to the Chilean economy.[14] Second, despite the general criticism of the negative social

13. In a speech to a seminar on foreign investment, President Patricio Aylwin stated: "The democratic government neither envisages nor desires a return to a state-based pattern of development. On the contrary, the government will stimulate private initiative, interfering as little as possible with market decisions. . . . It is also necessary to stimulate foreign investments. Fortunately, the ideological polarization that existed in the past in Chile on this matter has been overcome" (see El Mercurio, international edition, May 17–23, 1990, 1–2). Minister of Economic Affairs Carlos Ominami (a member of the Socialist Party) explained the economic philosophy of the new Chilean government in similar terms to a group of leading industrialists and investors in Tokyo (see El Mercurio, international edition, May 31–June 6, 1990, 4).

14. One must not minimize the impact of exile in Eastern European countries on many Chilean left-wing political leaders. Their negative personal experiences of the socialist economies

aspects of the neoliberal model, many people within the left-wing political parties admitted (openly or tacitly) that the Chilean economy was in better shape than at any other point in the previous twenty-five years. And third, the process of political and economic transformations in Eastern Europe following the fall of the Berlin Wall in 1989 was the coup de grâce for those who dogmatically and ideologically still insisted on the advantages of a centralized economic system.

Most Chilean leftist sectors—outside the Communist Party and the extreme Left—also accepted in the early 1990s the idea that the achievement of economic growth and the maintenance of financial equilibrium constituted a precondition to improve the living standards of the less favored segments of the population. This implied acknowledging the importance of maintaining an efficient administration of the economy.

Consumerism as an Instrument of Legitimation

The use of mass consumption by the Chicago Boys in order to legitimate the new political and economic order established by the Pinochet regime, and the eventual generation of a "consumer society," has had a profound impact in the nature of Chilean politics ever since. Mass consumerism has stimulated individualism and depoliticization among the population. In addition, Chilean governments are mainly evaluated by the people on the basis of their ability to satisfy their raising material expectations. In my view, this new consumeristic element in Chilean political culture and the subsequent people's demand for the further application of growth-oriented policies has strengthened even further the position of technocrats within the executive. In this section I analyze the strengths and the limits of the consumption-based strategy followed by the Chicago Boys during the military government.

As I have already said, one of the direct effects of the application of the neoliberal economic model since the mid-1970s has been the acquisition by the middle and upper classes of very sophisticated patterns of consumption, which has led to the configuration of a true "consumer society" in the country. As a result of the expansion of consumer credit, segments of the popular sectors also obtained some access to the "pleasures" of the developed world

---

finally convinced them that this was not the kind of economic system they wanted for Chile after the restoration of democracy.

by consuming foreign products, which symbolize "modernity" (see Halpern 2002).

The strengthening of a strong consumerist ethos among the population has been intimately related to the neoliberal economic policies applied by the military government since 1975. These policies deeply transformed both Chilean society and the Chilean economy, and openly stimulated the massive import into the country of foreign consumer goods. Before September 1973, the concept of "consumption" was rarely employed in the official political discourse of governments. And when it was used, it was rather applied in the sense of satisfaction of the basic needs of the poor in the fields of health, education, housing, and nutrition. In contrast, the "consumer societies" of the industrialized world have been traditionally seen by many Chileans as a very sad and negative aspect of the modernity achieved by Western societies, provoking the dehumanization of the people. This negative image of consumer societies was in fact also supported by left-wing sectors, as well as by Christian Democrats and even by extreme conservative Catholic groups. Because of this, it is not totally surprising that the *Declaración de Principios del Gobierno de Chile* of March 1974, the first major doctrinal document issued by the military government, openly attacked the consumer societies of the North: "Developed Western societies . . . have fallen into a materialism which has spiritually suffocated and enslaved man. The so-called consumer societies have come into existence, in which the dynamics of development seems to have been able to dominate the human being who feels himself innerly empty and unsatisfied, yearning with nostalgia for a more human and serene life" (Junta Militar 1974, 30). This document reproduced in fact the Catholic traditionalist criticism of consumer society, since at the time the *gremialistas* represented the most influential ideological stream among the forces that supported the military government. In the end, however, the *gremialistas* proved unable to prevent the rapid rise of their main ideological contenders, the neoliberal technocrats, who from 1975 on became the indisputable hegemonic force in the Pinochet government (see T. Moulian and Torres 1989 and Cristi and Ruiz 1992).

With the inauguration of the era of the Chicago Boys all official references (and certainly criticism) of "consumer societies" disappeared, since the process of modernization they put in motion represented in fact an open appeal to the population to liberate its consumeristic desires.

The process of authoritarian modernization was oriented toward the full opening of the Chilean economy to foreign competition and the total integration of the country into the world market. The neoliberal economic policies led to a full-scale privatization of the state-owned industries and to the near total elimination of the traditional role played by the state in the country's socioeconomic development. The idea was to replace the state with the alleged "impersonal rule of the market" as the main mechanism for the allocation of resources in society. Most of the studies dealing with the neoliberal modernization have focused on the economic and institutional dimension of this process. Some studies, for instance, stress the consequences of the opening of the Chilean economy to foreign competition, while others describe the process of privatization and modernization that took place in areas such as education, social security, and services (see Foxley 1983 and Ramos 1986).

Less attention, however, has been paid to the fact that as a result of the full integration of the Chilean economy into the world market, the Chilean upper and middle classes have dramatically enlarged their access to consumer goods from the core countries, which has led to the adoption of very sophisticated patterns of consumption. Although the import wave of consumer goods mainly benefited the dominant social sectors in society, the popular sectors were not entirely excluded from the new phenomenon of consumerism. In a sense this is true even for those who did not obtain *effective* access to those goods, since they at least ideologically assimilated the idea of modernity as almost synomymous with "consumerism" that the military regime was promoting. In an effort to depoliticize society and consolidate the personal rule of General Pinochet the regime had replaced political liberty with the "liberty to consume."

The attempt by the military government to redefine Chileans as *consumers* instead of *citizens* was mainly directed at privatizing the nature of the social relations within civil society. For this purpose, the regime tried to destroy such collective identities existing in Chilean society as party and neighborhood loyalties and social solidarity with the needy, which were officially seen as the unwanted legacy of a "socialistic" past. As a substitute for the search for collective goals, the military government offered a neoliberal ideology that promoted the achievement of *individual* goals (T. Moulian and Vergara 1980; Vergara 1985). In this manner, individual freedom was redefined as representing the free access to open markets, while the "pleasure of consumption" was presented as an instrument to express social differentiation and as a way to obtain personal rewards. From this perspective, the Chicago Boys pointed out that social mobility was in fact mainly a question of personal achievement. According to this conception of modernization, to be up-to-date in terms of the acquisition of consumer goods represented the single most important criterion for modernity. Moreover, the imitation of lifestyles and values imported from the core countries as a result of the free market policies became in fact the only way to participate in the experience of modernity—in other words, "to be modern."

As Brunner points out, the market is unable by itself to produce a normative consensus among the population or to generate social identities. In addition, the market does not accept the constitution of solidarity bonds and rejects any behavior not based on rational calculations. At most, the market can just create lifestyles that are crystallized in the consumption of particular goods (Brunner 1988b, 97, 119). In the end, the expansion of consumerist behavior in Chile generated a kind of passive conformism among the population, who eventually accepted the individualistic tenets of the neoliberal economic model based on the search for private satisfactions.

In order to understand the readiness of the Chilean people to accept and to support the open market policies that made possible the expansion of consumption, one has to take into account the following factors. To begin with, the consumption of *foreign* goods has always had a tremendous appeal for the Chilean upper and middle classes. This has mainly to do with the fact that since the 1930s until the military coup in 1973, foreign consumer goods were almost impossible to obtain because of the extremely high tariffs protecting national industries from foreign competition. As Ernesto Tironi indicates, the great interest of these social sectors in foreign goods had very little to do with their quality or utility. Their importance was rather related to the fact that they *symbolized* everything that was modern and new, because they came from societies that had prestige and were admired. So the structural scarcity of these products during those years did help to multiply the symbolic value given in the country to foreign goods. The consumption of these products created the illusion of participation in the developed world (Tironi 1986, 105).

The anxiety for consumer goods in the country reached its climax during the Unidad Popular government, when as a result of the economic and political crisis, the population was confronted with chronic shortages of all kind of goods, both foreign and national. In retrospect, one can state that the endemic scarcity of consumer goods constituted one of the main factors that provoked the increasing alienation of the middle class and other parts of the population from the UP government, thus facilitating the military coup of September 1973.

Consumption and Legitimacy

From the outset, the military government clearly understood the political importance of consumption. So, for instance, the official anti-Allende propaganda of the period following the coup was mainly focused on the scarcity issue. Television spots repeatedly showed pictures of unending lines of people waiting in front of stores followed by close-ups of empty shelves. This represented indeed, especially for the middle and upper classes, one of the most traumatic and hated memories of UP period. The official message was that the time of empty shopping bags was definitely over, and that from now on everyone (who could afford it) could enjoy unlimited access to consumer goods.

All this notwithstanding, the consumption of consumer goods was to experience for a while a severe contraction as a result of the application in 1975 of orthodox economic adjustment policies by the neoliberal economic team. As already mentioned, following the recession in 1975–76 the Chilean economy showed a vigorous dynamism in the period 1978–81. This was a triumphant era for the supporters of the military regime. Arnold Harberger, for instance, one of the main intellectual mentors of the Chicago Boys, proclaimed during those days: "One can predict that in ten years Chileans will enjoy a standard of living similar to that of Spain, which has a domestic product at the moment about double Chile's, while in 20 years Chileans will possibly be enjoying the same standards of living as Holland" (quoted in O'Brien and Roddick 1983, 68). General Pinochet, too, forecast in almost every speech a new era of unprecedented levels of consumption. Thus, for instance in 1980, in his annual speech of September 11 to commemorate the military coup, Pinochet promised that by the end of that decade one out of seven Chileans would own a car, one out of five would have a television set, and one out of seven would have a telephone (Vergara 1985, 185).

The media played a strategic role in broadcasting very optimistic projections of the future expansion of mass consumption, and in presenting mass consumption itself as synonymous with progress and modernization. The regime found television's aura of universality an especially effective tool for promoting individualistic acquisitiveness (Brunner 1988b). In the period

1978–81, Chile truly experienced a "consumption *boom*" as almost all consumer goods produced in the core countries became accessible to the Chilean upper and middle classes.

According to Banco Central figures, between 1976 and 1981 Chile imported 2,112,000 television sets, 154,000 kitchen stoves, 332,000 refrigerators, and 132,600 washing machines. In the peak years 1980 and 1981, Chile imported US$18.7 million in candy, US$26.5 million in leather and fur clothes, US$33.3 million in perfume and toiletries, US$50.3 million in alcoholic drinks and cigarettes, US$67.3 million in shoes, hats and umbrellas, and US$74.4 million in toys and amusement articles. In comparison with the country's import patterns of 1970, the import of perfume and toiletries represents an increase of 19,500 percent, and the import of television sets an increase of 9,357 percent (Ffrench-Davis 1982). Moreover, the number of cars in Chile increased from 262,000 in 1976 to more than 600,000 in 1985 (Lavín 1987).

Thousands of foreign goods became familiar and accessible to Chilean households, producing a fallacious image of progress and development in the country. This consumption boom was mainly made possible by factors such as the radical reduction of import tariffs (lowered to an average of 10 percent); the huge expansion of consumption credit for the population (in turn, made possible by generous foreign loans); the strong concentration of income at the upper social echelons (as a result of the regressive effects of the free market policies), and the maintenance of a overvalued national currency, which made foreign goods relatively cheap.

The import boom of consumer goods led to a radical transformation of Chilean streets and shops, as hundreds of thousands of new cars invaded the roads, and a large number of giant shopping centers appeared in the country's main cities with products from all over the world (see Délano and Translaviña 1989, 59–64). Although the main beneficiaries of this consumption boom were the middle and upper classes, it would be a serious mistake to underestimate the extent to which the rest of the population also participated in it. Many people who were not able to afford these consumer goods did finally also obtain access to them by contracting consumer credits, or more often by paying for them in monthly installments. For instance, by 1982, 42 percent of the families of Santiago were paying back one or more consumer loans (Martínez and Tironi 1985). So while the higher social sectors obtained access to modern European cars and very sophisticated U.S. or Japanese electronic products, the poorer segments of the population experienced, in a sense, their own consumption boom by acquiring products such as radios, television sets, battery watches, and cheap foreign clothes and gym shoes, which they previously had never had access to. Chile had in fact become a consumer society, this despite the country's strong social stratification and inequalities.

The internationalization of the Chilean economy has not only strengthened consumerism in the local culture, but also has led to the adoption of values, beliefs, ideas, and even patterns of behavior and cultural orientations similar to those of the core countries. Indeed, one can state that Chilean society has been deeply shaken by the modernizing neoliberal project. Actually, with the relative expansion of market relations the patterns of behavior regulated by economic calculations have also been expanded. In addition, many people availed themselves of a system of meritocratic and individualistic mobility that was replacing the old system in which one had to be part of a group (mainly political parties) and in which mobility was conditioned mainly by the capability of the group to exert political pressure on the state. More generally, the "discovery" of this new world of consumption convinced several social forces that there were direct advantages in the continuation and deepening of the ongoing process of transnationalization of Chilean society.

The Limits of Consumption-Based Legitimacy

The consumption-oriented model introduced by the military government had from the very beginning a structural weakness. To wit, the expansion of consumption was not based on sound economic development and real production, but on the expansion of foreign debt. The economic growth experienced by the Chilean economy in the period 1977–81 was far from sufficient to cope with the country's increasing financial indebtedness to the international banks. Politically, the military government had linked its legitimacy to the continuous expansion of the consumption of consumer goods. In 1981, however, the neoliberal model collapsed as a result of a wave of financial speculation and the enormous foreign debt that Chile had incurred (of almost 20 billion dollars). A deep economic recession followed, which suddenly interrupted the consumerist boom. This produced great discontent and frustration among the upper and middle classes because the crisis had destroyed the lifestyles that they had developed in previous years. The crisis actually produced a dramatic reduction in the import of consumer goods, which fell more than 50 percent in comparison with the pre-crisis period (Tironi 1988, 105).

The economic crisis also activated opposition to the military government, which in the boom years had proved unable to counteract the neoliberal ideological machine. From 1983 on, Chile experienced a true resurrection of the old political parties, who mobilized the population around demands for the restoration of democracy. From 1983 on the opposition was able to get growing support from the population despite the fact that the neoliberal technocrats were able to put an end to the economic crisis and guide the Chilean economy into a remarkable recovery in 1984–89. The regime ideologues were convinced that this should be sufficient to obtain the support of the majority of the Chilean electorate in the scheduled referendum in 1988 to extend Pinochet's rule for another eight years (see Drake and Jaksic 1991). Official opinion-makers propagated through the radio, television, newspapers, and even in books the idea that Chile was "on the eve" of definitively becoming a member of the developed world (see Lavín 1987 and Lavín and Larraín 1989). Dissident scholars, however, countered this overoptimistic view of the country's reality by stressing the growing gap existing between the rich and the poor in the country and the unequal distribution of the benefits of the process of modernization initiated by the neoliberal model (see Tironi 1988). Nevertheless, the opposition forces were realistic enough not to ignore the fact that Chile as a whole had indeed experienced a profound process of modernization since the late 1970s. Thus, during the 1989 presidential elections, which followed as a result of Pinochet's defeat at the 1988 referendum, they did not center their campaign around the modernization question or economic issues, but on the human right abuses of the military for which the Pinochet government had no clear-cut justification or explanation.

On the eve of the opposition's electoral victory in December 1989, it was clear that Chilean society had been radically modernized, and not only in the economic sphere. The new pattern of accumulation introduced by the neoliberal technocracy had indeed helped reduce the traditional dependence of society on the state, and had stimulated a process of individualization and diversification, enlarging the distance between public and private life. In addition, social organizations had become less politicized, and political parties had become less dependent on corporate interests. In short, the Chilean culture had become, in general terms, more pragmatic, more secular, and more individualistic (Tironi 1990).

As Van der Ree (2007) has conclusively established, the goal of making Chile a modern country has been a common objective pursued by Frei Montalva, Allende, and Pinochet as well as by the Concertación governments. Despite their divergent ideological backgrounds and their emphasis on different dimensions of modernity (social, political, economic, or cultural domains), time and again the banner of modernity has been demonstrated to have a formidable mobilizing power among the Chilean population at large. It is for this reason that the ability of the Chicago technocrats to produce a profound modernization of Chilean society was received not only with fervor by the Pinochet supporters, but also with at least tacit approval by the moderate sectors of the opposition.

The Rise of a Technocratized Opposition

The increasingly political role played by technocrats after 1973 was by no means a phenomenon confined exclusively to government circles. This trend was also visible in opposition quarters, where an increasing technocratization of the formulation and implementation of strategy had taken place. Since 1973, a large number of (oppositional) research institutes and nongovernmental organizations (NGOs) had been established and played a key role in the struggle against the authoritarian regime.[15] In 1985, for instance, there existed around forty private research institutes in the social sciences employing 543 researchers (not including research assistants and grant holders), of whom 30 percent had earned master's or doctoral degrees abroad. Around 65 percent of these researchers worked on a full-time basis. The impact of these institutes on national academic "production" was also enormous. During those years, with the exception of economics, the majority of social science articles and books written by Chilean scholars and published in Chile and abroad were by researchers associated with these private institutes. So, for example, in 1980–84 a total of 101 books was published by the thirteen private research institutes that had regular publication programs (Brunner 1986). This professionalization of the political opposition was, in my view, the result of several interrelated social dynamics that came into operation after the breakdown of democracy in 1973, such as the experience of exile, the academization of many political leaders, and the emergence of many private institutes and think tanks run by opposition forces.

15. For a list of private research centers in social sciences established in Chile after 1973, see Lladser 1986. On the role played by the NGOs opposing the military regime, see Taller 1989.

Immediately after the coup the new regime began to persecute intellectuals very severely. Many of them were imprisoned or killed by the military, while a larger group were dispersed all over the world as political exiles (see D. Kay 1987). Many Chilean academics exiled abroad found new lives teaching, pursuing research, or taking postgraduate courses in their new countries of residence. Others, with the support of local authorities and political organizations, created their own research centers dedicated to the analysis of the Chilean reality.[16]

What is important to stress here is the fact that many political leaders (the professional *políticos,* who in Chile had lived from party resources) were often obliged by circumstances to become incorporated into academic circles. Although most of them were academically trained (mainly in law, sociology, or economics), they had not worked as academics before, or for only a very short time. In many cases, the new academic experiences influenced their political outlook or, at least, changed their "political style." They became more scholarly and technocratic, and more involved with new theoretical debates taking place in the world. Many of these political figures learned for the very first time to work (and to achieve common goals) together with people who did not share their philosophical and political vision. This was after years of having inhabited semi-ghettoes within the narrow margins of their own political organizations.

Those politicians and intellectuals who were able to remain in Chile were expelled from the universities and the public institutions where they had worked. For the first time, Chilean intellectuals were radically cut off from their traditional source of income: the state. Their second source of subsistence, the political parties (who in turn also lived from state resources), was

16. That is the case of centers such as ASER-Chile (Paris), Casa Chile (Antwerp), Casa de Chile (Mexico City), Centro de Estudios y Documentación Chile-América (Rome), Centro Salvador Allende (Mexico City), CETRAL (Paris), CIPIE (Madrid), and the Institute for the New Chile (Rotterdam). See Angell and Carstairs 1987, 148–67. The so-called *proceso de renovación* experienced by several Chilean left-wing political parties since the late 1970s (which led to a definitive break with Leninism and toward a revaluation of democracy) is also directly related to the exile question. The exile of many Chilean political leaders in Eastern European countries was rather traumatic. There they directly confronted the dark side of "real socialism." This was, for instance, the case for political figures such as Jorge Arrate (current leader of the Socialist Party), who moved after several difficult years in former East Germany to the Netherlands, where he initiated a profound theoretical and programmatic discussion within the Chilean socialist movement (see Arrate 1983 and 1985). For an analysis of the significance of the socialist renovation for Chile's process of democratization, see Garretón 1987, 243–92.

also attacked by the security forces. The repression of the intellectuals produced a marked dispersal with each individual fighting literally for his or her
own life. After a couple of very repressive years, however, a difficult process
of regrouping and reorganization started. Intellectuals from similar academic
disciplines and with congenial political outlooks began to establish research
institutes as a means of surviving (in terms of income). They were mainly
financed by Western European and North American organizations for international cooperation, as a way of keeping alive an intelligentsia opposed to
military totalitarianism.[17] Some of these institutes also received funds
obtained from time to time by the Chilean political parties in exile.

The academic status of these institutes and the scholarly content of their
activities initially constituted their only "right of existence" within an
extremely repressive environment. Any criticism of the military government
had to be carefully formulated in academic terms and presented in an abstract
manner. This led to the almost complete disappearance of the slogans and
rhetoric that had characterized party politics before the coup.

In 1975 the Catholic Church founded the Academia de Humanismo Cristiano (AHC), to ensure the legal status of several research centers and to protect
them from direct state repression. In addition new research centers were created under the AHC umbrella to shelter persecuted academics and to monitor
the policies applied by the military government in different fields (labor legislation, agrarian policy, education, human rights, and so on).

Many of the research institutes initially tolerated by the military had a
Christian Democratic orientation and basically specialized in macroeconomic
and financial themes. From mid-1974 on the Christian Democratic Party—
which initially had supported the coup and offered technical assistance to the
military government—began to move into the opposition. Those Christian
Democratic academics who were still teaching at the universities were pressured by *gremialista* and neoliberal forces to resign their posts. Such was the
case of the members of the Centro de Estudios y Planificación Nacional
(CEPLAN), an institute associated with the Faculty of Economics of the Uni-

---

17. Thus, an evaluation made by the Swedish Agency for Research Cooperation with Developing Countries (SAREC) reads as follows: "We succeeded in preserving research capacity under
conditions of repression and political crisis. Support for private national centers has enabled
people to continue research projects after military intervention in the universities. These centers
also house researchers expelled from academic or government agencies because of political perse-
cution" (Spanding et al. 1985, 1; see also Brunner 1990, 180–91).

versidad Católica. CEPLAN was formed in 1970 as an alternative to the Chicago Boys when they acquired a dominant position within that university. In 1976 the academics associated with CEPLAN decided to break their links with the Universidad Católica and to establish themselves as a private institute under the new name of Corporación de Investigaciones Económicas para América Latina (CIEPLAN).

This research institute concentrated on monitoring the economic policy of the Chicago Boys. Paradoxically, the first open (tolerated) opposition to the military government and the neoliberal technocracy came from this group of technocrats, who were experts in financial and macroeconomic matters. This team of highly qualified academics accepted the neoliberal challenge ("the theme of economic policy can only be treated by specialists") and began to elaborate very sophisticated technical studies, in which they expressed their criticism of the economic policy of the military government (see Foxley 1983). The scholarly tone utilized by many opposition research institutes in their criticism of neoliberalism made possible the dissemination of their ideas (although in a limited way) through the publication of working papers and the organization of academic symposia on specific matters. For many years this constituted the only authorized way of diffusing ideas other than the official ones (Cavallo 1992, 146).

After a couple of years, CIEPLAN became a true think tank of the Christian Democratic Party. It expanded its activities from monitoring economic policies to the elaboration of proposals for an alternative socioeconomic model and for a new political system to be adopted after the expected departure of the military. The CIEPLAN "Monks" also began to occupy the few spaces left open to the independent press to expand their ideas and criticism to a broader public, by publishing articles and comments in *Mensaje* (owned by the Catholic Church), and later in *Hoy*, the first authorized opposition weekly (of Christian Democratic orientation).[18] During the last years of the military government Alejandro Foxley, director of CIEPLAN, became a well-known public figure who, bolstered by his economic expertise, successfully ventured into the field of political science and in particular the study of political consensus (Foxley 1986, 1989).

18. See Arellano 1982. This is a selection of the articles published between 1977 and 1981. This book became very controversial at that time, because it showed that since 1977 the researchers at CIEPLAN had been predicting the eventual collapse of the neoliberal economic model, which finally occurred in 1981.

Democratic Transition and Technocratization in Chile

From 1983 on, the room for political activities became broader, and scholars associated with several think tanks controlled by the democratic opposition began to criticize the Pinochet regime more openly. In this manner, new mechanisms of cooperation and consultation were created between academics and intellectuals associated with the different research institutes. They were initiated by experts on specific subjects who held similar political views (mostly members of the same political party). Through the organization of regular meetings and workshops, these professional collectives (the so-called *equipos técnicos*) worked out a common diagnosis of the existing situation in a specific field and formulated proposals to be implemented after the expected restoration of democratic rule. Thus, a group of socialist-oriented economists worked together for many years in an attempt to formulate a new economic policy, which was later adopted by the Socialist Party as its official economic program. The same was done by the other political parties and in other areas such as housing, social security, health care, defense, agriculture, education, foreign policy, and so on. This technocratization of party policymaking was facilitated by the fact that, at that time, open consultation with the party rank and file through a congress was unthinkable for security reasons.

In 1984 the Christian Democrats, together with the moderate wing of the Socialist Party and other minor center-left political organizations, formed the Alianza Democrática, an opposition coalition which aimed to defeat the military regime by political means at a plebiscite in a few years' time. According to the 1980 constitution, a national referendum was to be held before the end of 1988. The people had to choose between the prolongation of Pinochet's rule till 1997 (the "yes-option") or the holding of free elections within a year after the referendum (the "no-option").

The campaign for the "no-option" led to very productive cooperation among the different *equipos técnicos* of the political parties in this coalition. For the first time in modern Chilean politics, technocrats from the Center and from the Left worked together to formulate a common political program and to elaborate sectorial policies for a future democratic government. This exercise was especially fruitful for two reasons. First, it reduced—if not eliminated—the historical fears and prejudices existing between them. This was made easier by the fact that they shared similar technical and professional approaches and in many cases had studied at the same academic centers both in Chile and abroad. This cooperation at the technocratic top strongly contributed to the initiation of the rapprochement among supporters of different parties at the bottom, who for many decades had inhabited separate and even antagonistic political subcultures. Second, the existence of these multiparty technical teams greatly facilitated the formulation of a coherent governmental program for the presidential elections held in December 1989, and the subsequent formation of multiparty *equipos técnicos* to occupy positions in ministries and state agencies upon achieving electoral victory. In this way many technocrats from the different political parties who were appointed to official positions after the installation of the government of Patricio Aylwin in March 1990 had already worked together for more than seven years.

In short, these technocrats became important "bridge builders" between the several political and social forces who supported the Concertación alliance following the restoration of democratic rule in 1990.

6

The Emergence
of a Technocratic Democracy

The political developments in Chile since the 1990 democratic restoration provide, in my view, an excellent example of how democracy can coexist with technocratic groups occupying key positions in government. My contention here is that the present-day Chilean democracy not only "tolerates" the presence of technocratic groups, but that the latter have played a fundamental role in facilitating its consolidation.

In my opinion, the vital role played by technocrats in the four Concertación governments has been facilitated by the existence of a kind of "empate político," a political tie between the center-left forces in power and a strong right-wing opposition, including the business community and the military institutions. This situation shows many similarities with the political scenario existing in the late 1930s described in Chapter 3, which forced the various political forces to come to a basic "agreement on fundamentals" that facilitated the functioning of the Estado de Compromiso. Already in the transitional years 1988–90, the democratic opposition tried to calm down the entrepreneurial sectors that feared that democratic restoration would lead to the elimination of the free market economy and a total repoliticization of public policies. The democratic forces were placed in a difficult situation, for they were confronting a self-conscious military visibly proud of the modernization of the country and the economic development achieved during the Pinochet administration and a strong and extremely assertive business community, which was not willing to observe passively the destruction of the general's "oeuvre." The fact is that the Right and the military government were still able to generate support among a considerable part of the Chilean population, for this sector still obtained 43 percent of the votes in the 1988 referendum and 44.8 percent during the 1989 presidential elections.[1] In addition to this, from 1990 on the right-wing sectors could count on a comfortable overrepresentation in parliament because of the inclusion of the "designated senators" and the introduction of a binominal electoral law.

In this particular scenario the Concertación coalition was almost forced to "demilitarize" economic policymaking by putting it in the hands of renowned economists with technocratic credentials. In this manner, as in the late 1930s, the presence of competent technocrats in charge of the government's economic and financial decisions constituted a valuable guarantee for the business community, the army, and the political Right in general, that the Concertación coalition would not introduce fundamental changes in the economic model. However, this relative "equilibrium of forces" reached between the Center-Left and the Right since the late 1980s is not the only major factor that explains the adoption of technocratic formulas by the Concertación forces. What has been in my view even more important in facilitating the strong technocratic presence in the democratic era has been the long and painful process of "political learning" that took place among Concertación leaders about the causes of the breakdown of democratic rule in 1973. After years of retrospective analyses many among them came to the conclusion that one vital factor in the fall of Allende and the subsequent destruction of democracy was the extreme politicization of the state agencies, which had hindered the application of rational and coherent policies. Thus, I believe that the technocratization of the government's economic management during the Concertación years has mainly been the result of political necessity as well as of conviction.

As this chapter also shows, the Concertación governments have been constantly confronted with the tension between their objectives of high rates of economic growth and an efficient administration of the state on the one hand, and the need to encourage popular participation on the other. What the Chilean case reveals is that achieving notable success in the social and economic

---

1. Since 1990 the electoral support for right-wing candidates for president has been maintained at similar levels, and on two occasions they almost won the contests. See Angell 2007 for an in-depth study of the electoral process since 1990.

fields (sharp reduction of poverty, high levels of economic growth and prosperity, and so on) does not necessarily legitimate the technocratic structures that contributed to that success. The growing demands for participation, which have become manifest during the Bachelet government, have forced the authorities to search for consultative formulas that combine the technocratic rationale with certain spaces for civil society representation. I will return to this point in the final chapter.

Finally, the Concertación experience provides a classical case of covert and overt confrontations between technocrats and politicians within the government because the latter feel displaced by the former as the major actor in the decision-making process. After 1990 there followed a period of tacit "truce" in which the Concertación politicians actively facilitated the work of Aylwin's economic team in order to preserve economic stability in the country. Since the Frei Ruiz-Tagle administration, however, the animosity between politicians and technocrats has become public; the former have often openly attacked the presence of technocrats in the government. As we shall see in the final section of this chapter, during the Bachelet government the attacks coming from Concertación politicians against the technocratic inner circle around the president reached unprecedented highs, since the president in her first two years of government has kept most of the Concertación political leaders off her cabinet. Thus in recent years technocrats have tended to overshadow politicians within the government. The politicians' counterattack, however, has not been easy. They have been repeatedly accused of corruption and other irregularities that have damaged even further the already low reputation of political parties and the parliament among the Chilean population.

The triumph of the Concertación coalition at the December 1989 presidential elections marked the beginning of a new era in Chile's political history. Since the installation of the Aylwin government in March 1990, Chilean society has indeed experienced profound transformations in the socioeconomic, political, institutional, and even cultural realms. Despite these changes, however, the manifestly technocratic nature of governmental decision-making in the economic, financial, and administrative fields has been a constant feature of all the Concertación governments. It can be said that the Concertación governments of Patricio Aylwin (1990–94), Eduardo Frei (1994–2000), Ricardo Lagos (2000–2006), and Michelle Bachelet (2006–10) have privileged the formation of powerful technocratic teams in charge of the economic policies. These governments have also adopted, in different degrees, a technocratic discourse based on the modernization of the economy and the public sector, the search for efficiency, and a government "of the best." The Concertación's objectives of simultaneously accomplishing economic growth and financial stability on the one hand, and the reduction of social inequality in the country on the other (embraced in its slogan "growth with equity") have constantly strained the relations between technocrats and politicians within the governmental block.

In this chapter I analyze how Presidents Aylwin, Frei, Lagos, and Bachelet have formed their political and technical teams, stressing the main factors that since 1990 have influenced the balance of power between politicians and technocrats within the Concertación governments. Special attention is given to the personal political styles characterizing each of the four Concertación presidents, which in my view constitutes an important factor that explains their personal inclination to strengthen or weaken the presence and power of technocratic groups within their administrations. In addition, it will be argued that the position of technocrats within the governments has also been conditioned by how each president has conducted relations with the political parties. As will be shown in this chapter, the existence of open and concealed clashes between politicians and technocrats over power and influence within the government has been a common feature of all the Concertación governments.

Aylwin: From the CIEPLAN Monks to the "Transversal Party"

From the very beginning the Concertación coalition conferred great importance on providing a solid control of the economy, expressed in the achievement of high levels of economic growth and financial stability. This was seen as a necessary condition for the achievement of political stability in the country. There was an urgent need to eradicate the initial fears among some influential sectors in society that the restoration of democratic rule could lead to economic volatility and decline. For these reasons, the composition of the economic team under the Aylwin government reflected the government's desire to reassure[2] both local entrepreneurial groups and the international

---

2. On the importance of the signaling of messages of professional reputation and good credentials for obtaining or keeping the investors' confidence, see B. Schneider 1998.

business community that the administration of the Chilean economy would be conducted by experts.

The ascendancy of technocrats under the Aylwin government was facilitated by several factors. To begin with, the new democratic authorities required a clear and legitimate *modus operandi* for government appointments because of the coalitional nature of the new government. President Aylwin announced at the very beginning of his administration that he did not intend to distribute posts on the basis of "party quotas." As already indicated in Chapter 4, the distribution of posts according to party membership (rather than merit) constituted one of the most criticized features of the Allende government. Thus, following democratic restoration, everyone (including the parties that were part of the former Popular Unity coalition) wanted to avoid this danger at any cost. Accordingly, Aylwin stated that governmental posts would be awarded to "the most capable" in their specific technical fields. So in general terms it can be said that Aylwin's democratic government had implicitly accepted the principle introduced by the neoliberal technocracy under Pinochet, namely, that technical rather than political skills had to be the main selection criterion.

Second, the phenomenon of exile in the period 1973–89 certainly contributed, among other things, to the overall academic upgrading of the dissident intelligentsia and the political class in general. Many of the figures who since 1990 have held government positions, particularly those who served during the Aylwin government, spent the authoritarian period in exile, where they obtained specialized academic and technical training (Angell and Carstairs 1987). In addition, those who remained in Chile during the Pinochet government gained access to postgraduate programs in industrialized nations as a result of the institutional links developed between many dissident research institutes and foreign university centers (see Brunner and Barrios 1987 and Puryear 1994). Thus the high degree of technocratization of governmental decision-making since 1990 has been made possible by the existence of a large number of individuals with a high level of specialized academic training among the leading figures of the political forces participating in the Concertación coalition.

Last but not least, one of the major concerns of the Aylwin government was the preservation of financial and economic stability in the country to guarantee governability (Moreno 2006). The new democratic authorities were well aware of the fact that it would be almost impossible to consolidate the democratic system in a climate of economic instability.[3] In addition, the achievement of economic success in terms of economic growth, increasing exports, and guaranteed economic and financial stability was seen as essential for the prolongation of the Concertación coalition's rule in the country.

Therefore, when we look at the main figures chosen in 1990 to lead the *equipo económico* during the Aylwin administration, we find that almost all the officials appointed to high-level positions had undertaken postgraduate studies abroad. Never before had a democratic government in Chile had so many highly specialized technocrats at the ministerial level. Second, almost all the high-ranking officials had worked during the military regime at private research institutes founded by the opposition. The same trend can be observed in other ministries and state institutions. Even more significant is the fact that former members of the private research center "Corporación de Investigaciones Económicas para Latinoamérica" (CIEPLAN) occupied many of the most strategic positions within the economic team. Finance Minister Alejandro Foxley, founder and president of this Christian Democratically oriented think tank, proved able to make his CIEPLAN Monks[4] assemble into a cohesive team, whose strong *esprit de corps* shows many resemblances to the Chicago Boys.[5]

President Aylwin, an old-fashioned politician and former professor of law, showed little interest in becoming directly involved in the management of the economy. He was particularly concerned with the open wounds produced by the human rights violations of the previous regime and sought to find the truth and to do justice "within the limits of what was possible" as he put it. So Aylwin made public his full confidence in Alejandro Foxley and his collaborators and left the command of the economic policies entirely in the hands of the former CIEPLAN director. Thus, from the very beginning, Foxley enjoyed "relative autonomy" within the cabinet, demanding the right to choose his nearest collaborators in the *equipo económico* personally. He argued

3. The economic program of the Concertación stated that "there will be no growth, no peace or social justice if macroeconomic equilibria are broken because of an inadequate management of the economy, or because the goals are incompatible with available resources" (see Concertación 1993).

4. Fernando Henrique Cardoso dubbed the members of CIEPLAN "Monks" following the announcement of Aylwin's cabinet in March 1990. See "CIEPLAN Monks Take Command in Chile," *Southern Cone Report*, April 19, 1990, 4.

5. At that time the CIEPLAN technocrats were often referred to by the press as the "CIEPLAN boys," to stress the technocratic similarities with their predecessors (see, e.g., *El Mercurio*, May 11, 1990).

that this was the only way to achieve the needed coherence in the formulation and application of his financial policies (see Giraldo 1996, 256). As Montecinos points out, "The economic team requested and obtained significant leverage in order to resist pressures for increased government spending. The high level of cohesiveness in the government contributed to maintain its stability. Against the complaints of sectorial ministries, but with the support of the President, the jurisdiction of Foxley's team encompassed policy areas that were well beyond the traditional boundaries of the Finance Ministry" (1998a, 119). As a result of the excellent management of the economy, Foxley's prestige and popularity among the population became very high, and at one point, he was seen by many as the "natural successor" to Patricio Aylwin.[6]

Despite their relative autonomy from the traditional party structures, one must still bear in mind that the Concertación technocrats continued to work within the framework of political parties. The technocrats' prominence during the Aylwin government was possibly also facilitated by the fact that since March 1990 the political parties had a difficult restart after many years of inactivity in the public sphere. But as early as the mid-1990s it had become clear that traditional politicians would not be able to restore their old pivotal position within the Chilean political system. Many of them found a redoubt in Parliament and were no longer in leading positions at ministerial level, as had been the case before September 1973.

Preserving economic stability was certainly not the sole concern of the Aylwin government. The new authorities also had to deal with the extremely sensitive question of the human rights abuses committed by the military forces during the Pinochet regime. The specific nature of the Chilean transition made it very difficult to find an adequate solution for the human rights problem without producing a negative impact on military-civil relations and the political stability in the country. On this matter, technocrats were of little use. Therefore, during his administration, Aylwin also recruited a large team of legal experts and experienced politicians to monitor this process and to reduce the frictions produced by this reopening of the painful recent past. He also counted among his ministers on the valuable support of experienced *políticos* such as Enrique Correa, Edgardo Boeninger, Enrique Krauss, and Patricio Rojas, who coordinated the sensitive relations with the opposition parties and the armed forces.

6. See, for instance, "Foxley, el hombre fuerte," *HOY*, April 9–15, 1990, 3–5.

Table 2   Members of the economic team of the Aylwin government: foreign university affiliation

Name	Position	University
Ministry of Finance		
Alejandro Foxley[a]	Finance minister	University of Wisconsin
Pablo Pinera[a]	Deputy finance minister	University of Boston
Andrés Velasco[a]	Chef de cabinet	Columbia University
José Pablo Arellano[a]	Budget director	Harvard University
Javier Etcheverry[a]	Tax director	University of Michigan
Manuel Marfán[a]	Policy coordinator	Yale University
Ministry of Economic Affairs		
Carlos Ominami	Minister of economic affairs	Université de Paris
Jorge Marshall	Deputy minister of economic affairs	Harvard University
Alejandro Jadresic	Coordinator of sectorial policies	Harvard University
Juan Rusque	National Fisheries Service	University of Wales
Fernán lbáñez	Secretary of foreign investments	MIT
Other institutions		
Andrés Sanfuentes	President of Banco del Estado	University of Chicago
Eduardo Aninat	Coordinator of foreign debt	Harvard University
Ernesto Tironi*	General manager of CORFO	MIT
Hugo Lavados	Supervisor of stock markets	University of Boston
Roberto Zahler	Adviser to Central Bank	University of Chicago
Ricardo Ffrench-Davis*	Director of studies at Central Bank	University of Chicago
Alvaro Briones	Operations manager of CORFO	U. Autónoma de México
Ernesto Edwards	Vice president of Banco del Estado	University of Boston
Alvaro García	Subdirector of ODEPLAN	University of California
Fernando Ordoñez	Subdirector of ODEPLAN	University of Edinburgh

* Former members of CIEPLAN.

SOURCES: *El Mercurio*, April 11, 1990, p. (B) I; *Southern Cone Report*, April 19, 1990, p. 4.

It is also important to stress that figures such as Alejandro Foxley and other former members of CIEPLAN proved to have both great technical ability and good political skills, and thus came to play the role of what Roderic Camp (1985) has called "political technocrats." By way of example, Foxley played a key role in establishing mechanisms of consultation between the state, entrepreneurs, and labor representatives. In turn, Labor Minister René Cortázar, another CIEPLAN Monk, convinced many labor leaders about the absolute need to moderate their socioeconomic demands in order to avoid labor unrest and the increase of social tensions, which could lead to economic instability.[7] With this, Foxley and Cortázar did in fact shape the basis for the establishment of what Peter Evans calls an "embedded autonomy." These economists in charge of the economic policies and labor issues kept fluid contact with the actors involved, yet at the end of the day made the final decisions with a large degree of independence.[8]

The members of Aylwin's cabinet and their closest associates were very conscious of the historical significance of their actions for the future of democratic rule in the country: they were writing history and knew it. This helped to generate a sphere of close cooperation and increasing trust among them, despite their different political affiliations. The political style that characterized President Aylwin was crucial in producing this high level of affinity among the members of his cabinet. He made it clear that they were working for the entire Chilean people and not for the parties of the Concertación coalition. Hence, his direct collaborators consciously transferred their loyalties from their political parties to his government (Fuentes 2000).

What we see during the first Concertación government is the constitution of a close and successful cooperation between technocrats and some leading *políticos* at the highest levels of decision-making. A cross-fertilization phenomenon took place in which politicians adopted a more technocratic approach (talking in more technical manner, often referring to statistics and the like), while technocrats strengthened their political skills (by establishing links with representatives of civil society and by referring to the goal of consolidating democratic rule in the country). The degree of mutual understanding achieved among the main collaborators of President Aylwin was such that it resulted in the natural emergence of a very close companionship among the technico-political team within his cabinet. This became known as the "partido transversal," as it cut across formal party differences. This phenomenon was in fact the expression of the broad consensus achieved since the early 1990s

---

7. Foxley and Cortázar summarize their experiences in attempting to improve industrial relations in the country in Foxley 1993 and Cortázar 1993.

8. As Evans has pointed out, "Having successfully bound the behavior of incumbents to its pursuit of collective ends, the state can act with some independence in relation to particularistic societal pressures. . . . 'Embeddedness' is as important as autonomy. Embeddedness . . . implies a concrete set of connections that link the state intimately and aggressively to particular social groups with whom the state shares a joint project of transformation" (1995, 59).

among the different forces forming the Concertación on the main economic and political objectives ahead and the ways to achieve them.

While some warmly welcomed the emergence of "transversality" within Aylwin's cabinet—they saw it as a sign of political maturity and a sound basis to maintain political stability in the country—others saw in it the possible surfacing of a self-conscious and closed clique that could hinder democratic accountability. Transversality was also be seen by some sectors of the political class as the result of the adoption of a technocratic approach by which the country's main social and economic problems were removed from their political dimension and presented as being basically technical problems that simply required technical solutions. The emergence of this transversal party was seen by the leaders of the main Concertación political parties as a danger to their own position and their ability to maintain their influence on government decisions through "their" ministers and high officials within the cabinet and their representatives in Parliament. Although transversality was less cultivated by the following Concertación governments, this experience during the Aylwin government would continue to be nostalgically remembered within the most moderate and technically oriented sectors of the Concertación coalition in years to come.

The Iron Circle Versus the Top Ten: The Frei Years

The end of Patricio Aylwin's presidential term of office brought to a close the first period of the Concertación era, which revolved primarily around the transition to democracy. When Eduardo Frei Ruiz-Tagle became president of the Republic in December 1994, there was a visible shift toward a modernizing agenda. In the official analysis of the Concertación parties, the two greatest fears of the transition period (economic crisis and another military coup) had not materialized. It was felt that the second government of the Concertación should address its energies to the modernization of the state apparatus, the judicial system, and the infrastructure, and seek to integrate Chile more fully into the world economy.

The new president, an engineer by profession, with a markedly entrepreneurial profile, had not engaged in much party politics in the past. He only became politically active at the time of the 1988 referendum and was later elected senator in the elections of 1989. President Frei sought to give his government agenda a more technical and economic slant. He summarized his modernizing project, which was prepared by a team of intellectuals and technocrats, in his electoral platform, "Un Gobierno para los Nuevos Tiempos: Bases Programáticas del Segundo Gobierno de la Concertación de Partidos por la Democracia" (A Government for the New Times: The Platform of the Second Government of the Coalition of Parties for Democracy). The terms "modernity" and "modernization" abounded in his program, which highlighted the need to modernize the state apparatus and eliminate inefficacy and inefficiency from public administration. In an evidently technocratic and meritocratic vein, it was argued that

> At present, the Chilean state has lagged behind in tackling the great challenges of development and modernity, in taking advantage of the historic opportunity that opens itself up to the country . . . and in gradually moving toward a truly modern style of governance and management. . . . A performance-oriented management style . . . presupposes a change in the culture of [public] administration, which will make it possible to improve the quality of services. . . . The incorporation of technologies and modern management principles will make it possible to give prompt and quality solutions to the problems of Chileans, while avoiding bureaucracy. . . . We shall assign maximum importance to the quality of the persons who hold posts of responsibility within the state. We shall set up a system for the appointments to top management posts, which includes technical suitability.

As Alfredo Joignant (2003, 87) puts it, "It is the expectation of economic transformation generated by President Frei as well as the explicitly modernizing 'nuevos tiempos' proposal that has led to the spread of powerful depoliticizing currents among the population, in view of which the promise of more and better democracy could not but succumb to the onslaught originating in the technocratic sectors of the Concertación elites."

Despite his emphasis on appointing technically qualified individuals to his administration, Frei was, at first at least, also obliged to strengthen the political sector within his cabinet. The belief at the time was that Aylwin's successor would have to deal with an increased level of unrest from the popular sectors and from urban laborers. The trade unions had honored their agreement with Aylwin's government to moderate their demands in order to facilitate the consolidation of democracy in the country (Cortázar 1993). However, by the end of his administration there already was a generalized feeling that the existing political stability and economic prosperity had removed all serious threats to the new democracy and that the time had come to share the fruits of economic progress. To head off any problems and protect the gains made during the Aylwin government, Frei appointed the general secretaries of the member parties of the Concertación to his cabinet: Germán Correa (Socialist Party) was made minister of the interior; Víctor Manuel Rebolledo (Partido por la Democracia, PPD), minister of government affairs; and political expert Genaro Arriagada (Christian Democratic Party), minister of the presidency. In addition, Frei appointed Socialist Jorge Arrate as minister of labor in order to hold the trade unions back. Thus Frei put an end to the existence of Aylwin's "transversal party," which had alienated both the top brass and grassroots of the government coalition parties.

However, with the exception of some attempted strikes by teachers and the public health sector, the much anticipated labor and social tensions did not materialize, and bringing the parties' general secretaries into the cabinet only served to replicate within the cabinet itself the internal party political skirmishes between rival factions. Frei tolerated this state of affairs for six months, then in September 1994, restructured his cabinet. He replaced Germán Correa with Carlos Figueroa as minister of the interior, and appointed Edmundo Pérez Yoma minister of defense. These two ministers, together with Genaro Arriagada, all personal friends of the president, were to become his main advisers and the wielders of a large amount of influence and power within the government. The press referred to this threesome as Frei's "Iron Circle." They not only exerted a great of influence on Frei's decisions but also acted as a presidential "buffer," reducing to a minimum Frei's appearances in the mass media and before the people. They were moved by the conviction that Frei was a very poor communicator and that the achievements and objectives of his government were better conveyed to the citizens through his main ministers.

In the same cabinet reshuffling President Frei also appointed José Joaquín Brunner, an outstanding sociologist and intellectual, to replace Víctor Manuel Rebolledo as minister of government affairs. Brunner was not a member of Frei's circle of friends, but he soon came to be much trusted by the president, with the consequent gradual weakening of the position and influence of the

Iron Circle. Obviously, this gained him the enmity of the Iron Circle.[9] Brunner imposed order on the cabinet, demanding accountability from and defining the limits of the sphere of influence of each of the ministers within the administration. With this, he put a limit on how much the members of the Iron Circle could interfere in issues that were beyond their remit.[10] Brunner's presence on the cabinet also implied a strengthening of the more "liberal" wing of the Concertación, which staunchly supported the modernizing agenda seeking the professionalization and technification of the government and the modernization of the economy through more privatizations and a larger degree of internationalization of the Chilean economy.

President Frei knew that in order to undertake the much awaited modernization of the state and the Chilean economy, he would need the collaboration of a large group of technocrats to formulate and implement the necessary measures to make the "New Times" take shape. The star of the economic team was Finance Minister Eduardo Aninat, who had privileged access to the person of the president, but always had to contend with actions by the Iron Circle intended to limit his power and influence. This prestigious economist, who had worked at CIEPLAN in the 1980s, was the main negotiator with the international banks in the process of restructuring the Chilean foreign debt during the Aylwin administration. He did his postgraduate work at Harvard University and for many years acted as consultant for the World Bank and the Inter-American Development Bank (IDB), advising on the application of several structural adjustments in countries of the region.[11] Aninat teamed up with his undersecretary Manuel Marfán, another of Alejandro Foxley's CIEPLAN Monks, who had a doctorate from Yale. During the Aylwin administration, Marfán had acted as coordinator between the Ministry of Finance and the Banco Central and had headed the technical team that carried out the tax reforms in 1990 and 1993.

In addition to the Finance Ministry senior incumbents, Frei also availed himself of the enthusiastic support of a vast group of young technocrats (see Table 3). They were mainly between forty and forty-five years old; most of

9. See "Los conflictos de palacio," *La Tercera,* May 17, 1997.

10. On the strengthening of Brunner's position within Frei's government, see "La victoria del afuerino," *Qué Pasa,* May 6–12, 1997. See also "José Joaquín Brunner Ried," *Qué Pasa,* July 1–7, 1997.

11. See "La ruta de Aninat para llegar al FMI," *La Tercera,* September 19, 1999.

Table 3 Leading technocrats under the Frei administration

Name	Position	Degree/profession	Accrediting institution
Jorge Rosenblut	Deputy minister of telecommunications	Ph.D. in economics	Harvard University
Pablo Halpern	Director secretary of communication	Ph.D. in communications and culture	University of Pennsylvania
Eduardo Bitrán	Chief executive officer, CORFO	M.A. in economics	Boston University
José Pablo Arellano	Minister of education	Ph.D. in economics	Harvard University
Claudio Hohmann	Minister of transportation	Civil engineer	Universidad Católica de Chile
Carlos Mladinic	Minister of agriculture	Economist	Universidad de Chile
Germán Quintana	Minister of planning, MIDEPLAN	Civil engineer	Universidad de Chile
Felipe Sandoval	Vice president, CORFO	Civil engineer	Universidad de Chile
Mario Marcel	Executive secretary, Committee for Modernization of Public Management	Ph.D. in economics	Cambridge University
César Oyarzo	Director, National Health Fund	M.A. in economics	Georgetown University
Jorge Rodríguez	Deputy minister for regional development	M.A. in economics	Boston University
Claudio Orrego	Executive secretary, Committee for Modernization of Public Management	M.A. in public policy	Harvard University
Daniel Fernández	Director, Santiago underground	Civil engineer	Universidad de Chile
Alex Figueroa	Minister of health	Physician	Universidad Católica de Chile
Oscar Landerretche	Deputy minister of economic affairs	Ph.D. in economics	University of Oxford
Guillermo Pickering	Deputy minister of infrastructure	Lawyer	Universidad de Chile
Roberto Pizarro	Minister of planning and international cooperation	Ph.D. in economics	University of Sussex
José de Gregorio	Coordinator of economic policies	Ph.D. in economics	MIT
Sergio Galilea	Deputy minister of the presidency	M.A. in urban planning	Universidad de Chile

SOURCES: Several newspapers and institutional Web sites.

them had studied economics or engineering, and had done postgraduate studies abroad. Some of them had already worked in Aylwin's government, others came from the private sector and the world of academia. Among those who made names for themselves under Frei were Jorge Rosenblut, Eduardo Bitrán, and Pablo Halpern, who were often identified as the *de facto* leaders of this new generation of technocrats referred to by the media as the "Frei Boys," as a parallel to Pinochet's Chicago Boys.

Jorge Rosenblut, a civil engineer with a doctorate in economics from Harvard had been the director of interministerial coordination during the Aylwin administration, working in close collaboration with Edgardo Boeninger, at the time secretary general of the presidency and gray eminence of the transition during this government (see Boeninger 1997). Frei initially appointed Rosenblut deputy minister of telecommunications and later, in May 1995, undersecretary general of the presidency. He was one of the drivers of modernization and one of the technocrats most heeded by Frei. His strong visibility and evident privileged access to the president made him one of the most attacked targets by the members of the Iron Circle.

Because of his close connection with Jorge Marshall, Eduardo Bitrán, a civil engineer with a master's from MIT and a doctorate in economics from Boston University, began to collaborate in 1989 in the design of technological policies for the Concertación program, which eventually took him to the Finance Ministry in 1990. His initial work was that of Minister Foxley's adviser on sectorial policies during Aylwin's government, and he was the author of the Capital Market Bill, which was approved during this administration. Frei appointed him to be the CEO of CORFO. In this position, he became known as the advocate of privatization and a clear defender of market economy, full economic competition, and reduction of the entrepreneurial role of the state.[12]

Frei appointed Pablo Halpern director of the secretariat of communication and culture, with the mission of safeguarding the image of the president. Halpern had a doctorate in communications from the University of Pennsylvania, and was considered to be one of the main experts in Chile in the field because he had worked with the main public image builders of the United States. In the course of Frei's senatorial and presidential campaigns in 1989

12. See "Eduardo Bitrán: Liberal de tomo y lomo," *La Tercera*, May 26, 1997. See also "Un giro con tornillos," *El Mercurio*, July 7, 2006.

and 1994, both men worked in close contact; and in later years, when Frei was elected president, this rapport continued, with his consequent appointment. From this position, Halpern developed close links with the press and other mass media. This increased his visibility among the people at La Moneda Palace and generated some tension with the Iron Circle.

What these three officials—Rosenblut, Bitrán, and Halpern—had in common was their youth, their markedly technical profiles, professional expertise, and impressive academic credentials obtained in the United States. In addition, they shared a liberal vision of politics and the economy and were convinced of the need to strengthen the modernization of the country on all fronts. Although their identification with a specific political party was weak, these young men were united by a strong feeling of belonging to the Concertación. Their technical profiles and common aspects in their way of thinking and acting drew them together, and by 1996 they were already identified by the press as the "Top Ten," a group that on several occasions would see the president on his own, to discuss matters related to the modernizing agenda.[13] Frei valued their lack of party political attachment, their technical know-how, and their determination to see modernization through. Because of this, he gave them unlimited freedom to develop their ideas and implement their plans.[14]

In September 1996, President Frei decided on an important change in his cabinet. He replaced Genaro Arriagada with an economist, Juan Villarzú, as minister of the presidency. This was a sign that the Iron Circle was losing power in the eyes of President Frei. A front-line technocrat, Villarzú had in fact been one of the original Chicago Boys. He had a master's in economics from the University of Chicago and had participated actively in the initial years of the military government as director of the Budget Office (1973–75).[15] He later held executive positions in the private sector and on the return of

13. The name for this informal group was given by one of its members, as one of their meetings coincided with the tennis match on May 7, 1996, in which the Chilean tennis player Marcelo Ríos achieved a victory that brought him into the "Top Ten" of the Association of Tennis Professionals.

14. In a later interview, Rosenblut said: "During Frei's government the freedom of execution that he gave us ministers was extraordinary. In the economic, telecommunications, and energy spheres, he gave enormous space to manage things our way" (*Revista COSAS*, January 6, 2003).

15. In a later interview, Villarzú expressed an open support of technocracy: "I believe in a technocratic state, efficient at the level of execution, in which ministers, undersecretaries and the middle management should be professional, efficient, well paid, and so on" (*La Nación*, June 6, 2004).

democracy formed part of Aylwin's administration as executive vice president of CODELCO.

With this cabinet change six months before the midpoint of his term of office, Frei wanted to reactivate his modernizing agenda. In addition to Villarzú he appointed a series of young technocrats to key posts. Accordingly, he opted for economist José Pablo Arellano (forty-four) as his new minister of education. Arellano, who had a doctorate in economics from Harvard, started his professional career at CIEPLAN and was its executive director from 1984 to 1989. At the time of his appointment as education minister he was the budget director at the Ministry of Finance. Frei appointed civil engineer Claudio Hohmann (forty-one) transportation minister. Hohmann had previously worked on the privatization of the railways and had designed the plan for the access of private individuals to the passenger transport business. Commercial engineer Carlos Mladinic (forty-one), who had previously been CORFO's CEO, undersecretary of economy, and director general of international economic relations at the Ministry of Foreign Affairs, was appointed minister of agriculture. The last of the young technocrats recruited into the modernizing program was Roberto Pizarro (forty-two), who became the new minister of planning and international cooperation.[16]

Everybody expected that these appointments would be a sort of acknowledgment of the work done by the Frei Boys, but the arrival of Villarzú restricted the leeway and influence of people like Rosenblut and Bitrán. What must be borne in mind is that although Villarzú is considered to be a technocrat *pur sang*, he has always been a party man (PDC) and also had political experience in negotiations with the right-wing opposition. He was also a personal friend of Figueroa's, which also limited his inclination to develop a very close relation with the Frei Boys. Villarzú's arrival also overshadowed Aninat's position, who finally left the Ministry of Finance in 1998 to join the IMF.[17]

The cabinet change did not reduce the tension between the Frei Boys and Ministers Figueroa and Pérez Yoma. On the contrary, the latter intensified their attack on Rosenblut, Halpern, and Bitrán. At a meeting of the political team early in November of that year, Pérez Yoma is said to have referred to Rosenblut, Halpern, and Bitrán in very offensive terms as a "dangerous Jewish troika." This episode, which was leaked to the press, was later categorically

16. See "Cinco cambios en el gabinete de Frei," *La Tercera*, September 28, 1996.
17. See "Juan Villarzú: El plan maestro," *Revista HOY*, February 3–9, 1997, and "El hombre fuerte del gabinete: La estrategia Villarzú," *La Tercera*, September 28, 1997.

denied by the defense minister. Deputy Jorge Schaulsohn, also of Jewish ancestry, protested in person to President Frei, because he considered this an act of anti-Semitism.

Christian Democrats who sympathized with Pérez Yoma sprang to his defense and launched a series of accusations in the press against Rosenblut's performance. Such was the case of PDC deputy Juan Carlos Latorre, who in a press interview on November 7 hinted that Rosenblut's links with the entrepreneurial sector had led him to block all legislation meant to keep a controlling eye on private companies. In order to avoid a conflict with Minister Pérez Yoma, neither Minister Villarzú nor Brunner came to Rosenblut's defense. Ricardo Lagos, the public works minister, who distrusted the privatizing urge of the "Top Ten," also remained silent.[18] When Rosenblut realized how little support he had among key actors within the government, he submitted his resignation to Frei on the following day.[19] This was undoubtedly a victory for Pérez Yoma, but the strong efforts needed to remove the undersecretary were a proof of his own political weakness.

Amid a scenario of growing weakening of his influence, Defense Minister Pérez Yoma, stated in April 1997 that "there are schemers in La Moneda,"[20] implicitly referring to Brunner and Halpern, whom he always considered to be responsible for spreading his scathing remark about the Rosenblut-Bitrán-Halpern trio. The weakness of Pérez Yoma and Figueroa's position became clear when both Brunner and Halpern remained in their posts after Pérez Yoma's accusation. However, after Rosenblut's resignation, dismay set in among the technocrats, whose initiatives to push forward their modernizing plans were thwarted.[21] Thus, one year later, Bitrán was forced to resign from CORFO. He became the CEO of Fundación Chile.[22] Halpern was the only

18. As a minister, Lagos also had some clashes with the "Top Ten" on some specific issues, such as Bitrán's plans to privatize the water companies and so on. All this explains the fact that in the subsequent government of Ricardo Lagos such figures as Rosenblut, Halpern, and Bitrán held no public posts and kept a watchful eye on the situation from the entrepreneurial world. However, as we shall see later, after Bachelet's victory in January 2006, these three technocrats made a glorious comeback to the public scene.

19. See "La primera baja," in *Qué Pasa*, November 15, 1996. See also "El corazón de los tecnócratas," *La Época*, November 17, 1996, and "Políticos y tecnócratas," *La Tercera*, November 17, 1996. Rosenblut later became an important executive in several telecommunications companies.

20. See *La Tercera*, April 1997.

21. See "La épica modernizadora que no fue: Los desencantados de Frei," *La Tercera*, July 13, 1999.

22. He was to remember his departure from CORFO as follows: "We made enemies in differ-

member of the trio to survive the onslaught of the traditional politicians in the cabinet until the end of the Frei administration.[23]

The position of yet another member of the Iron Circle, that of Interior Minister Carlos Figueroa, was also on the wane. Figueroa was guilty of a faux pas of his own when, at the municipal elections of October 1996, he arrived at the polling station without his identity card, which he had left at home, and used his driver's license as identification. This aroused strong criticism from right-wing sectors and weakened his position. The escape of members of the Frente Patriótico Manuel Rodríguez in December 1996 from a maximum security prison made it impossible for him to continue as the minister.

What is important to make clear here is that opposition to the Frei Boys was not restricted to actions by the Iron Circle. Their autonomous behavior and their indifference to party guidelines had also provoked the fury of the socialist sectors in Parliament and the leaders of the Socialist Party. What lies behind all this hostility is the tension between two sectors within the government coalition (the so-called two souls of the Concertación), which had been building up since 1990 and was becoming more and more evident with every passing day. On the one hand, there is a sector (particularly, the most left-wing members of the coalition, but also including many Christian Democrats) that rejects the element of continuity in matters of pro-market economic policies that has been characteristic of the actions of the Concertación governments. On the other, there is a sector that, in general terms, is satisfied with the results obtained and intends to carry on along this road to development in which the market plays a leading role.

In 1998 this fight broke out in a rather violent way as the result of a series of factors. First, several studies were published that criticized diverse structural aspects of the political and social model prevailing in the country. This was particularly the case of the book by sociologist Tomás Moulian, *El Chile actual: Anatomía de un mito,* published in 1997. Moulian's book, which had many repercussions in public opinion, acidly attacks the Concertación governments for continuing policies established by the military regime.[24] The

---

ent camps with our reforms. And some lies were spread to discredit me" (*El Mercurio,* July 22, 2006).

23. During the Lagos administration, Halpern became the dean of the Faculty of Communication of Joaquín Lavín's Universidad del Desarrollo, and then went into business in the United States.

24. This book became an instant best seller, and several editions were sold out a mere few weeks after publication.

following year, the United Nations Development Program (UNDP) published an annual report on human development entitled *Las paradojas de la modernización,* in which it analyzes the darker side of the process of modernization in Chile, centered on the disenchantment of Chileans with the consumer society. Both books were best sellers in Chile.

All this prompted a strong response from the liberal sector of the Concertación, which was condensed in a document for discussion entitled "La fuerza de nuestras ideas," written by a group of ministers and former collaborators of the liberal wing of the Concertación led by José Joaquín Brunner.[25] The document countered every single one of the negative and pessimistic arguments about the trap of Chilean modernity. The publication of this document generated an ample debate with those sectors of the Concertación which were more critical of the results of the Chilean economic model and were demanding larger degrees of citizen participation. This alternative vision of the achievements and blunders of the Concertación was made public one month later with the publication of the document "La gente tiene razón," endorsed by a long list of Concertación politicians and intellectuals.[26] These two opposed sides within the Concertación came to be called the *autocomplacientes* ("self-complacent") and the *autoflagelantes* ("self-flagellant") by the press.[27] Although the heated debate no longer made the headlines, this dichotomy within the Concertación was reproduced in the subsequent administrations of Lagos and Bachelet.

It is interesting to note that if we consider the main criticism generated from within the government of the way the state policies are managed, the darts are often aimed at aspects related to their technocratic leaning. In different passages of "La gente tiene razón" there are instances of openly antitech-

---

25. See *El Mercurio,* May 17, 1998. This document was signed by sixty-two public personalities.

26. See *La Época,* June 14, 1998. This document was signed by more than 140 important Concertación members, including Socialists and Christian Democrats.

27. For an in-depth analysis of the struggle between *autocomplacientes* and *autoflagelantes,* see Navia 2004, 235–45. On the debate generated by these two documents, see "La guerra de los papeles," *Revista HOY,* June 8, 1998. It is important to point out that the division between *autocomplacientes* and *autoflagelantes* is not the same as the division between technocrats and politicians. Although most public technocrats do indeed defend self-complacent stances, one can find among Concertación politicians *autoflagelantes* as well as *autocomplacientes.* In my view, the main issues dividing the two groups are generally related to the question about what roles the state, the market, technocrats, and political parties should play in the decision-making process in present-day Chile.

nocratic criticism and reassessment of the role of political parties and the people:

> The political parties and the state have the responsibility to create the conditions for the development of forms of action and collective organizations . . . of civil society. This is a condition . . . to allow society to play its role of counterweight and limit . . . the power of technocracy. . . . The indispensable technical capabilities are not enough for suitable leadership of society; an ethics of democratic commitment is necessary in order to go beyond a mere book-keeping conception of the workings of democracy. . . . With the same emphasis as we defend the balance between public spending and taxes we declare that the absolute level of both variables is not a merely technical matter, but should also represent the preferences of the people, expressed through the democratic political system.[28]

President Frei attempted to put an end to the debate when he asked for "fewer words and more action" from his people in the government, so as to win the election of 1999 and thus pave the way for a third government of the Concertación.

On August 1, 1998, Frei suddenly announced his third and last cabinet reshuffle. Public Works Minister Ricardo Lagos and Economy Minister Álvaro García were to be replaced. This allowed Lagos to plunge into his campaign for the nomination as the Concertación candidate for presidency at the primary elections that would take place in mid-1999. García became one of his main campaign advisers. Also removed were Carlos Figueroa, Juan Villarzú,

---

28. This antitechnocratic criticism had begun to emerge the previous year. In an article, political expert Alfredo Joignant said that there is "a growing subordination of the political to the technical, which tends to be translated into a gap between party and government. The clear technical imprint of the Frei administration, with an emphasis on modernization, implies a persistent disregard for the political aspects of the agenda that is the natural consequence of such an imprint. . . . This technocratic leadership entails insensibility to the political risk proper, which is translated into the inability to anticipate unfavorable political scenarios" (*La Época*, November 23, 1997). In turn, Germán Gamonal, an outstanding political commentator, referred to the apoliticism of Frei's government as follows: "In 'the New Times' there is no political activity since that topic is not mentioned, it is taboo in the cabinet councils. [N]or do parties operate, as there are only meetings of the top echelons, or at most, of the political committees. In Congress there is no political debate and the members of Parliament restrict themselves to taking part in committees or, in the plenary room, to dealing with projects that are designed by the technical teams of the Executive" (*La Época*, June 10, 1998).

and José Joaquín Brunner, three figures that in previous years had had a key role in the battle—now coming to an end—between the members of the Iron Circle and the "Top Ten" technocrats.

Some time later, Frei's government ran into trouble. The Asian crisis had serious repercussions for the Chilean economy and threatened the sudden end of the uninterrupted economic growth that Chile had enjoyed ever since the return to democracy in 1990. This was compounded in October of that year by an unexpected major political crisis triggered by the arrest of General Pinochet in London, which sparked a severe confrontation in Chile between his defenders and his detractors (see P. Silva 2000). President Frei set aside his modernizing agenda and concentrated on day-to-day political survival and keeping together the two sectors of the Concertación, which were now arguing about the fate of the general. It was evident that as of October 1998 a new political cycle had begun in which the technocrats would be less active and less publicly visible.

Lagos and His "Second-Floor Advisers"

The 1999–2000 presidential election in Chile was a much harder contest than either of the previous presidential races since democratic rule was restored in 1990. Two candidates, Socialist Ricardo Lagos, representing the ruling Concertación coalition, and Joaquín Lavín, the candidate of the right-wing coalition *Alianza por Chile,* were equally matched and fought for every single vote. For the first time since 1990 two electoral rounds were needed to decide the outcome.[29] While in the first round Lagos and Lavín ended practically equal, in the second and decisive round Lagos just managed to obtain a slight advantage against his right-wing rival.[30]

For a long time it was expected that the December 1999 contest would bring an easy victory for the Concertación candidate, whoever he might be. This expectation was based on the excellent electoral performance showed by the Concertación coalition during the 1989 and 1993 presidential elections, when Patricio Aylwin and Eduardo Frei Ruiz-Tagle easily won in the first round with 55.2 and 57.9 percent of the votes cast. In addition, during the

29. The two rounds were held on December 12, 1999, and January 16, 2000.
30. In the first round Lagos obtained 47.9 percent of votes (against 47.51 percent for Lavín). In the second and final round Lagos obtained 51.31 percent (against 48.69 percent for Lavín).

1990s the right-wing opposition had been extremely divided and had proved unable to unite behind a single candidate. So when Ricardo Lagos won the Concertación's "primaries" from Christian Democrat Andrés Zaldívar on May 30, 1999, his victory in December 2000 seemed almost guaranteed. However, the need to hold these primaries just nine months before the elections did also reduce the unity and cohesion within the Concertación's coalition. The struggle between Lagos and Zaldívar for the coalition's candidacy produced some unavoidable confrontations between Socialists and Christian Democrats, which did not automatically vanish after the primary.

Between the primaries and Election Day the popularity of Joaquín Lavín increased to such a point that he had a real chance to win the presidency. Although he eventually lost, the huge support he obtained from the Chilean voters placed him automatically among the figures with the best chances to win the presidential elections in December 2005. Therefore, the most singular consequence of the 1999–2000 elections was the fact that for the first time since the restoration of democratic rule in 1990, the Chilean Right had become a real option to govern the country (see P. Silva 1991 and Angell 2005).

The great difficulties that Lagos had to surmount to win the presidency and his narrow margin over his rival to a large extent conditioned the attitude he was later to adopt with respect to the presence of technocratic groups in his government. In the first place, Lagos knew that his name and person awakened great fear in the political Right and in the economic and financial elites of the country, as became evident in the last months of the campaign (see E. Silva 2002). If he won, he would be the first socialist president since Salvador Allende. His candidacy was problematic even in the eyes of important sectors of the Christian Democrats, who also feared what might happen if the country elected a socialist president. Also, a not negligible part of them felt attracted to and represented by Joaquín Lavín's modernizing, technocratic, and apparently apolitical discourse (see P. Silva 2004). And, as a matter of fact, after the elections it was confirmed that many people who in 1989 and 1993 had voted for the Concertación candidate this time had transferred their allegiance to the candidate of the Right (Angell 2005, 85–86).

For this reason, Lagos was obliged to reassure the electorate that he would not transform the economic model and that there would be many elements of continuity with the two previous administrations. He had to further demonstrate that he had the necessary qualifications to steer the economy with a knowledgeable hand. In Patricio Valdivieso's words, "Lagos had to highlight his technocratico-entrepreneurial gifts and abandon an important part of the more traditional and republican discourse in the final pre-elections period and in the intervening time between the first and the second electoral round" (2002, 6). So, just as Lavín had boasted of his master's degree in economics from the University of Chicago, the people in charge of the Concertación propaganda had to splash Lagos's vast academic and intellectual experience. There was no shortage of credentials: Lagos had worked at the Faculty of Economics of the University of Chile, and had even served as the secretary general of the university. He later worked as researcher and consultant for several organizations of international renown such as FLACSO, ECLAC, UNDP, and UNESCO. During his exile he worked as visiting professor at Duke University, where he had earned a doctorate in economics. Also, it is important to bear in mind that in the second round Lagos was much indebted to Soledad Alvear, Frei's popular justice minister, who resigned her post to place her enormous popularity at the service of Lagos's candidacy as head of his campaign. All this seemed to anticipate that Lagos would be forced to give in to the PDC when designating the members of his cabinet and also that he would not be able to give his government an out-and-out leftist seal.

In fact, Lagos was essentially a politician with a strong academic and intellectual leaning, but he wanted to give his government the image of effectiveness that he had cultivated when he was the minister of public works in Frei's government. Lagos was to adopt a style that was a combination of pragmatic man of action, setting deadlines for his ministers to reach given targets,[31] and statesman, thinking of the Chile of the future and fascinated with the idea of the bicentennial to be celebrated in 2010. Also, it is worth noting that Lagos was an economist who had in some way been associated with the old structuralist-Cepalian mainstream of the 1950s and 1960s. In other words, he had little affinity with the more technocratized and management-oriented approaches taught at Chilean and U.S. universities that had indeed shaped and influenced many of the young economists who were taking part in the governments of the Concertación. This was mirrored by the slogan that he used for the first round, "growth with equity," a very Cepalian phrase that was somewhat distant from the explicit stress placed by Frei on modernization. The slogan

---

31. The most emblematic case was the appointment of Michelle Bachelet as minister of health, publicly assigning her the task of putting an end to queues in the public medical clinics in three months. Her good performance gave her great public exposure and acclaim and was her launching pad to the presidency.

disturbed the entrepreneurial sectors a great deal. The word "equity," they feared, might mean the radical transformation of income distribution in the country through tax increases on the wealthy.

Until the end of his government Lagos would always have an ambiguous position toward technocracy.[32] As minister of public works, he cohabited with technocrats because this ministry was a nesting-place for engineers. Lagos made his the idea of being a "doer," a man who accomplishes things, inaugurates bridges and highways, and so on, which he put to good use in his subsequent campaign. I have already referred to his clashes with the Top Ten during the Frei administration. However, he was careful not to take sides openly in the 1998 debate between the "self-complacent" and the "self-flagellating," for he knew that he would need the support of both factions to become president.[33]

In the composition of his cabinet, Lagos showed elements of continuity and of change with respect to the previous administration. There was continuity given that he inherited some figures that had already been ministers during Frei's government; there was change because he included six women in his cabinet. As Patricio Navia has pointed out (2004, 258–59), a careful look at the ministers in Lagos's first cabinet shows that he did not favor meritocracy, but rather a traditional approach bases on political "quotas." Even the integration of "new faces" was the result of the needs of and negotiations with the political parties. That was the case, for example, with the appointment of Mariana Aylwin (minister of education and the daughter of former President Aylwin) and Alejandra Krauss (minister of planning and international cooperation, and the daughter of the Christian Democratic leader Enrique Krauss), who professionally speaking were not the most suitable persons to hold those positions. However, allocating quotas was a gesture to mollify the parties of

32. Only later did he openly express his disapproval of technocracy. In a speech on the occasion of the inauguration of the School of Governance and Public Administration of the Universidad Alberto Hurtado in July 2006, Lagos referred to "technocratism" in decision-making in a harsh way. He insisted that "it is necessary to leave technocratism behind, together with the belief that decision-making is the task of technocrats and not of the representatives of a country. . . . Technicians are essential to introduce realism, but ultimately it is the politician who has to make the final decision. . . . As far as there is an integrated vision of how to create and implement the public policies, those responsible for ruling will have a clear road ahead to confront demagogy, because whether you are a technocrat or whether you are a demagogue, both are equally dangerous" (*La Tercera*, July 25, 2006).

33. It is very revealing, however, that in 1998 several of his closest advisers during his administration signed the self-flagellating document "La gente también tiene la razón," among them Guillermo Campero, Eugenio Lahera, and Francisco Vidal.

the Concertación and did not constitute a sign that Lagos would cogovern with the parties. Although Lagos was a member of the PPD, he never projected an image of himself as a party man and when he organized his presidential campaign he did not do it from the parties but from the think tank "Fundación siglo 21," which he created especially for this purpose.[34]

Also striking is the presence of so many ministers with law degrees (see Table 4), which indicates that from the very beginning Lagos privileged a political rather than a technical background in his cabinet. This was reflected in the appointment as minister of the interior of José Miguel Insulza, referred to as "Panzer" in the mass media because of his great political strength and his acknowledged ability as negotiator. All this notwithstanding, Lagos carried on with the unwritten rule already established in the two previous governments of leaving the conduct of the economy in the hands of prestigious economists. The new president knew that in view of the many existing apprehensions about his true intentions concerning the economy he had to send a strong signal to the local and international financial and economic communities that the conduct of the economy would be in good hands. Consequently, he appointed Nicolás Eyzaguirre as his minister of finance. Eyzaguirre had begun his career at CEPAL in the 1980s, followed by a stint at the Banco Central and later postgraduate studies at Harvard University. At the time of his appointment, he was one of the executive directors of the IMF. Eyzaguirre is an "atypical" technocrat, for he has a left-wing past and at some point in his life had been a card-carrying member of the Communist Party. In addition, he has a very good political nose, and is very much given to late nights and folk music. All this, combined with the use of plain and informal language and an excellent sense of humor, facilitated enormously his establishing rapport with the people during the Lagos administration.[35] Another member of Lagos's cabinet was young economist José de Gregorio, minister of the economy, energy, and mining. This technocrat *pur sang* with a doctorate in economics from MIT had been the coordinator of macroeconomic policies of the Ministry of Finance under Frei. At the time of his appointment, he was a

34. It is interesting to note that Lagos attracted mainly sociologists and political scientists and just a few economists of a nontechnocratic profile to that foundation.

35. When the Lagos administration was coming to an end, Eyzaguirre was one of the most popular ministers and was considered a potential candidate for the 2010 presidential elections.

visiting professor of economics at the University of California.[36] Other members of Lagos's first cabinet with technocratic profiles were Álvaro García (minister of the presidency), Mario Marcel (director of the Budget Office), and Claudio Orrego (minister of housing).

However, from the outset Lagos gave his ministers very little freedom or autonomy. Unlike Frei, who gave the members of his cabinet much decision-making leeway, Lagos's political style was more authoritarian and controlling. According to many analysts, this has to do with his strong character and his desire to make his administration one of the best of the Concertación. Others have characterized Lagos as having the personality of an orchestra conductor who tries to play every instrument himself (see Navia 2004).

In fact, Lagos put himself above the political parties that formed the Concertación and sought to be seen as someone his South American peers and the rest of the world would acknowledge as a statesman. After a few years in the government several political analysts began to compare his almost regal style to that of French president François Mitterrand.[37] Lagos's background, which was more intellectual than technical, made him distrust the technocratic sectors. Possibly, he also drew lessons from his experience as a minister in Frei Ruiz-Tagle's cabinet. The most severe criticisms leveled at Frei Ruiz-Tagle were that he, as president, had not provided the necessary leadership to keep the administration from becoming somewhat disorganized, and that he had not put a timely end to the struggle between technocrats and politicians within his government.

Lagos opted for setting up a structure more similar to that of the United States, in which a group of close advisers or members of the presidential staff, the members of the so-called kitchen cabinet, advised him directly and monitored what the ministers did to put some kind of order in the government's actions.[38] This was the origin of the mythical "second floor" of La

36. The press engaged in speculation about whether his extremely technical profile and his lack of political and party political experience would not prove to be a great disadvantage for his performance. A political column thus expressed this view: "Holding three ministerial posts at once will not be easy. . . . His great capacity to overcome the challenges of his portfolio are acknowledged . . . yet, the fact that he is a technocrat and not an old hand at party life may also play against him" ("El perfil del nuevo 'superministro,'" *La Tercera*, February 1, 2000).

37. See "Monsieur le Président o el modelo no confesado de Lagos," *La Tercera*, August 27, 2005.

38. Lagos had already made public his plan of forming the committee of advisers during his presidential campaign. See "Traje a la medida de Lagos," *Qué Pasa*, January 24, 2000.

Table 4 Members of Lagos's first cabinet: professional training

Name	Position	Profession
José Miguel Insulza	Minister of the interior	Lawyer
Soledad Alvear	Minister of foreign affairs	Lawyer
Mario Fernández	Minister of defense	Lawyer
Nicolás Eyzaguirre	Minister of finance	Economist
Alvaro García	General secretary of the presidency	Economist
Claudio Huepe	General secretary of the government	Lawyer
José de Gregorio	Minister of economy and energy	Economist
Alejandra Krauss	Minister of planning and cooperation	Lawyer
Mariana Aylwin	Minister of education	Lawyer
José Antonio Gómez	Minister of justice	Lawyer
Ricardo Solari	Minister of labor	Economist
Carlos Cruz	Minister of public infrastructure, transport, and telecommunications	Economist
Michelle Bachelet	Minister of health	Physician
Claudio Orrego	Minister of housing	Economist
Jaime Campos	Minister of agriculture	Lawyer
Alfonso Dualto	Minister of mines	Mine engineer
Adriana Delpiano	Minister of women's affairs	Social assistant
José Weinstein	Minister of culture	Sociologist

SOURCES: Several ministerial Web sites.

Moneda, for that was where the offices of Lagos's main advisers were located. Among them were Ernesto Ottone, Agustín Squella, Guillermo Campero, Carlos Vergara, and Javier Martínez,[39] all of them loyal friends of the president. Most of them were sociologists by profession and during Pinochet's dictatorship had operated from different private research institutes or from FLACSO or CEPAL, analyzing the social and political reality of the country. They contributed to the formulation of policies to be implemented if democracy was ever restored. Such was the case of Guillermo Campero, a sociologist of renown, expert in labor relations, with an in-depth knowledge of entrepreneurial organizations, who during the dictatorship had done postgraduate studies at the EHESS, Paris, and back in Chile had worked at the Instituto Latinoamericano de Estudios Transnacionales (ILET). Another member of the group of advisers was Javier Martínez, a prominent sociologist who worked at the Corporación de Estudios Sociales y de Educación (SUR) and has written

39. Apart from having similar social backgrounds and being roughly the same age, and apart from the fact that some of them had studied in Paris, they were all from Valparaíso and avid fans of the Wanderers football club. See "¿Que significa ser wanderino? Verde que te quiero verde," *El Mercurio de Valparaíso*, April 29, 2001.

extensively on the changes in social relations in Chile as a result of the economic and cultural transformations brought about by the neoliberal system.

Yet another of his closest advisers was Eugenio Lahera, who had a doctorate in public affairs from Princeton. Lahera had already worked with Ricardo Lagos in the early 1980s and also in the two rounds of the presidential campaign. Before that, he had worked at the Fundación Chile 21, of which he was the director, and was the editor of the *CEPAL Review*. The head of Lagos's group of advisers was sociologist Ernesto Ottone, who has a doctorate in political science from the University of Paris and in his youth had been a member of the Chilean Communist Party. He and Lagos are long-standing personal friends, who share a common past at CEPAL, of which Ottone was secretary general.[40]

From the very beginning, Lagos's group of advisers opted for keeping a low profile. They avoided publicity and did not give interviews. Although the public heard little or nothing from them, within the cabinet their presence was strongly felt from the very beginning. As pointed out by Carlos Huneeus, during the Lagos administration the relation of the members of the advisory committee and the ministers was not at all easy. Very often the president had one of his advisers accompany him to a meeting with one of his ministers to take notes.[41] In fact, one of the main tasks assigned by Lagos to his advisory committee was to act as the controlling organ of the tasks assigned to each of the ministries. In addition, they delivered strategic information and analyses to President Lagos and always had to be consulted by the other ministers and government officials on important issues.

Although Lagos had the technocrats firmly in check on the domestic front, he was obliged to give them free rein in the area of international foreign trade. A cohort of modern professionals at the Ministry of Foreign Affairs proved their worth when they designed and negotiated free trade agreements with countries in North America, Europe, and Asia. The result of this was the strengthening of the influence of the Directorate of International Economic Affairs within the ministry, where a throng of young economists were in charge of formulating Chile's commercial strategies, and of representing Chile in the specialized commissions of international bodies like APEC.[42]

40. See "Ernesto Ottone: El ocaso del consejero," *Qué Pasa*, August 27, 2005.

41. Carlos Huneeus, "Los asesores presidenciales," *La Tercera*, July 2, 2006.

42. For example, I find quite revealing the interview with Ricardo Lagos Weber (speaking of how his experience as a negotiator abroad might be of use to his plans to go into national

Bachelet: Technocracy *cum* Citizen Participation?

In the final phase of Lagos's term of office there emerged a climate of uncertainty and doubt about the future of the ruling coalition. Indeed, many had begun to entertain the idea that there would not be a fourth Concertación government. This prospect was the topic of "La ceremonia del Adiós," a paper restricted to Concertación circles written by socialist sociologist Antonio Cortés Terzi. In addition, there was veiled criticism of Lagos for having done too much to strengthen his personal popularity, and too little to transfer that popularity to the government coalition that had taken him to power.

Simultaneously, there was a growing belief in the right-wing opposition that its candidate, Joaquín Lavín, could beat the government coalition in the elections of December 1999. Lavín's thesis, namely, that any Concertación candidate would only represent "more of the same" and that he, on the contrary, was the candidate of change, was beginning to take root in public opinion. However, the appearance at the end of 2004 of two women seeking to become the Concertación's candidate for the presidency ensured Lavín's defeat. The emergence of Soledad Alvear and Michelle Bachelet as possible future leaders of the country did indeed represent a truly revolutionary change in Chilean politics. It attracted a great deal of attention from national and international mass media and aroused great expectations among the population.

The duel between Alvear and Bachelet to be the Concertación candidate for the presidency revived the friction between Christian Democrats and Socialists that had marked the contest between Andrés Zaldívar and Ricardo Lagos in 1999. This time, however, the possibility of a victory by the Socialist torchbearer created many more hard feelings among the Christian Democrats than before. On the one hand, a Bachelet victory would mean that a Socialist candidate would represent the government coalition for the second time running, which was extremely difficult to accept. Besides, Bachelet represented the so-called New Left, the hard-liner wing within the Socialist Party, and this

---

politics) in the September 26, 2004, issue of *La Tercera*. On that occasion he declared: "We have done a big job to insert Chile in the world but the task ahead is even greater than the agreements signed. My link with politics is there. We need public policies to orient the development of Chile. And I consider that Parliament should be further professionalized contributing with views from people who come more from technocracy and can transfer their experience to the political world. With great humility I believe that one can make a contribution, give a different emphasis, some freshness to politics."

generated misgivings within the PDC about the ideological orientation of a Concertación government under her leadership.

What is important to note here is that Bachelet's candidacy was not the result of a decision made by either Lagos or the leadership of the Socialist Party, but was rather imposed on the party by the candidate herself. She had had an excellent performance as minister of health and defense in the Lagos administration and had won (most) Chileans over because of her warm personality, her sunny disposition, her contribution to the reconciliation of Chileans, and her use of plain and down-to-earth language. It was the mass media that identified her as a potential presidential candidate, whereas the leaders of her party, the so-called Socialist barons, hesitated for quite some time before endorsing a candidacy they had had no hand in creating.[43] Her campaign for the nomination met with resistance not only from the Christian Democrats but also from the top echelons of her own party because they feared that they would have no or little influence in any government she headed. It was Soledad Alvear's withdrawal from the presidential contest in May 2005 that gave Bachelet the green light to represent the Concertación.

In the early days of her campaign Bachelet resorted to an antitechnocratic discourse that boded ill for the state techno-bureaucracy if she was victorious in the December elections.[44] Partly, her stress on this antitechnocratic discourse was directed against her right-wing rival, Joaquín Lavín, who embodied the liberal technocrat of the Chicago school. In addition, in May 2005 another right-wing candidate made his unexpected appearance at the starting gate of the Chilean presidential race. It was economist Sebastián Piñera, who also had a technocratic track record, at whom it was necessary to charge.

Bachelet's slogan in the campaign to represent the Concertación was quite significant: "No a los tecnócratas, sí a la gente" (No to technocrats; yes to the people). Both her campaign spokesperson and Ricardo Solari, a Socialist leader and one of her closest advisers, had insisted on emphasizing the nega-

43. Andrés Velasco said, without mincing his words, in an interview in October 2005: "Michelle Bachelet did not attain candidate status thanks to the establishment, but did so despite the Concertación establishment. If the party structures had had the power of veto at the moment of nominating a presidential candidate, it wouldn't have been Bachelet" (*La Nación*, October 9, 2005).

44. In an improvised debate Bachelet declared: "I'm betting on a different kind of politics, a more participatory democracy; for more capability, evolution, and participation in public policies going beyond a group of technocrats" (*La Nación*, August 3, 2005).

tive aspects of technocracy and the existing tension between it and the objective of strengthening citizen participation in public policies.[45]

It is interesting to note that just as the 1998 UNDP report on human development had an important impact on the controversy between the self-flagel lating and the self-complacent, the 2004 UNDP report on power in Chile published in January 2005 was to exert a strong influence on the leaders of Bachelet's campaign.[46] This report criticized the technocratic character of the state elite and made an urgent appeal to strengthen the mechanisms for citizen participation in Chile.

> While some are oriented to the construction of a collective project that may integrate society through a more open democracy, others adhere to a vision oriented toward individual projects and to a more technocratic leadership. . . . The challenge is to go from a representative to a participative democracy. This will allow social actors who are not connected to the state and political society to participate in politics from civil society. (UNDP 2004, 208, 242)

From mid-2005 on, Bachelet and her campaign team began to shift their emphasis to citizen participation. This involved a notable change from what until then had been the position of the Concertación on participation. Before Bachelet the government coalition had favored the consolidation of democratic structures and institutions and the principle of representative, not participative, democracy.[47] What is interesting is that the newly introduced figure of "the citizenry" would come to be privileged at the level of discourse to the detriment not only of technocratic cadres but also of the political parties.

45. Thus, in the essay written in 1996 on the administration of the state, both of them concluded that "satisfying the new demands of public institutions in the sphere of management with mere technical specialized [know-how] is an illusory simplification. . . . The limitations of technocracy in the sphere of public management are evident. . . . It provides no response to problems that require the fulfillment of democratic commitments and the consideration of factors that are of a political type. In addition, the good performance of the specialists in the state is not sufficient if it is unaccompanied by getting in touch with the social reality, the concerns and perceptions of the citizens" (Toha and Solari 1996, 15).

46. "The intelligentsia of the campaign team is studying and quoting the report 'El poder: Para qué y para quién?' of the United Nations Development Program as if it were the Jerusalem Bible" (El Mostrador, July 25, 2005). See also "El baile de los que mandan," La Nación, January 16, 2005.

47. The criticisms against technocratism and the demand for a more participative and direct democracy had until then been a banner mainly restricted to the extraparliamentary Left and to some "self-flagellating" members of the Concertación, particularly from the Socialist Party.

Bachelet seemed more and more inclined to dispense with the support of the political parties of the Concertación. The adoption of this supraparty political strategy by Bachelet was to generate gradually increasing friction with the leaders of the political parties that made up the Concertación, who were frustrated by how little influence they had over the candidate and her campaign. This became evident when after visiting Prime Minister Rodríguez Zapatero in July 2005, Bachelet suddenly declared that following the Spanish example, she would also apply a strict parity of gender in her choice of ministers and top officials. This measure meant that the leaders of the Concertación parties, practically all of whom were men, at one stroke had lost access to half the key posts in a future government of this coalition. This was compounded by Bachelet's announcement at the end of her campaign that there would be "no second helpings" for anybody during her government, in the sense that there would be an end to continuity, as she would not summon the ministers or top functionaries of the previous government to form part of her cabinet. With both measures Bachelet wanted to make good her promise of making way for "new faces" in order to bring about a generational *aggiornamento* within the Concertación.

To accomplish this, however, Bachelet would first have to win the election. To do that, she would have to win the trust and support of that wide sector of the electorate and the world of trade and industry in general which had some misgivings about her much-too-left-wing credentials. And second, she would have to find these new faces outside party circles. Bachelet found the solution to both problems in her decision to establish a tacit strategic alliance with the think tank "Expansiva," which had gathered together a large group of young thinkers, intellectuals, and technocrats of liberal inspiration yet confirmed Concertación inclination. Like Lagos, Bachelet made it clear that despite her socialist leanings, the economic policy in any government she formed would be in the hands of prestigious economists of a liberal imprint, who would continue to develop the economic model upheld so far. For this reason, she began to attend different forums on economic matters accompanied by Expansiva economists.

The origins of Expansiva are to be found at Harvard University, where in January 2002 there was a meeting convened by Chilean economist Andrés Velasco, which gathered together about forty young Chilean scholars and professionals, among them economists, political scientists, and sociologists working at different U.S. universities to think about "the Chile to come." Velasco convened another, similar meeting a year later, this time in a private lodge at a ski resort on Cerro Nevado, near Santiago, and received much mass media coverage.[48] It was there that the idea jelled of creating Expansiva, a think tank of young professionals who wished to contribute to the creation of better public policies for the country. Expansiva is a modern organization, with no physical premises, whose main instrument is a Web site where its members publish their papers on the most varied topics and areas of the national reality. Its leader, Andrés Velasco, has an impressive curriculum vitae. He holds a doctorate in economics from Columbia University. He was the director of the Department of Latin American studies of Columbia University, and in 1996 he received tenure as a professor of economics at Harvard. He took his initial steps as an economist at CIEPLAN in the 1980s, where he worked quite closely with the director, Alejandro Foxley. After the return to democracy in 1990, he followed Foxley to the Ministry of Finance, where he worked as coordinator of international finance. When President Lagos was forming his cabinet, Andrés Velasco's name was mentioned as possible finance minister. Eventually, Lagos chose Nicolás Eyzaguirre, and Velasco returned to academia in the United States. Velasco has an out-and-out technocratic profile and has defined himself as politically independent. He is a staunch upholder of free trade and the search for technical excellence in the formulation and application of public policies.[49]

Jorge Marshall, another CIEPLAN Monk, was among the most important members of Expansiva. Marshall has a doctorate in economics from Harvard University, and in March 2006 became Aylwin's undersecretary of the economy. He was later appointed minister of the economy and is currently one of the members of the board of BancoEstado. The most outstanding members of the "Top Ten" group who had worked in Frei Ruiz-Tagle's government— Jorge Rosenblut, Pablo Halpern and Eduardo Bitrán—also joined Expansiva. Jorge Rosenblut, who after his exit from Frei's government had turned into a successful businessman both in Chile and the United States, became a privi-

48. See for example, "New Kids en el Poder," *La Nación*, February 2, 2003, and "Shiny Happy People," *La Nación*, February 23, 2003. As suggested by both headlines, the U.S. training of most of these young professionals is being highlighted.

49. In an article of July 1997, Velasco made an overt defense of technocracy. "Modern democracy operates on two principles: delegation and competence. We delegate certain decisions to an elite because they are technically complex and it is efficient to resort to the opinion of experts. With them in charge, the rest of the citizens can take a holiday and feel no qualms. . . . The Chilean democracy is elitist, closed, technocratic, aesthetically not presentable, yet it works" (*La Tercera*, July 19, 1997).

leged intermediary between Bachelet and Chilean entrepreneurs, and was also in charge of raising funds for her presidential campaign.[50] Halpern became the candidate's main media adviser.[51] And Eduardo Bitrán became a member of her cabinet.

The emergence of Expansiva as an important source of advice and support for Bachelet meant that the CIEPLAN Monks and the Top Ten had returned to the political center of gravity of the country after a period of "cooling off" during Lagos's six years in office, when they remained distant from the public scene. With this choice, Bachelet also restored the principle of transversality that had operated during Aylwin's government, and had been abandoned by Frei Ruiz-Tagle.

Bachelet's rapprochement with the liberal leaders of Expansiva early in 2005 was followed by much misgiving by the leaders of the Concertación, particularly the members of the Socialist think tank Fundación Chile 21, directed by economist, former minister of economy, and current PPD senator Carlos Ominani.[52] This foundation, associated with the PPD-PS world, had played a key role in Ricardo Lagos's presidential campaign in 1999. Its members were confident that Bachelet would seek their support to design her government program, which would involve their attaining a privileged niche for the recruitment of experts for her government. However, Bachelet appeared determined to keep her distance from Lagos's cadres and party-political structures. In any case, the tug of war between these two think tanks, Expansiva and Chile 21 somehow or other replicated the old struggle, ongoing since 1998, between the "self-complacent" and "self-flagellating" sectors of the Concertación.

But how could Bachelet reconcile her choice of the *Expansiva* technocrats to put together her economic program in particular and the government program in general with her initial antitechnocratic discourse? In my opinion, the key to this contradiction lies in the fact that Bachelet became aware that there was much that she wanted to accomplish and she had a relatively short

---

50. It was Rosenblut who organized the meeting that Bachelet had in New York in January 2005 with some top executives of banking conglomerates such as J. P. Morgan and Citigroup to send off reassuring signals concerning her future management of the economy. This was Bachelet's first trip abroad as a presidential candidate. See "El hombre de Bachelet en Miami," *Qué Pasa*, March 26, 2005, and "El hombre de las platas de Bachelet," *Qué Pasa*, December 31, 2005.

51. See "Pablo Halpern: El regreso a las grandes ligas," *Qué Pasa*, August 27, 2005.

52. See "Vínculos Bachelet-*Expansiva* generan anticuerpos en el PS," *La Tercera*, March 27, 2005; "La pugna por el corazón y la mente de Bachelet," *La Tercera*, April 3, 2005; and "Pugna entre asesores de la candidata," *La Tercera*, May 14, 2005.

time in which to do it.[53] Therefore, it was indispensable to have a well-designed government program with a clear economic and social strategy that identified the most emblematic reforms of her administration. All this was taking place before her installation in March 2006. Apparently, she may also have realized that it was possible to reconcile the presence of technocracy in her government with her objective of strengthening citizen participation. This became clear by the way in which, as a candidate for the nomination, Bachelet structured her government program early in January 2005. Several working committees were formed, with the participation of scholars and experts in each subject, and representative figures of certain sectors and organizations of civil society were also invited to participate.[54] Bachelet continued to use this same style of work after securing the nomination in May 2005.

In addition, and as a result of her experience as an exile in Europe, her professional training as a physician, and above all, her postgraduate studies in military matters in Washington in 1997–98, Bachelet was in fact much less distant from the technocratic universe than was generally assumed. Her studious attitude, her good marks as a student, and her recognized pragmatism and down-to-earth approach to tasks and problems made her from the outset compatible with technocrats such as Andrés Velasco and Jorge Marshall, whose working styles and ways of acting are quite similar to hers.[55]

Thus after the results of the first round of the presidential elections on December 11, 2005, had made it clear that Sebastián Piñera and Michelle Bachelet would have to go to a run-off; at the end of that same month Bachelet unveiled her "Plan 100 days: 36 commitments." In the best technocratic style, the candidate committed herself to meet specific objectives in a preestablished period of time. On this occasion she was accompanied by a select group of economists among whom were Andrés Velasco and Alejandro Foxley, who gave a detailed account of how much the application of the plan would cost and how the thirty-six measures to be adopted in the first hundred days of government would be funded. Bachelet proudly referred to the high professional quality of the members of the technical team that had formulated the

53. In March 1994 Parliament passed a constitutional reform that reduced the presidential term from six years to four.

54. See "Los nuevos nombres y estilo de Bachelet," *La Nación*, January 8, 2005.

55. See "Como Andrés Velasco conquistó a Bachelet," *Qué Pasa*, February 4, 2006. Thus, as Patricio Navia, a Chilean political scientist working at New York University, has suggested, "Since Bachelet privileges pragmatism, she prefers horizontal relations and wishes to promote inclusion, diversity and participation, her style adjusts easily to that of U.S.-trained technocrats" ("Los yankees de Bachelet," *Qué Pasa*, February 11, 2006).

plan and concluded that "no other political sector than the Concertación, can convene such a highly qualified group of people."[56]

However, the greatest surprise that Bachelet sprang came after her victory at the run-off on January 15, 2006. Although the comfortable difference in votes that she achieved over her opponent Sebastián Piñera (53.5 percent against 46.5 percent) strengthened her relative autonomy from the parties of the Concertación, it is no less true that the party machinery and even Lagos's government itself that were actively mobilized between the first and the second round helped secure that victory.[57] Thus in official circles there was some confidence that Bachelet would remember the parties of the Concertación, especially her own Socialist party, when naming the members of her cabinet.[58]

But Bachelet played her political cards quite close to her chest and prolonged the suspense about who would form part of her cabinet until the very last. Her autonomy from political parties in the formation of her cabinet was so complete that she informed the general secretaries of the parties who would be on her cabinet only a few minutes before she informed the rest of the country. Although the parties had proposed some names to the president elect, she took next to no notice of the petitions and proposals and produced a list of ministers that left everybody gasping—from the political elite of the Concertación to the country in general.[59] The first big surprise was that Bachelet fulfilled her promise of appointing women to half the cabinet posts and of not appointing overly experienced politicians.[60] Most of the members of her cabinet were indeed relatively young and had a marked technico-professional profile, which in many cases included postgraduate studies in the

---

56. *La Nación*, December 28, 2005.

57. Thus, for example, Lagos freed his experienced minister of education, Sergio Bitar, to resign his ministerial post after the first round, so that he could lead Bachelet's campaign for the run-off.

58. Amid expectation about whom Bachelet would choose, most of political analysts, including prestigious political scientists like Ricardo Israel and Carlos Huneeus, were inclined to believe that Bachelet would in the end not distance herself from the political parties because of the active and decisive role that they played in the campaign for the run-off election. See "¿Innovará tanto con su estilo?" *El Mercurio de Valparaíso*, January 17, 2006.

59. One of the main newspapers carried the following headline with the news of the announcement of the cabinet members: "The style of the President Elect: Dissociates from party political pressure" (*El Mercurio*, January 31, 2006). According to sociologist Eugenio Tironi, after the announcement of the designation of ministers, the political parties were in a "state of shock." See interview in *La Tercera*, April 2, 2006, "Bachelet ha creado su propia transversalidad."

60. Much to almost everyone's surprise, the names of distinguished leaders of the Concertación, such as Sergio Bitar, José Antonio Viera-Gallo, and Jorge Schaulsohn, whom everybody assumed would get cabinet appointments, did not appear on the list of the president elect.

United States.[61] However, the most salient feature of her cabinet, which generated much debate within the parties of the Concertación and in the mass media, was the large number of members of Expansiva in the cabinet and the rest of the government apparatus.[62]

Andrés Velasco, the finance minister, was at the top of the list and had thus become the new strong man of the Chilean economy.[63] Bachelet also appointed members of Expansiva to two of the heavyweight ministries in Chile, namely, the Defense Ministry, to which she appointed Vivianne Blanlot, and the Ministry of Public Works, which she gave to former "Top Ten" Eduardo Bitrán. Members of Expansiva were also appointed as undersecretaries and were well represented in several special committees she created (see Table 5). One of the few points of contact between Lagos's and Bachelet's administrations was Ricardo Lagos Weber, the former president's son, who was appointed minister secretary of the government, thus becoming the official spokesperson of the administration.

Bachelet soon demonstrated her modern management style as president: as the new ministers were sworn in, much to everyone's surprise, she presented them with individual files in which she had listed the different targets of their respective portfolios and the respective deadlines to be observed in the four years of her government. At the same time, Bachelet set up a series of study committees to submit proposals to the president within a certain period of time. Thus, Edgardo Boeninger was put in charge of a committee to study the binomial system, and Mario Marcel in charge of a commission on the welfare and pensions system. Most of the members of these committees were experts in their respective fields,[64] and among them there were also

61. The high technical level of Bachelet's cabinet was noticed worldwide. In the Argentine press, an article entitled "El gabinete más globalizado de América Latina" enthusiastically highlighted the fact that "some 70 percent of the ministers appointed by Bachelet speak English and most of them hold doctoral degrees from the most important universities in the United States and Europe." The article concludes that these people "did not spend their years of exile in the United States and Europe crying over their personal dramas, but instead were getting ready for the future in some of the best universities in the world" (La Nación, Buenos Aires, March 11, 2006).

62. See "Nuevo grupo de pensamiento irrumpe en el poder: ¿Qué es Expansiva?" La Nación, February 12, 2006.

63. This appointment generated much unease in Socialist circles, which had given their support to Mario Marcel, another talented young technocrat with a doctorate in economics from the University of Cambridge, and who had worked quite closely with Bachelet during the campaign.

64. The committee studying the reform of the welfare system was questioned by some sectors precisely because of its marked technocratic character. An article in El Mostrador said: "President Bachelet's team has missed the wonderful chance of putting into practice their project for citizen government close to the vast majority. Its composition is eminently technocratic, that is,

members of the civil society. Through their inclusion, Bachelet tried to fulfill her promise that her administration would be a "gobierno ciudadano" (government of the citizens). However, as she began to stress in her discourse the issue of "citizen participation," an academic discussion also began in Chile on what should be specifically understood by "participation" of the citizenry in public policies and possible impacts both on the effectiveness of policies and political stability in the country.[65]

The acid test of citizen participation came abruptly at the end of May 2006, when the organizations of secondary school students in Santiago called for school takeovers and an indefinite strike to demand improvements in the quality of education. This generated a series of violent clashes between students and the police. The action of the secondary school students also unleashed a series of demonstrations by social movements and radical sectors of the extraparliamentary Left, who expressed their solidarity with the students' struggle and also took to the streets of Santiago. The images of violence in the streets and the high degree of radicalization and intransigence of the leaders of the students caused not a few Chileans to fear that the climate of relative peace and political stability that the country had enjoyed since the restoration of democracy in 1990 had come to an end. There was even fear that there might be a recreation of the climate of political and social violence of the early 1970s.

The students demanded the creation of a committee, similar to the welfare committee, to analyze the problems of education in Chile and formulate proposals for change, with a majority of student participation. The appeals from some right-wing sectors for the government to assert its authority and from some Concertación sectors for the government to defuse the crisis led Bachelet to impose her voice in the composition of the committee. Qualified experts were in the majority, although there was ample student representation.[66]

---

most of the members are experts whose opinions will not be expressed as such, but will be intended to be placed in the sphere of technical expertise and neutral know-how, uncontaminated by the political and economic interests at play" ("Comisión de Reforma Previsional y la tecnocracia," El Mostrador, August 10, 2006).

65. Thus, since March 2006 there has been a series of meetings and symposia on this issue, as, for example, "Participación ciudadana en la gestión pública en Chile," jointly organized by FLACSO-Chile and the University of Leiden in Santiago at the beginning of May 2006.

66. When she presented her proposal for educational reforms, Bachelet made it clear that she, not the students, had final say on the matter and states in the initial part of her speech that "this is a government that engages in dialogue and that after listening and talking makes decisions. I have resolved to take new measures to guarantee that our young may study at ease and in the right conditions" (La Segunda, June 1, 2006).

Table 5   Members of "Expansiva" within the Bachelet administration

Name	Position	Degree	Field	Accrediting institution
Andrés Velasco*	Minister of finance	Ph.D.	Economics	Columbia University
Eduardo Bitrán**	Minister of public infrastructure	Ph.D.	Economics	Boston University
Vivianne Blanlot	Minister of defense	M.A.	Economics	American University
Karen Poniachik	Minister of mining and energy	M.A.	International relations	Columbia University
María Olivia Recart	Deputy minister of finance	M.A.	Economics	ILADES-Georgetown University
Pilar Romaguera	Deputy minister of education	Ph.D.	Economics	Boston University
Pablo Bello	Deputy minister of telecommunications		Economics	Universidad de Chile
Carlos Álvarez	Executive vice president of CODELCO	M.A.	Public administration	Harvard University
Jean Jacques Duhart	Innovation manager, CODELCO	M.A.	Public administration	ENA-France
Jorge Marshall*	Vice president of BancoEstado	Ph.D.	Economics	Harvard University
Pilar Armanet	Ambassador to France	M.A.	Public studies	Universidad de Chile
Luis Felipe Céspedes	Coordinator of financial policies, Ministry of Finance	Ph.D.	Economics	New York University
Marcelo Tokman	General coordinator of the minister's advisers, Ministry of Finance	Ph.D.	Economics	UC Berkeley
Heidi Berner	Coordinator, Budget Office (DIPRES)	M.A.	Public administration	Harvard University
Jorge Rodríguez	Director, study department, Budget Office (DIPRES)	M.A.	Economics	Harvard University
Pablo Halpern**	Chief strategic adviser, Bachelet's presidential campaign	M.B.A.	Business administration	Kellogg School of Management, Northwestern University

Name	Role	Degree	Field	University
Jorge Rosenblut**	Liaison with business community and budget adviser during presidential campaign	M.A.	Public administration	Harvard University
José Miguel Benavente	Member of the National Council for Innovation		Industrial engineering	Universidad de Valparaíso
Cristóbal Aninat	Member of the Boeninger presidential commission (binomial electoral system)	M.A.	Political science	New York University
Axel Christensen	Member of the Marcel presidential commission (pension system)	M.A.	Business administration	Stanford University
Andrea Repetto*	Member of the Marcel presidential commission (pension system)	Ph.D.	Economics	MIT
Alfredo Joignant	Member of the García presidential commission (educational system)	Ph.D.	Political science	Université de Paris I Pantheon-Sorbonne
Carolina Toha	Member of the García presidential commission (educational system)	Ph.D.	Political science	Università di Milano
Alejandra Mizala	Member of the Marcel and the García presidential commissions	Ph.D.	Economics	UC Berkeley
Daniel Fernández	Executive director of the Televisión nacionál		Civil engineering	Universidad de Chile
Bernardita Escobar	Adviser to the minister of economy	M.Phil.	Economics	Cambridge University
Luis Eduardo Bresciani	Chief of urban development division, Ministry of Housing	M.A.	Urban design	Harvard University

* Ex CIEPLAN Monks.

** Ex Top Ten.

SOURCES: Several newspapers and institutional Web sites.

However, the crisis reduced considerably the large degree of autonomy from political parties that Bachelet had managed to establish. As a matter of fact, it was the Concertación parties and not the government that managed to pacify the strikers and put an end to the crisis through their internal structures and party links with the organizations of students and the other social movements involved. The symbol of this was a meeting of Bachelet and all the leaders of the Concertación parties at the end of the crisis as an act of unity that evoked the image of the return of the prodigal daughter.

The crisis of the secondary school students, which in practice represented a sort of "overdose" of direct citizen participation, seriously damaged the newly installed government of Bachelet and undoubtedly weakened the supporters of the "citizenry" discourse within the government.[67] In particular, the crisis had undermined the position of Andrés Zaldívar, the minister of the interior, and of Martin Zilic, the minister of education, who were accused from different sectors of not having managed the crisis properly. In the long run, Bachelet was forced to remove these two ministers only four months after having been sworn in. In addition, her government's public approval rating dropped significantly.[68]

The crisis provoked by the secondary school students also made some public opinion circles openly come to the defense of representative democracy and question the possible benefits of participative democracy. In July 2006, there was an article by the influential opinion shaper Patricio Navia demanding that Bachelet should explain what she understood exactly by participative democracy and warning about the dangers that a mob democracy might involve for political stability.

> The tension between representative democracy and participative democracy is today at the center of our political system. . . . Bachelet has expressed her preference for the government of citizens. Yet, although

67. Thus, even Camilo Escalona, the president of the Socialist Party and a loyal supporter of the president, asserted that "Bachelet formed her cabinet and organized her government inviting participation, yet this participation has materialized the wrong way. The demands are so numerous and in some cases so out of proportion that instead of dialogue we have disorder" (*La Segunda*, August 12, 2006).

68. In April 2006, one month after being installed, Bachelet enjoyed a 62.1 percent approval rating. In May, that had dropped to 54.2 percent, and in June 2006 to 44.2 percent, the lowest popularity rating of any president since 1990. Yet this decline in approval of the government did not imply increased approval of the opposition parties by the population. This state of affairs is a reflection of the very poor image that citizens have of political parties in general.

participative democracy appears to be a reasonable and appealing mod-
ality . . . those who shout the loudest or cast the most stones are likely
to win in a participative democracy. . . . Our country has already suf-
fered because of an irresponsible contempt of representative democracy.
We must not make the same mistake again. No doubt, representative
democracy needs improving and the introduction of mechanisms that
facilitate and strengthen control by the citizenry. But to idealize the
man in the street and express a nostalgic preference for popular power
over representative democracy is the worst mistake that the Left in Chile
can make today.[69]

In any case, it might seem that after the student crisis Bachelet's modus operandi was to tackle national issues by soliciting both the judgment of experts
on each topic and the opinion of the appropriate sectors of the civil society.
In other words, she strove to establish some kind of effective articulation
between a technocratic management style and a particular type of referendum. This approach might be leading to the sort of situation that Peter Evans
(1995) has defined as "embedded autonomy," in which the government technocracy opens up real channels of communication and consultation with representatives of the social sectors involved in each type of decision, but in
which, at the end of the day it is the technical cadres and the public policymakers that, preserving a relative autonomy from the pressure groups of society, make the final decisions.[70]

   After the end of the student crisis, the antagonism between the various
political parties also diminished. Although after the onslaught by the students
Bachelet's degree of autonomy was visibly reduced, she has been able to preserve a high degree of independence, as reflected in how she and her minister
of foreign affairs, Alejandro Foxley, have approached international relations,

---

69. Patricio Navia, "Poder popular," *La Tercera*, July 1, 2006.

70. Criticism of these ad hoc committees was not long in coming. Carlos Huneeus, for
example, has argued that "the student protest was a major blow not only to the government but
also to the political system. . . . The young have made politics come back to the frontline of
democracy, [instead of being] passed over by technocratism and its conservative bias. The student
protest generates tension in the Concertación, because there is a confrontation of two ways of
understanding the action of the government: a 'technical' view, with a series of prescription
policies, susceptible of being shared by 'experts' of different ideologies, or a political view. . . .
The technical view ignores the conflicts of interests existing in society whereas the political view
acknowledges them, seeks to regulate them through a consensus or the norm of the majority"
(*Qué Pasa*, June 10, 2006).

particularly with Chile's immediate neighbors. However, Bachelet has been increasingly confronted with a growing rebellion among Concertación senators and deputies who have not supported several important bills presented by the executive such as the release of additional funds to finance the Transantiago transport system. In this manner the Parliament has become the main redoubt from which Concertación politicians can exert pressure on Bachelet and increase their degree of influence on her government.

What is indeed clear after the announcement of Bachelet's cabinet in January 2006 is that the "Expansiva effect" has strongly eroded the traditional function of political parties as the main recruitment entity of the ruling class.[71] A series of new think tanks has been established, with the object of giving the necessary technical and political support to future presidential candidates by generating ideas and formulating future public policies.[72] In view of the technico-professional nature of these private centers, obviously this boom of think tanks favors individuals of a technocratic profile, with expertise in specific fields and issues, over traditional politicians and their political organizations.[73]

71. There are analysts who see Expansiva as a sort of proto-party or a sui generis political party because even without traditional party political structures or representation in Parliament, this think tank has been able to appropriate a good share of power in Bachelet's government. Others are of the opinion that in the future Expansiva might become a sort of "Bacheletista" party.

72. Such is the case of the foundation "ProyectAmerica," led by former senator José Antonio Viera-Gallo, which gathers together several figures of the Concertación who were not incorporated into Bachelet's government. Former president Ricardo Lagos has created "Democracia y Desarrollo," whose official objective is to look after the legacy of his work and its international projections, but which is seen as a possible electoral platform for the presidential elections of 2009. In turn, Joaquín Lavín created the research center "Vanguardia," while UDI leader Pablo Longueira, who has expressed his interest in becoming the presidential candidate of the Right for 2009, has created the foundation "Chile Justo." In addition, CIEPLAN, which has been practically paralyzed since 1990 when Foxley and his team joined Aylwin's administration, has been renewed and reinforced with the appointment of Ignacio Walker, Lagos's minister of foreign affairs and a political expert of renown, as its new director. See "¿Para qué sirven los think tanks?" (La Tercera, April 2, 2006); "El efecto Expansiva en la derecha" (La Nación, April 22, 2006); "¿Todo el poder a los think tank?" (La Nación, April 27, 2006).

73. At the beginning of the Aylwin administration there were already signs that political think tanks would have a great future in the Chilean political reality. At the time, I concluded that "the key role played by the technocrats of CIEPLAN in the new government also shows the increasing importance that research institutes have attained within Chilean politics, to the detriment of political parties, as reservoirs of an alternative techno-political class. The Chicago Boys have also received the message, establishing a CIEPLAN-like think tank in order to monitor the performance of the Aylwin government and to wait for political change in the future for the deployment of their policies. The struggle for political power between competing technocratic groups entrenched in their respective think tanks has become a new feature of Chilean politics" (P. Silva 1991, 409–10).

The battle between technocrats and politicians within the Concertación reached a high point with the expulsion from the Christian Democratic Party of the influential Senador Adolfo Zaldívar in December 2007. For years, he had become one of the most visible opponents of the growing influence of technocrats within the Concertación governments. He criticized the existence of the "partido transversal," as the technocratic forces within the executive have been called, almost daily. He has openly demanded the end of the technocrats' excessive influence and the strengthening of the role played by political parties in government affairs.[74] However, his departure produced a profound political crisis within the PDC; some members of the Parliament also left the party in solidarity with the senator, and the position of the PDC leader, Senator Soledad Alvear, became severely questioned by the party members. In response, Bachelet sent a strong signal of support to her leadership by appointing in January 2008 Edmundo Pérez Yoma, a close associate of Alvear, as the new minister of the interior.[75] With this move, which clearly fortified the position of politicians to the detriment of technocrats, Bachelet seemed to be trying to make some concessions to the former in an attempt to reduce the tensions within the ruling coalition and to help to defuse the crisis within the Christian Democratic Party.

In the final phase of her government, most probably Bachelet will have to face constant pressure from the sectors of the Concertación further to the Left to reverse the trend toward technocracy and strengthen the mechanisms for citizen participation. At the same time, her government will be permanently besieged by the leadership of the PDC and the PS-PPD axis, which will continue to apply pressure in order to recover the share of power that they have lost to the technocratic sectors.

74. "Because no political checks and balances have been applied on it, the transversal power exercised by technocrats has run totally out of control" (Rodolfo Zaldívar to *El Mercurio*, July 8, 2007).

75. Curiously enough, in the same cabinet reshuffle (January 8, 2008), Bachelet announced the departure of the minister of public infrastructure, Eduardo Bitrán, a representative of the hardcore technocracy, with whom Pérez Yoma had had a series of conflicts during the Frei administration.

7

Technocracy in Chile:
Past, Present, and Future

In this final chapter I summarize the main features of the technocratic phenomenon in Chile on the basis of the long-term historical analysis and theoretical reflections provided in the previous chapters. I will particularly focus
on the continuities as well as the changes that can be observed in the political
role played by Chilean technocrats since the 1920s, putting emphasis on the
most recent period. Drawing conclusions from past and current experiences
I will also refer to possible scenarios that the Chilean technocrats might face
in the years to come.

The chapter is organized in three sections. In the first I elaborate further on
the close relationship existing between the middle class and the technocratic
phenomenon in Chile and highlight some important sociopolitical factors
that for a long time made possible their mutual identification. The second
deals with the ever problematic relation existing between technocrats and
political parties, including their relations with the president and the political
class at large. This section concludes with a brief analysis of the current competition between political parties and think tanks in their efforts to influence
the government. The final section discusses the technocrats' insulation, relative autonomy, and embedded autonomy vis-à-vis other social and political
actors in Chile. I particularly emphasize their traditional function as a buffer
zone between progressive and conservative forces in Chile, contributing by
this to the achievement of political stability in the country. As it has been

shown in the previous chapter, however, in recent years their relative autonomy has become severely questioned by some political forces and representatives from civil society organizations, which demand more participation in the decision-making process.

Technocrats and the Middle Class: A Marriage for Life?

One of the central arguments developed in this book is that both the origin and further development of the technocratic phenomenon in Chile during most of the twentieth century have been intimately related to the emergence and further ascendancy of the middle class. As this study has shown, technocratic ideas came into the country with French positivism and were soon incorporated in the thought and writing of influential Chilean thinkers and important representatives of the middle class like Lastarria and Letelier. They defended ideas such as the need to establish a government based on merit, to break with traditional cultural patterns, to make science instead of religion the main guide for state affairs, to expand education, and to strengthen citizenship. These ideas were identical to the main claims and aspirations of the emerging Chilean urban middle class in the second part of the nineteenth century. These demands were also central in the battle by Chilean liberals against the oligarchic rule. They aimed to put an end to the legacy of the old colonial order, the dominance of aristocratic families, and the suffocating presence of the Catholic Church in all facets of public life.

At the center of the struggle of the Chilean middle class for social emancipation was a demand for access to higher education as a way to social advancement. For this reason, the Universidad de Chile attracted the young Lastarria, Letelier, and many others who were eager to demonstrate their talents and well disposed to lead the cultural and ideological struggle against oligarchic mediocrity. This specific historical context helps us understand why in Chile technocratic positivism initially had a rather libertarian and anti-oligarchic character. Other important vehicles for spreading technocratic ideas among middle-class circles have been the Radical Party and the Freemasons, who were intimately connected with liberal and radical scholars within the academic structures. In Letelier, as was the case for many others, all these institutions were embodied in a single individual.

When in the early decades of the twentieth century the oligarchic order came to an end, a visible change took place in the position adopted by techno-cratically oriented groups vis-à-vis the state. In the early years they saw the state as the main bastion of the conservative forces and, hence, an entity to be profoundly distrusted. After the turn of the century, however, the state came to be increasingly regarded by reform-oriented representatives of the middle class as a formidable institution from which a series of radical changes could be introduced in Chilean society. The expansion of the state also implied a welcome enhancement of employment opportunities for people with middle-class backgrounds in the growing number of state institutions and agencies created since the mid-1920s.

The authoritarian government of Colonel Carlos Ibáñez (1927–31) elevated many young engineers with middle-class backgrounds into very influential positions within the state machinery. At the same time, the middle-class elec-torate, as well as important sectors of the Radical Party and the Freemasons could not resist the quite appealing pledge made by the Ibáñez regime to put an end to political corruption and build up a modern Chile. Mesocratic fig-ures such as Pablo Ramírez played a strategic role in both recruiting techno-cratic personnel for the expanding state agencies and formulating a technocratic discourse to present the Ibáñez regime as the embodiment of the modern meritocratic state. The fall of Ibáñez in 1931, however, did not lead to the elimination of technocrats from the state apparatus or to the decline of state interventionism in Chile. On the contrary, since the early 1930s the state continued to expand its functions and size, allowing the incorporation of new contingents of middle-class technicians and professionals into the public administration and in the running of state-owned enterprises.

The creation of the Development Corporation (CORFO) in 1939 constituted an important landmark in the ascendancy of technocracy in Chile. This large and powerful state institution was managed almost entirely by engineers from largely middle-class backgrounds. Since its foundation until the early 1970s CORFO was the main actor in fostering industrialization in the country and supporting all the productive sectors of the economy. This resulted in the formulation of a veritable "industrialization ideology" in which the ideal of economic modernization and social progress were well integrated. This pro-industrialization project was one of the main expressions of the mesocratic rule established since the mid-1920s. In the mid-1950s, however, pro-business interests began to criticize openly the model of state-led industrialization and the central role played by the state in the Chilean economy. Instead, they advocated the adoption of policies more in tune with free trade principles. This had important consequences for the tacit alliance existing for decades between technocrats and the middle class. This "state versus free market" dichotomy generated serious cleavages within the middle class and divided the technocratic estate itself. The Alessandri administration (1958–64) launched a purge against the technocrats in CORFO and other state agencies. They were soon replaced by another group of technocrats coming from the private industry.

While some sectors of the middle class supported the efforts of the Alessandri government to reduce the presence of the state in the Chilean economy, others became inclined to support the recently established Christian Democratic Party (PDC) and its project to reshape the social and economic structures of the country by an active state. By the end of the 1950s the PDC had replaced the Radical Party as the main representative of the Chilean middle class.

Following the victory of Eduardo Frei in the 1964 presidential elections, hundreds of young Christian Democratic technocrats were incorporated into the state institutions. In contrast to the old engineers from CORFO, who had permanently kept an aura of apoliticism and neutrality, these young technocrats were more militant and enthusiastically embraced the call to bring about a deep transformation of the Chilean socioeconomic structures. As I have argued, the relative power of technocrats within the state was dramatically reduced following the election of Salvador Allende and the installation of the Unidad Popular government in 1970. The process of political polarization experienced in the country strengthened the position of radical politicians and intellectuals. The explicit self-identification with the working class (*obrerismo*) adopted by the Allende government alienated large sectors of the middle class. In a climate of extreme political polarization the mutual identification that had existed between the state technocrats and the middle class since the late 1920s came to a dramatic end.

The dissociation between technocracy and the middle-class ethos became absolute during the military government. Although most of the Chicago Boys also had middle-class roots, the openly pro-business policies they deployed rapidly eliminated any trace of self-identification of this social sector with the state technocracy. The forced reduction of the number of civil servants and the free trade policies had severely affected the middle-class sectors. In addition, the Chicago Boys' complete identification with orthodox neoliberalism made their self-proclaimed apoliticism totally unbelievable. In this manner, the polarization and divisions among Chileans produced during the governments of Salvador Allende and Augusto Pinochet also divided the middle class profoundly along almost irreconcilable political and ideological lines.

Since the democratic restoration in 1990 the political divisions among Chileans have been gradually reduced. The relatively good administration of the economy and the search for consensual policies has facilitated the establishment of a new political climate. Although technocratic groups have also played a strategic role during the Concertación administrations, the middle class–technocratic nexus of the past has not been reestablished.

To sum up, it can be said that the middle class became an important supporter of technocratically oriented policies on their way to social emancipation. For a long time the state technocracy expressed many aspirations of the middle-class sectors, such as meritocratic rule and a government of the most capable instead of the most affluent. However, since the mid-1960s this implicit alliance rapidly eroded as the middle class also became affected by the deep political and ideological divisions experienced by the entire country until the end of military rule in 1990. During the Concertación era the Chilean technocracy has generally defended universal principles of efficiency and good governance that are not aligned along specific class boundaries. In addition, today the state no longer represents an important source of employment, and its actions seem not to affect too much the daily life of the Chilean middle class. Because of this, it is very unlikely that in the near future this important sector of society will look again to the state as its main vehicle for social advancement.

Technocrats, Presidents, and Political Parties: An Uneasy Triangular Relation

As I have suggested before, the president of the Republic plays a decisive role in the degree of power and influence attained by technocrats within a particular administration. This is particularly true in the case of Chile, where there is a strong presidentialist tradition. As a general rule, the technocrats can operate undisturbed and exert their decision-making power within the government and state agencies provided that they have the staunch support of the president. No sooner is presidential support withdrawn, or the president no longer appears to be willing to defend technocrats from the pressure and criticism of political parties and public opinion in general, than the technocratic groups can see the writing on the wall. In order to understand the decision made by some presidents to surround themselves by technocrats at times (or to take the wind out of their technocratic sails at other times), the analysis must account for the tricky relation between president and supporting political parties.

There is no doubt that Chilean presidents very often appoint ministers or other officials with a markedly technocratic profile in order to reduce the capacity of the political parties that elevated them to power to apply pressure on their administration or policies. In other words, technocrats can be said to constitute a buffer zone between the president and the political parties. In addition, there is the initial assumption that technocrats should be able to formulate and apply state policies with a long-term perspective and to seek successful results, regardless of the pressure or opposition that may be generated in certain groups because of some policies. Conversely, the presence of ministers and collaborators with a markedly political seal might lead those very same groups to defend narrowly partisan political interests. This has the added inconvenience that political and electoral factors may come into play that do not always correspond to the interests of the government as a whole. In other words, their presence may affect the internal cohesion of the government, impairing the effectiveness of governmental action.

In governments with an authoritarian imprint like the regimes of Ibáñez and Pinochet, the presidents gave their resolute support to their technocratic teams, since they sought to thus "depoliticize" the public apparatus. Yet, by doing so, these authoritarian regimes had to face the criticism of their distinct technocratic orientation from sectors otherwise not entirely opposed to their rule. Thus, Ibáñez gave his permanent support and protection to his minister, Pablo Ramírez, who from the day of his appointment was the object of harsh criticism by influential political and social circles because of his determined manner to operate and introduce changes in the administration of the state without consulting the sectors affected. The same thing happened in the case of the Chicago Boys under the Pinochet regime. This group of technocrats was strongly criticized by some business and corporate sectors in the first years of application of his neoliberal model, as their interests were negatively affected. Also within the armed forces there was veiled criticism of the course to be steered by the economic policy, as it implied a break with the nationalist and statist tradition of the military institutions. Pinochet extended his full support to his finance minister, Sergio de Castro, and his Chicago Boys, and gave a latitude approaching carte blanche for the execution of their economic reforms. However, after the economic crisis of 1982 and the rise of a massive opposition to the regime and its economic policies, Pinochet dismissed his team of Chicago technocrats without hesitation. They were replaced by a more moderate and heterodox group of economists, who applied a more pragmatic policy to weather the economic storm.

During the Concertación era, each president has had his or her own motives and reasons to incorporate technocrats into the inner circles of government.

Patricio Aylwin understood perfectly that his was a transition government during which he should keep a watchful eye on both political stability and economic welfare, given the enormous uncertainty about what was to become of the country after the return to democracy. There were fears about the possible emergence of a painful cycle of political and social conflict, associated with a worsening of the economic situation. The first democratic government sought to prove that it was better able to manage the political sphere, create a national consensus, and increase further the economic growth and well-being of the country in general than the dictatorship had proved to be. To generate guarantees and confidence in all the sectors of the country—including entrepreneurs, right-wing parties, and the armed forces—Aylwin opted for governing above political parties, without giving them a very direct and visible influence in his administration. His closest advisers were characterized not by their political leanings but by their great professional prestige. In turn, they managed to implement a professional and technocratic approach that would point out the way for future Concertación governments.

During the Aylwin administration the political parties of the government coalition also realized the importance of counting on that core of technocrats in key positions, as high-quality governance guaranteed the consolidation of the democratic regime—and of the Concertación as the government coalition—for a long time. What is apparent is that during the Aylwin administration there was a useful "division of labor" between the technocrats and politicians of the Concertación. While the former took over the task of demonstrating the economic efficiency and good housekeeping of the state institutions, the politicians were in charge of dealing with a series of complex issues inherited from the dictatorship, such as human rights, civil-military relations, and so on. The good job done by the technocratic government team drew its members closer together, despite their being formally affiliated with different political parties. This fact originated what came to be called the "transversal party," in which the technocratic and liberal ideology is the common denominator.

The second president of the Concertación, Frei Ruiz-Tagle initially privileged the strengthening of the political team, although he himself was an engineer by profession and an advocate of the technocratic way by conviction. He was forced in this direction by the resurgence of social and salary demands from the more disadvantaged groups. During the Aylwin administration the trade unions had zealously kept a truce with the government to contribute to a smoother transition and maintain the political and social stability in the country. By the end of the Aylwin administration, however, Chile's prospects included political stability and, above all, a fair share of economic bonanza. Thus, the time seemed ripe for a wave of social demands that would have to be negotiated by figures with political influence and good relations with the leaders of the trade union and social movements. Yet the expected resurgence of social unrest never came to be. This moved Frei Ruiz-Tagle to concentrate on attaining a greater degree of internationalization and modernization of the Chilean economy, which were among his main objectives. To do so, he gave maneuvering room to a new group of technocrats known as the "Top Ten," who for some time had a privileged position and much influence on the president's strategic decisions. However, this technocratic ascendancy was strongly resented by the "Iron Circle" formed by old politicians, who waged ruthless war on the Top Ten, and finally made Frei Ruiz-Tagle turn them out.

Ricardo Lagos, the third president of the Concertación, had always had strong misgivings about technocrats, with whom he had several disagreements during his term as minister in the Frei Ruiz-Tagle cabinet. Because of his socialist credentials, Lagos's presidential victory aroused strong uncertainty in the business and financial sectors. For this reason, Lagos made sure to send off unequivocal confidence-inspiring signals by appointing Nicolás Eyzaguirre as his new minister of finance—a technocrat both known and trusted by the financial community. However, Lagos's closest circle was a group of sociologists with whom he had long-standing ties of friendship, and whom he housed near his presidential office in La Moneda.

With the election of Michelle Bachelet, there has appeared an entirely new angle in the positioning of the president in relation to the technocrats. As can be seen, there is a paradox here: when Bachelet was the Concertación presidential candidate, she deployed a markedly antitechnocratic discourse, and yet she eventually appointed the most technocratic cabinet that Chile has had since the restoration of democracy in 1990. To understand this situation it is necessary to consider the strained relations between Bachelet and the leaders of the parties making up the Concertación prior to her victory at the polls. Bachelet was always an outsider to the upper party political echelons, and her candidacy was mainly the result of her enormous personal popularity, not the resolute backing of the parties of the Concertación. Bachelet wished to continue to keep her distance and relative independence from the political upper ranks, so she decided to recruit her cabinet from outside the party political structures and thus resorted to a select group of technocrats from the think tank Expansiva. From that moment on, the government officials recruited from Expansiva have been systematically criticized by the Concertación party political leaders, who demand that the prevailing rule of technocracy should come to an end. Particularly, the secondary school student rebellion in 2006 (known as "the penguins' revolution"); the failure of Transantiago, the public transport system launched in February 2007; and the economic team's refusal to authorize a substantial increase in social expenditure, with the allocation of part of Chile's surplus revenue resulting with the hike in the price of copper, triggered open criticism of the Expansiva technocrats, focused mainly on their leader, Finance Minister Andrés Velasco.

In Chile party politicians and technocrats have rarely gotten along, with the exception of the Radical Party, which practically assimilated all the technocratic tenets originating in Comtean positivism. Thus, under the leadership of Valentín Letelier, technocratic ideas were officially incorporated into the ideology of the Radical Party. However, when mesocratic rule arrived hand in hand with Arturo Alessandri's election as president in 1920, it was above all an antipolitical discourse or one of scientific neutrality that prevailed in the technocrats of the state machinery. This became even more evident under Ibáñez, who shared these antiparty political feelings.

After the severe crisis of the 1930s, the coming into power of the Frente Popular in 1938, and the creation of CORFO in the following year, it was evident that the continued operation of an efficient technocracy in charge of the state enterprises and of CORFO would become a central element for the preservation of the Estado de Compromiso. This was understood by both the center-left and the left-wing parties. Hence, on the whole, the parties did respect the relative autonomy of technocrats within the state and, in fact, abstained from criticizing the job they were doing until the mid-1960s.

Once the PDC came into power in 1964, the young technocracy that joined the state machinery consisted of out-and-out party militants and defenders of Frei Montalva's political platform. Although this made them become attuned with the ruling party, it inevitably generated the criticism of the opposition left-wing parties, which questioned the effectiveness of the policies applied by Frei Montalva in the economic and financial sphere and in such areas as the agrarian reform, housing policy, and so on.

Something similar happened during the government of Salvador Allende, in which the official technocracy sported the colors of the parties of the Unidad Popular. What was most striking was the presence of a large number of people from the Izquierda Cristiana and the MAPU, two PDC splinter groups, who had acquired government experience during Frei Montalva's administration. During Allende's government, the technocrats lost practically all decision-making influence. This became the preserve of the leaders of the government coalition parties and of some intellectuals who played the role of ideologists of the doctrine, in charge of defining the line of action of all militants, including that of the technocrats within the government.

The military government abruptly dismantled the bureaucratic scaffolding inherited from the previous administration by dismissing most of the technocrats who had joined the public administration at the time of Frei and Allende. The Chicago Boys were thus able to operate within the state with no concern for political parties: the parties on the center and left of the political spectrum were banned, and those on the right chose voluntarily to cease their political activities in acknowledgment of their support of, and subordination to, the new military authorities. Although some of the Chicago Boys had taken part in Jorge Alessandri's presidential campaign in 1970, they had no clear party political background.

I have already referred to the fact that during the military regime the government promoted the ascendancy of the neoliberal technocracy and avoided a much too open association with right-wing parties. Among those opposed to this regime, the harsh repression prevented for many years the reconstitution of the political parties that made up the old Unidad Popular. The only opposition that was accepted was the academic diversity organized around private research institutions. This is the reason why these institutes and the researchers working there began to gain the upper hand over the political parties in the final phase of the military regime, on the occasion of the 1988 referendum, and during the campaign to regain democracy for the elections of 1989. I also argued that these institutes gradually adopted a technocratized discourse that countered the neoliberal discourse.

It is important to note that after the experience of the Unidad Popular and seventeen years of antiparty official propaganda, the Chileans were wary of political parties and politicians in general, and that this distrust was quite pervasive. On the whole, the strengthening of technocracy has been not only the result of processes that have taken place within the government; the collective frame of mind of public opinion and its widespread rejection of the political class have also been contributory factors. As we have seen before, these factors were clearly present in the period preceding the ascent of Ibáñez in 1927, Alessandri in 1958, Pinochet in 1973, and to a certain extent from 1990 on after the restoration of democracy.

During the first two governments of the Concertación, the political parties that form this government coalition managed to preserve their internal unity and play an important role in the consolidation of democracy. There is no denying that the fear of a possible regression to authoritarianism and the need to present a united front before Pinochet and his supporters contributed to maintain party discipline translated, among other things, in the full support of the government actions by the Concertación members of the Chilean parliament. However, the growing discredit of party political activity and politicians, the increased depoliticization of Chilean society, and the rise of technocracy and of the importance of expertise have led to a gradual weakening of the internal cohesion and the appearance of open disagreements within the political parties.

This weakness has generated an opportunity for the so-called think tanks, which have acquired increased visibility in the public scene and have challenged the function of political parties as centers of political influence and as recruiting grounds for upper-level government officials. As we saw in the previous chapter, this phenomenon of the ascent of think tanks in political activity has become strongly manifest during the government of Michelle Bachelet, who recruited an important part of her cabinet from the think tank Expansiva. Ever since this happened, several influential figures with technico-professional profiles, both from the government and the right-wing opposition have become members of different think tanks in order to reinforce their political weight. Unlike political parties, membership in think tanks is limited to people with advanced degrees and vast professional experience who also coincide to a large extent in their diagnosis of the problems of the country and their possible solutions.

Although in the near future the think tanks will continue to grow stronger, to the detriment of political parties as the main source of ideas and candidates for government posts, the role of political parties in national politics is not quite over. The weakening of the discipline and hierarchical structures within the parties on the one hand and the growing tensions between the political parties and governmental technocracies on the other have generated an unexpected reactivation of the Chilean Congress, which looms up as a political actor that is gaining weight. What we have observed is that the Concertación members of parliament no longer necessarily vote in favor of projects presented by the government and that the government must negotiate parliamentary support on an almost case-by-case basis. In other words, the legislative branch of government appears to be generating an important political counterbalance to the power and influence of the state technocracy, which until the early months of Bachelet's government seemed to be boundless.

Technocrats and the Citizen: From Insulation to Embedded Autonomy

Citizen participation in politics in Chile has been traditionally channeled through a solid political party system, which for many decades exerted an effective control on initiatives put forth by the people. This explains why Chile, unlike other countries in the region, is characterized by a nearly complete absence of populisms or *caudillismos* based on the manipulation of the masses by popular leaders lacking strong party political or ideological foundations. As a result of this strong institutionalization of politics, even in the periods of greatest political unrest during the administrations of Frei Montalva and Allende, the political parties in power continued to exert effective control on the masses.

Thus, historically the creation of more effective and direct mechanisms for citizen participation in decision-making was never actually a pressing demand from the social grassroots themselves. The slogans "promoción popular" under Frei Montalva and "poder popular" under Allende were in fact initiatives with a strong discursive component, which did not emerge from the social grassroots but were articulated "from the top down" by the political forces in power. This explains why the relative isolation that has characterized the Chilean technocracy of state ever since its birth in the initial decades of the twentieth century until the present did not emerge as an attempt to inhibit the influence of the popular masses or of the electorate on the government. As I have suggested elsewhere in this study, the state technocracy in Chile has played the important role of intermediary or buffer between the political forces of the Center-Left and the Right, which feel a deep mutual mistrust, and which for many decades found themselves to be in a political tie. The mesocratic sectors accessed governmental power in the decade of the 1920s, but they were unable to break the Right entrenched in Parliament thanks to its overrepresentation in the farming provinces. In addition, this strong and influential Right continued to control most of the economy and the world of finance.

The isolation from day-to-day political activity of the strategic sectors of the state machinery, such as the ministries responsible for the country's economy and finance, and CORFO, is therefore the result of a dramatic balancing act of the forces of both sectors. Paradoxically, it was the very existence of this equilibrium that made possible and accounts for the constitution of the so-called Estado de Compromiso. We have already seen that this democracy of basic general agreements was created in the late 1930s, began to show signs of fracture in the mid-1960s, and came to an end with the fall of Allende's government in 1973. Thus, despite its apolitical orientation and convictions, the state technocracy ended up by playing an extremely important role in the working of Chilean democracy during the Estado de Compromiso. In fact, its very presence in the state administration became a guarantee for the political Right and the dominant social sectors that the governments of the Center-Left of those years would not eventually indulge in the politicization and ideologization of the enterprises belonging to the state and of the general policies for the promotion of production.

As I argued in the previous section, this role as buffer zone became diffuse and eventually disappeared during the decade of the reforms under the governments of Frei Montalva and Allende, when a new generation of young technocrats of Social-Christian-cum-Socialist inspiration joined the civil service with the mission of implementing a program of profound socioeconomic reforms. This change in the role of the state technocracy—from buffer zone to actor actively committed to the government platform—coincides with the strong shifts in the balance of power that took place in the country beginning in the early 1960s. We must remember that the political Right lost so many seats in Parliament to the Christian Democrats and the Left that the political tie that had led to the need for a compromise state was broken. This new scenario also wiped out the conviction—and the need— to preserve an independent state technocracy between the right-wing and center-left forces.

The situation changed once again under Pinochet's regime. The military authorities were bent on evicting from the state machinery the technical cadres that had identified themselves with the previous governments. However, at the same time, they were trying to prevent this same machinery from falling into the hands of the political forces that supported the coup (the Christian Democrats, the Partido Nacional, the *gremialistas*, Patria y Libertad, and so on). With this objective in mind, they appointed a series of military officers to strategic positions (ministries, regional governments, state companies, and so on) and paved the way for the Chicago Boys, who avowed themselves to be completely apolitical and only interested in the application of public policies supported by scientific evidence. This latter point reinforced the image that the military government wished to project: a technical and apolitical government that was above party politics and aimed at long-range national objectives.

No sooner were the neoliberal Chicago Boys commissioned to take over economic policy in April 1975 than they were armor-plated and insulated from external pressures by Pinochet and the rest of the cabinet. Thus, both the entrepreneurial sectors affected by the trade opening (the industrial and traditional agricultural sectors) and the sectors of the political Right that did not look kindly on the application of free market policies were prevented from getting access to the economic team to persuade them of the need to adhere to more protectionistic policies. The fact that the neoliberal technocrats were shielded against pressures from the political and entrepreneurial elite, together with the absence of an effective left-wing opposition because of the existing climate of extreme repression, made it possible for the neoliberal technocracy to operate practically under laboratory conditions. In fact, the Chicago Boys were able to implement their neoliberal model for a number of years without having to deal with the political and social pressures and generalized criticism that would no doubt have come their way under democratic circumstances.

Curiously enough, after the restoration of democracy in 1990 the position of relative autonomy from political and social pressures attained by the economic team became even more solid. In fact, it was possible to observe a situation of political balance that in some aspects was reminiscent of the years of the Estado de Compromiso. The context was one in which the forces of the Concertación took over the political power via the elections, but were confronted by a very strong right-wing opposition that included an important sector of the population: professional sectors, practically the whole of the corporate/entrepreneurial class, the mass media, the armed forces, and last but not least, a Congress controlled by the opposition. In addition, the Concertación was getting ready to deal with pressures from left-wing sectors (both from within the Concertación and from the extraparliamentary Left) and from the trade unions, originating in claims to abandon the neoliberal policies and adopt more distributive measures.

In this complex and uncertain political scenario, the state technocracy once again has positioned itself as a symbol of stability by implementing public policies underpinned by practical and theoretical international experiences with a high technical component. The good performance attained by Chile since 1990 in terms of public and financial policies, which has been acknowledged worldwide by a diversity of official agencies and bodies, has increased the prestige of technocracy and its degree of influence within the governments of the Concertación. However, the growing technocratic profile of the governments of the Concertación began to generate negative reactions from some sectors within the governmental coalition, demanding renewed appreciation for, and revaluation of, political action and politicians as the foundation of the decision-making process. As already mentioned in this study, during the governments of Frei Ruiz-Tagle and Lagos, there was a series of clashes within the government team between the technocratic sectors and old guard political figures who opposed the hegemony of the former.

As Bachelet excluded from her government nearly all of the most influential political figures and opted for a cabinet made up of technocrats, the antitechnocratic struggle moved into the streets and parliament. The impervious and arrogant attitude initially adopted by the technocrats in charge of the educational policies when they were forced to deal with the massive and radical demonstrations organized by the secondary school students from May 2006 on generated a strong antitechnocratic feeling in wide sectors of society. The extensive media coverage of the so-called penguins' revolution and their demands for better education installed the issue of technocracy and demands for citizen participation in public policies firmly in the national political agenda. Also, some Concertación members of parliament who so far had obeyed and passively supported the orders of the president began to demand radical changes in education policies.

Finally, the secondary school students' movement forced the government to give in and agree to a series of their demands. Among them was the creation of an Education Commission, which would include teachers, education experts, government technocrats, and representatives of the students, tasked to draft and submit to the president a proposal on how to reform and improve education in Chile. In my opinion, this experience in which technocrats and representatives of society gather together to hold discussions about the public policies, but in which the former, on behalf of the government, have the final say, represents a clear example of the embedded autonomy of the Chilean technocracy. Thus, decisions are made only once the sectors affected by such policies are consulted and their opinions taken into account.

Although the government and its technocracy were forced by some sectors of society to adopt consultation mechanisms that guarantee a higher degree of citizen participation in the definition of the public policies, I believe that the embedded autonomy of the government technocracy vis-à-vis the civil society may become a viable decision-making model for important national issues (such as education, health, welfare, and so on). Embedded autonomy could in fact represent the cornerstone of a new "compromise" in the Chilean political system. This would make it possible to attend, at least in part, to the growing demands for a greater degree of citizen participation in public affairs and policymaking. In addition, it would be a guarantee that, at the end of the day, these policies would have a technical design that would make them realistic and compatible with the human and financial resources available, and in line with other general objectives of the government. In other words, embedded autonomy may make it possible to attain an equilibrium between citizen participation and administrative efficiency.

The credibility and prestige of the Chilean governmental technocracy experienced a severe blow as a result of the grave failings of Transantiago, the new public transport system launched in February 2007. This episode has revealed the urgent need for the governmental technocracy to be more receptive to how the people and the sectors involved will be affected at the moment of designing the public policies. This would make it possible not only to prevent planning mistakes, but also to generate a stronger commitment among the people to the new policies and their successful implementation. In this way, public policies would no longer be exclusively "top down" initiatives, as has been the rule ever since the return to democracy in 1990, and would, in a certain sense, become everybody's.

For a long time, the Chilean technocracy lived under the strong protection of governments and presidents, who have by this attempted to reduce the influence of pressure groups on the formulation of public policies. Although in my opinion, the insulation of technocracy contributed in a positive way to the functioning of the old Chilean democracy, and has been most effective in the consolidation of the current democratic regime, the present moment appears to demand closer links between technocracy and the citizens. This rapprochement, far from weakening technocracy, will give it increased visibility in the eyes of the population and will help it to reinforce its function as the rationalizing entity of the main demands of the people within the framework of a modern democracy.

In the coming years political parties and politicians will probably be able to increase their amount of power and influence in the highest governmental circles, to the detriment of the position of the state technocrats. However, I think that even if this occurs, the marked technocratic nature of the post-1990 Chilean democracy will not be significantly altered. As has been the case for most of the twentieth century, in the near future the state technocrats will most likely continue to play their important role of mediators between contending social and political forces.

References

Ahumada, Jorge. [1958] 1973. *En vez de la miseria*. Santiago: Editorial del Pacífico.

Akin, William E. 1977. *Technocracy and the American Dream: The Technocrat Movement, 1900–1941*. Berkeley and Los Angeles: University of California Press.

Alessandri, Arturo. 1967. *Recuerdos de gobierno*. 3 vols. Santiago: Editorial Nascimento.

Ames, Barry. 1987. *Political Survival: Politicians and Public Policy in Latin America*. Berkeley and Los Angeles: University of California Press.

Angell, Alan. 1972. *Politics and Labor Movement in Chile*. New York: Oxford University Press.

———. 1988. "Some Problems in the Interpretation of Recent Chilean History." *Bulletin of Latin American Research* 7, no. 1: 91–108.

———. 1993. *Chile entre Alessandri y Pinochet: En busca de la utopia*. Santiago: Editorial Andrés Bello.

———. 2005. *Elecciones presidenciales, partidos políticos y democracia en el Chile post Pinochet*. Santiago: Ediciones Centro de Estudios Bicentenario.

———. 2007. *Democracy After Pinochet: Politics, Parties, and Elections in Chile*. London: Institute for the Study of the Americas.

Angell, Alan, and Susan Carstairs. 1987. "The Exile Question in Chilean Politics." *Third World Quarterly* 9, no. 1: 148–67.

Arancibia, Patricia, and Francisco Balart. 2007. *Sergio de Castro: El arquitecto del modelo económico chileno*. Santiago: Editorial Biblioteca Americana.

Arellano, José Pablo, ed. 1982. *Modelo económico chileno: Trayectoria de una crítica*. Santiago: Editorial Aconcagua.

———. [1985] 1988. *Políticas sociales y desarrollo: Chile 1924–1984*. Santiago: CIEPLAN.

Arias, Raúl, Jesús Fresno, Nuria Ordovás, and Hilda Sánchez. 1981. "El monetarismo como ideología." *Economía de América Latina* 6, no. 1: 159–76.

Arrate, Jorge. 1983. *El socialismo chileno: Rescate y renovación*. Rotterdam: Institute for the New Chile.

———. 1985. *La fuerza democrática de la idea socialista*. Barcelona and Santiago: Ediciones Documentas.

Ascher, William. 1984. *Scheming for the Poor: The Politics of Redistribution in Latin America*. Cambridge: Harvard University Press.

Baño, Rodrigo, ed. 1982. *Las modernizaciones en Chile: Un experimento neoliberal*. Rome: Centro de Estudios y Documentación Chile-América.

Barr-Melej, Patrick. 2001. *Reforming Chile: Cultural Politics, Nationalism, and the Rise of the Middle Class*. Chapel Hill: University of North Carolina Press.

Bauer, Arnold J. 1990. "Industry and the Missing Bourgeoisie: Consumption and Development in Chile, 1850–1950." *Hispanic American Historical Review* 70, no. 2: 227–53.

Bell, Daniel. 1960. *The End of Ideology*. Glencoe, Ill.: The Free Press.

———. 1973. *The Coming of Post-Industrial Society.* New York: Basic Books.

Bernedo, Patricio. 1989. "Prosperidad económica bajo Carlos Ibáñez del Campo, 1927–1929." *Historia* 24:5–105.

Bilbao, Francisco. 1897. *Obras Completas.* 4 vols. Santiago: Imprenta de "El Correo."

Bitar, Sergio. 1986. *Chile, Experiment in Democracy.* Philadelphia: Institute for the Study of Human Issues.

Blackmore, Harold. 1974. *British Nitrates and Chilean Politics, 1886–1896: Balmaceda and North.* London: The Athlone Press.

———. 1993. "From the War of the Pacific to 1930." In *Chile Since Independence,* ed. Leslie Bethell, 33–85. Cambridge: Cambridge University Press.

Boeninger, Edgardo. 1997. *Democracia en Chile: Lecciones para la gobernabilidad.* Santiago: Editorial Andrés Bello.

Borzutzky, S., and L. Hecht Oppenheim, eds. 2006. *After Pinochet: Chile's Road to Capitalism and Democracy.* Gainesville: University Press of Florida.

Bradford Bruns, E. 1990. *The Poverty of Progress: Latin America in the Nineteenth Century.* Berkeley and Los Angeles: University of California Press.

Bresser-Pereira, Luiz Carlos, and Peter Spink, eds. 1999. *Reforming the State: Managerial Public Administration in Latin America.* Boulder, Colo.: Lynne Rienner.

Brunner, José Joaquín. 1986. "Las ciencias sociales en Chile: El caso de la sociología." *Documento de Trabajo* 325. Santiago: FLACSO.

———. 1988a. *El caso de la sociología en Chile: Formación de una disciplina.* Santiago: FLACSO.

———. 1988b. *Un espejo trizado: Ensayos sobre cultura y políticas culturales.* Santiago: FLACSO.

———. 1990. "La intelligentsia: Escenarios institucionales y universos ideológicos." *Proposiciones* 18:180–91.

Brunner, José Joaquín, and Alicia Barrios. 1987. *Inquisición, Mercado y Filantropía: Ciencias sociales y autoritarismo en Argentina, Brasil, Chile y Uruguay.* Santiago: FLACSO.

Brunner, José Joaquín, Alicia Barrios, and Carlos Catalán. 1989. *Chile: Transformaciones culturales y modernidad.* Santiago: FLACSO.

Brunner, José Joaquín, and Angel Flisfisch. 1985. *Los intelectuales y las instituciones de la cultura.* Santiago: FLACSO.

Burnham, James. 1943. *La revolución de los gerentes.* Buenos Aires: Editorial Claridad.

Calcagno, Eric. 1989. *El pensamiento económico latinoamericano: Estructuralistas, liberales y socialistas.* Madrid: Ediciones de Cultura Hispánica.

Camp, Roderic Ai. 1980. *Mexico's Leaders: Their Education and Recruitment.* Tucson: University of Arizona Press.

———. 1983. "El tecnócrata en México." *Revista Mexicana de Sociología* 45, no. 2: 579–99.

———. 1985. "The Political Technocrat in Mexico and the Survival of the Political System." *Latin American Research Review* 20, no. 1: 97–118.

Cancino, Hugo. 1988. *Chile: La problemática del Poder Popular en el proceso de la vía chilena al socialismo.* Odense: Odense University Press.

Cardemil, Alberto. 1997. *El camino de la utopía: Alessandri, Frei, Allende, Pensamiento y obra.* Santiago: Editorial Andrés Bello.

Cardoso, Fernando Henrique, and Enzo Faletto. 1969. *Dependencia y desarrollo en América Latina.* Mexico City: Siglo XXI.

Castillo, Fernando, Lía Cortés, and Jordi Fuentes. 1999. *Diccionario histórico y biográfico de Chile*. Santiago: Zig-Zag.

Castro, Sergio de. 1992a. *"El Ladrillo": Bases de la política económica del gobierno militar chileno*. Santiago: Centro de Estudios Públicos.

———. 1992b. "Prólogo." In *"El Ladrillo": Bases de la política económica del gobierno militar chileno*, 7–12. Santiago: Centro de Estudios Públicos.

Cavallo, Ascanio. 1992. "Alejandro Foxley." In *Los hombres de la transición*, 141–54. Santiago: Editorial Andrés Bello.

Cavarozzi, Marcelo. 1975. "The Government and the Industrial Bourgeoisie in Chile, 1938–1964." Ph.D. diss., University of California at Berkeley.

———. 1992. "Patterns of Elite Negotiation and Confrontation in Argentina and Chile." In *Elites and Democratic Consolidation in Latin America and Southern Europe*, ed. John Higley and Richard Gunther, 208–36. Cambridge: Cambridge University Press.

Centeno, Miguel A., and Sylvia Maxfield. 1992. "The Marriage of Finance and Order: Changes in the Mexican Political Elite." *Journal of Latin American Studies* 24, no. 1: 57–85.

Cerda Albarracín, César. 1998. *Historia y desarrollo de la clase media en Chile*. Santiago: Ediciones Universidad Tecnológica Metropolitana.

Chonchol, Jacques, and Julio Silva Solar. 1951. *Hacia un Mundo Comunitario: Condiciones de una política social-cristiana*. Santiago: Editorial del Pacífico.

Cleaves, Peter. 1974. *Bureaucratic Politics and Administration in Chile*. Berkeley and Los Angeles: University of California Press.

Cochrane, James. 1967. "Mexico's New Científicos: The Díaz Ordaz Cabinet." *Inter-American Economic Affairs* 21, no. 1: 61–72.

Collier, David, ed. 1979. *The New Authoritarianism in Latin America*. Princeton: Princeton University Press.

Collier, Simon. 2003. *The Making of a Republic, 1830–1865: Politics and Ideas*. Cambridge: Cambridge University Press.

Collier, Simon, and William F. Sater. 1996. *A History of Chile, 1808–1994*. Cambridge: Cambridge University Press.

Concertación. 1993. "Un Gobierno para los Nuevos Tiempos: Bases Programáticas del Segundo Gobierno de la Concertación de Partidos por la Democracia." Santiago: Comando de la Concertación.

Contreras Guzmán, Víctor. 1942. *Bitácora de la Dictadura: Administración Ibáñez, 1927–1931*. Santiago: Imprenta Cultura.

CORFO (Corporación de Fomento de la Producción). 1965. *Geografía económica de Chile: Texto refundido*. Santiago: CORFO.

Correa Prieto, Luis. 1962. *El presidente Ibáñez, la política y los políticos: Apuntes para la historia*. Santiago: Editorial del Pacífico.

Correa Sutil, Sofía. 2004. *Con las riendas del poder: La derecha chilena en el siglo XX*. Santiago: Sudamericana.

Cortázar, René. 1993. *Política laboral en el Chile democrático: Avances y desafíos en los noventa*. Santiago: Dolmen.

Crawford, William R. 1971. "Positivist Thought in Chile: Lastarria and Bilbao." In *Positivism in Latin America, 1850–1900: Are Order and Progress Reconcilable?* ed. Ralph L. Woodward, 17–24. Lexington, Mass.: D. C. Heath.

Cristi, Renato, and Carlos Ruiz. 1992. *El pensamiento conservador en Chile.* Santiago: Editorial Universitaria.

Crowther, W. 1973. "Technological Chance as Political Choice: The Civil Engineers and the Modernization of the Chilean State Railways." 3 vols. Ph.D. diss., University of California at Berkeley.

Cruz, Pedro N. 1944. *Bilbao y Lastarria.* Santiago: Editorial Difusión Chilena.

Délano, Manuel, and Hugo Translaviña. 1989. *La herencia de los Chicago Boys.* Santiago: Ediciones del Ornitorrinco.

Devés Valdés, Eduardo. 2004. "La circulación de las ideas y la inserción de los cientistas económico-sociales chilenos en las redes conosureñas durante los largos 1960." *Historia* 37, no. 2: 337–66.

De Vylder, Stefan. 1976. *Allende's Chile: The Political Economy of the Rise and Fall of the Unidad Popular.* Cambridge: Cambridge University Press.

DIPRE (Dirección de Presupuesto). 1978. *Somos realmente independientes gracias al esfuerzo de todos los chilenos: Documento de política económica.* Santiago: DIPRE.

Domínguez, Jorge I., ed. 1994. *Parties, Elections, and Political Participation in Latin America.* New York: Routledge.

———. 1996. *Technopols: Freeing Politics and Markets in Latin America in the 1990s.* University Park: Pennsylvania State University Press.

Donoso, Ricardo. 1946. *Las ideas políticas en Chile.* Mexico City: Fondo de Cultura Económica.

Drake, Paul W. 1978. *Socialism and Populism in Chile, 1932–52.* Urbana: University of Illinois Press.

———, ed. 1989. *The Money Doctor in the Andes: The Kemmerer Missions, 1923–1933.* Durham: Duke University Press.

Drake, Paul W., and Iván Jaksic, eds. 1991. *The Struggle for Democracy in Chile, 1982–1990.* Lincoln: University of Nebraska Press.

Edwards, Agustín. 1931. *Recuerdos de mi persecución.* Santiago: Editorial Ercilla.

Edwards, Alberto. [1924] 1952. *La fronda aristocrática: Historia política de Chile.* Santiago: Editorial del Pacífico.

Edwards, Alberto, and Eduardo Frei. 1949. *Historia de la los partidos políticos chilenos.* Santiago: Editorial del Pacífico.

Edwards Matte, Ismael. 1937. "Los 'cabros' de Pablo Ramírez y la reconstrucción nacional: Apuntes para la historia." *Hoy,* March 4, 11–13.

Ellul, Jacques. [1954] 1964. *The Technological Society.* New York: Alfred A. Knopf.

Encina, Francisco. [1911] 1981. *Nuestra inferioridad económica.* Santiago: Editorial Universitaria.

Evans, Peter. 1995. *Embedded Autonomy: State and Industrial Transformations.* Princeton: Princeton University Press.

Falcoff, Mark. 1989. *Modern Chile, 1970–1989: A Critical History.* New Brunswick, N.J.: Transaction Publishers.

Fernández de la Mora, Gonzalo. 1986. *El crepúsculo de las ideologías.* Madrid: Espasa-Calpe.

Ffrench-Davis, Ricardo. 1982. "El experimento monetarista en Chile: Una síntesis crítica." *Colección Estudios CIEPLAN* 9:5–40.

———. 2003. *Entre el neoliberalismo y el crecimiento con equidad: Tres décadas de política económica en Chile.* Santiago: J. C. Sáenz Editor.

Figueroa, Virgilio. 1931. *Diccionario histórico*. Santiago: Establecimientos Gráficos Bakells.

Fischer, Frank. 1990. *Technocracy and the Politics of Expertise*. Newbury Park, Calif.: Sage.

Fontaine, Arturo. 1989. *La historia no contada de los economistas del presidente Pinochet*. Santiago: Zig-Zag.

Foxley, Alejandro. 1983. *Latin American Experiments in Neoconservative Economics*. Berkeley and Los Angeles: University of California Press.

———. 1986. *Para una democracia estable*. Santiago: Editorial Aconcagua/CIEPLAN.

———. 1989. "Economic and Political Transitions in South America." In *Democratization and the State in the Southern Cone*, ed. Benno Galjart and Patricio Silva, 75–101. Amsterdam: CEDLA.

———. 1993. *Economía política de la transición*. Santiago: Dolmen.

Frank, André Gunder. 1969. *Capitalism and Underdevelopment in Latin America: Historical Studies of Chile and Brazil*. New York: Monthly Review Press.

Friedman, Milton. 1962. *Capitalism and Freedom*. Chicago: University of Chicago Press.

———. 1975. *Milton Friedman en Chile: Bases para el desarrollo económico*. Santiago: Fundación de Estudios Económicos.

Fuentes, Claudio. 2000. "After Pinochet: Civilian Policies Towards the Military in the 1990s Chilean Democracy." *Journal of Interamerican Studies and World Affairs* 43, no. 3: 111–42.

Fuenzalida Grandon, Alejandro. 1911. *Lastarria i su tiempo*. 2 vols. Santiago: Imprenta Barcelona.

Galbraith, John Kenneth. 1967. *The New Industrial State*. New York: Mentor.

Galdames, Luis. 1937. *Valentín Letelier y su obra*. Santiago: Imprenta Universitaria.

———. 1964. *A History of Chile*. 1941. Reprint. New York: Russell & Russell.

Garretón, Manuel Antonio. 1987. *Reconstruir la política: Transición y consolidación democrática en Chile*. Santiago: Editorial Andante.

———. 1989. *The Chilean Political Process*. Boston: Unwin Hyman.

———. 2000. *La sociedad en que vivi(re)mos: Introducción sociológica al cambio de siglo*. Santiago: LOM.

Gazmuri, Cristián. 1999. *El '48' chileno: Igualitarios, reformistas radicales, masones y bomberos*. Santiago: Editorial Universitaria.

Gerth, H. H., and C. Wright Mills. 1946. *From Max Weber: Essays in Sociology*. New York: Oxford University Press.

Gil, Federico. 1966. *The Political System of Chile*. Boston: Houghton Mifflin.

Giraldo, Jeanne K. 1996. "Development and Democracy in Chile: Finance Minister Alejandro Foxley and the Concertación Project for the 1990s." In *Technopols: Freeing Politics and Markets in Latin America in the 1990s*, ed. Jorge I. Domínguez, 229–75. University Park: Pennsylvania State University Press.

Góngora, Mario. [1981] 1988. *Ensayo histórico sobre la noción de estado en Chile en los siglos XIX y XX*. Santiago: Editorial Universitaria.

Gouldner, Alvin W. 1979. *The Future of Intellectuals and the Rise of the New Class*. London: Macmillan.

Graciarena, Jorge. 1984. "El estado latinoamericano en perspectiva: Figuras, crisis, perspectivas." *Pensamiento Iberoamericano* 5:39–74.

Gramsci, Antonio. 1971. *Selections from the Prison Notebooks*. London: Lawrence and Wishart.

Grindle, Merilee S. 1977. "Power, Expertise, and the 'Tecnico': Suggestions from a Mexican Case Study." *Journal of Politics* 39, no. 2: 400–426.

Haggard, Stephan, and Robert R. Kaufman, eds. 1992. *The Politics of Economic Adjustment*. Princeton: Princeton University Press.

Hale, Charles A. 1996. "Political Ideas and Ideologies in Latin America, 1870–1930." In *Ideas and Ideologies in Twentieth Century Latin America*, ed. Leslie Bethell, 133–205. Cambridge: Cambridge University Press.

Halpern, Pablo. 2002. *Los nuevos chilenos y la batalla por sus preferencias*. Santiago: Planeta.

Haring, Clarence H. 1931. "Chilean Politics, 1920–1928." *Hispanic American Historical Review* 11, no. 1: 1–26.

Harrison, David. 1988. *The Sociology of Modernization and Development*. London: Unwin Hyman.

Herf, Jeffrey. 1984. *Reactionary Modernism: Technology, Culture, and Politics in Weimar and the Third Reich*. Cambridge: Cambridge University Press.

Hernández Parker, Luis. 1945. "En la piscina entrevisté al nuevo mago: Pablo Ramírez." *Ercilla*, 22 May, 9.

Hira, Anil. 1999. *Ideas and Economic Policy in Latin America: Regional, National, and Organizational Case Studies*. Westport, Conn.: Praeger.

Hirschman, Albert. [1963] 1965. *Journeys Toward Progress: Studies of Economic Policy-Making in Latin America*. New York: Anchor Books.

Huneeus, Carlos. 2000. "Technocrats and Politicians in an Authoritarian Regime: The 'ODEPLAN Boys' and the 'Gremialists' in Pinochet's Chile." *Journal of Latin American Studies* 32, no. 2: 461–501.

———. 2007. *The Pinochet Regime*. Boulder, Colo.: Lynne Rienner. [First Spanish edition, 2001.]

Huneeus, Jorge. 1910. *Cuadro histórico de la producción intelectual de Chile*. Santiago: Imprenta Barcelona.

Huntington, Samuel P. 1968. *Political Order in Changing Societies*. New Haven: Yale University Press.

Ibáñez Santa María, Adolfo. 1984. "Los ingenieros, el estado y la política en Chile: Del Ministerio de Fomento a la Corporación de Fomento, 1927–1939." *Estudios Históricos* 7. Instituto de Historia, Universidad Católica de Chile.

———. 2003. *Herido en el ala: Estado, oligarquías y subdesarrollo en Chile, 1924–1960*. Santiago: Editorial Biblioteca Latinoamericana.

Jobet, Julio César. 1955. *Ensayo crítico del desarrollo económico-social de Chile*. Santiago: Editorial Universitaria.

Joignant, Alfredo. 2003. "La democracia de la indiferencia: Despolitización, desencanto y malestar en el Gobierno de Eduardo Frei Ruiz-Tagle." In *El período del Presidente Frei Ruiz-Tagle*, ed. Oscar Muñoz and Carolina Stefoni, 83–106. Santiago: FLACSO–Editorial Universitaria.

Jones, H. S., ed. 1998. *Comte: Early Political Writings*. Cambridge: Cambridge University Press.

Jorrín, Miguel, and John D. Martz. 1970. *Latin-American Political Thought and Ideology*. Chapel Hill: University of North Carolina Press.

Junta Militar de Chile. 1974. *Declaración de Principios del Gobierno de Chile.* March 11, 1974. Santiago: Publiley.

Kaufman, Robert R. 1972. *The Politics of Land Reform in Chile, 1950–1970: Public Policy, Political Institutions, and Social Change.* Cambridge: Harvard University Press.

———. 1979. "Industrial Change and Authoritarian Rule in Latin America." In *The New Authoritarianism in Latin America,* ed. David Collier, 165–253. Princeton: Princeton University Press.

Kay, Cristóbal. 1989. *Latin American Theories of Development and Underdevelopment.* New York: Routledge.

Kay, Cristóbal, and Patricio Silva, eds. 1992. *Development and Social Change in the Chilean Countryside: From the Pre–Land Reform Period to the Democratic Transition.* Amsterdam: CEDLA.

Kay, Diana. 1987. *Chileans in Exile: Private Struggles, Public Lives.* Basingstoke: Macmillan.

Kellner, Hansfried, and Frank W. Heuberger, eds. 1992. *Hidden Technocrats: The New Class and New Capitalism.* New Brunswick, N.J.: Transaction Publishers.

Konrad, Georg, and Ivan Szelenyi. 1979. *The Intellectuals on the Road to Class Power.* Brighton: Harvester Press.

Lagos, Ricardo. 1961. *La concentración del poder económico.* Santiago: Editorial del Pacífico.

Lastarria, José Victorino. [1875] 1891. *Lecciones de política positiva.* Paris: Librería de Ch. Bouret.

———. [1878] 2000. *Literary Memoirs.* New York: Oxford University Press.

Lavín, Joaquín. 1986. *Miguel Kast: Pasión de vivir.* Santiago: Zig-Zag.

———. 1987. *Chile: Revolución silenciosa.* Santiago: Zig-Zag.

Lavín, Joaquín, and Luis Larraín. 1989. *Chile: Sociedad emergente.* Santiago: Zig-Zag.

Lechner, Norbert, ed. 1987. *Cultura política y democratización.* Santiago: FLACSO.

Letelier, Valentín. 1886. *De la Ciencia Política en Chile.* Santiago: Imprenta Gutenberg.

———. 1892. *La filosofía de la educación.* Santiago: Imprenta Cervantes.

———. 1895. *La lucha por la cultura: Miscelánea de artículos políticos y estudios pedagógicos.* Santiago: Imprenta Barcelona.

Levy, Daniel C. 1996. *Building the Third Sector: Latin America's Private Research Centers and Nonprofit Development.* Pittsburgh: University of Pittsburgh Press.

Lindberg, Leon B. 1976. *Politics and the Future of Industrial Society.* New York: David McKay.

Lladser, María Teresa, ed. 1986. *Centros privados de investigación en ciencias sociales en Chile.* Santiago: Academia de Humanismo Cristiano–FLACSO.

Lomnitz, Larissa A., and Ana Melnick. 2000. *Chile's Political Culture and Parties: An Anthropological Explanation.* Notre Dame: Notre Dame University Press.

Loveman, Brian. 1976. *Struggle in the Countryside: Politics and Rural Labor in Chile, 1919–1973.* Bloomington: Indiana University Press.

———. 1979. *Chile: The Legacy of Spanish Capitalism.* New York: Oxford University Press.

———. 1992. "Rural Unionisation and Party Politics." In *Development and Social Change in the Chilean Countryside,* ed. Cristóbal Kay and Patricio Silva, 55–74. Amsterdam: CEDLA.

Loveman, Brian, and Thomas M. Davies, eds. 1997. *The Politics of Antipolitics: The Military in Latin America.* Wilmington, Del.: Scholarly Resources.

Malloy, James M. 1979. *The Politics of Social Security in Brazil.* Pittsburgh: University of Pittsburgh Press.

Mamalakis, Markos J. 1965. "Public Policy and Sectorial Development: A Case Study of Chile, 1940–1958." In *Essays on the Chilean Economy,* ed. Markos Mamalakis and Clark W. Reynolds, 1–200. Chicago: Richard D. Irwin.

Mannheim, Karl. [1936] 1976. *Ideology and Utopia.* London: Routledge & Kegan Paul.

Martínez, Javier, and Ernesto Tironi. 1985. *Las clases sociales en Chile: Cambio y estratificación, 1970–1980.* Santiago: Ediciones SUR.

Martner, Gonzalo, ed. 1971. *El pensamiento económico del gobierno de Allende.* Santiago: Editorial Universitaria.

———. 1973. "The Popular Unity Government's Efforts in Planning." In *The Chilean Road to Socialism,* ed. Ann Zammit, 69–75. Sussex: IDS University of Sussex.

McBride, George. 1971. *Chile: Land and Society.* 1936. Reprint. New York: Octagon Books.

McClelland, David. 1961. *The Achieving Society.* New York: Van Nostrand.

Medina, Eden. 2006. "Designing Freedom, Regulating a Nation: Socialist Cybernetics in Allende's Chile." *Journal of Latin American Studies* 38, no. 3: 571–606.

Melfi, Domingo. 1931. *Dictadura y Mansedumbre.* Santiago: Imprenta Universitaria.

Meller, Patricio. 1984. "Los Chicago boys y el modelo económico chileno, 1973–1983." *Apuntes CIEPLAN* 43. Santiago: CIEPLAN.

———. 2000. *The Unidad Popular and the Pinochet Dictatorship: A Political Economy Analysis.* London: Macmillan.

Menges, Constantine C. 1966. "Public Policy and Organized Business in Chile: A Preliminary Analysis." *Journal of International Affairs* 20, no. 12: 343–65.

Meynaud, Jean. 1968. *Technocracy.* London: Faber and Faber. [First French edition, 1964.]

Miller, Daniel. 1987. *Material Culture and Mass Consumption.* Oxford: Blackwell.

Miller, Nicola. 1999. *In the Shadow of the State: Intellectuals and the Quest for National Identity in Twentieth-Century Spanish America.* London: Verso.

Molina, Sergio. 1972. *El proceso de cambio en Chile: La experiencia 1965–1970.* Santiago: Editorial Universitaria.

Montecinos, Verónica. 1988. "Economics and Power: Chilean Economists in Government, 1958–1985." Ph.D. diss., University of Pittsburgh.

———. 1998a. *Economists, Politics, and the State: Chile, 1958–1994.* Amsterdam: CEDLA.

———. 1998b. "Economists in Party Politics: Chilean Democracy in the Era of the Markets." In *The Politics of Expertise in Latin America,* ed. Miguel A. Centeno and Patricio Silva, 126–41. Basingstoke: Macmillan.

Montero, René. 1937. *Ibáñez: Un hombre, un mandatario, 1926–1931.* Santiago: Imprenta Cóndor.

———. 1952. *La verdad sobre Ibáñez.* Santiago: Zig-Zag.

Moreno, Marco. 2006. "Emergencia del Paradigma de la Gobernabilidad en América Latina: Aprendizajes de la transición y consolidación democrática para la gobernabilidad en Chile." Ph.D. diss., Leiden University.

Moulian, Luis, and Gloria Guerra. 2000. *Eduardo Frei: Biografía de un estadista utópico.* Santiago: Editorial Sudamericana.

Moulian, Tomás. 1982. "Desarrollo político y estado de compromiso: Desajustes y crisis estatal en Chile." *Estudios CIEPLAN* 64. Santiago: CIEPLAN.

————. 1983. "Los frentes populares y el desarrollo político de la década del sesenta." *Documento de Trabajo* 191. Santiago: FLACSO.

————. 1997. *Chile actual: Anatomía de un mito.* Santiago: LOM.

Moulian, Tomás, and Isabel Torres. 1989. "La problemática de la derecha política en Chile, 1964–1983." In *Muerte y resurrección: Los partidos políticos en el autoritarismo y las transiciones del Cono Sur,* ed. Marcelo Cavarozzi and Manuel Antonio Garretón, 335–93. Santiago: FLACSO.

Moulian, Tomás, and Pilar Vergara. 1980. "Estado, ideología y políticas económicas en Chile, 1973–1978." *Colección de Estudios CIEPLAN* 3. Santiago: CIEPLAN.

Munizaga, Giselle. 1988. *El discurso público de Pinochet: Un análisis semiológico.* Santiago: CESOC/CENECA.

Muñoz, Oscar. 1982. "La CORFO y el desarrollo nacional." In *Modelo económico chileno: Trayectoria de una crítica,* ed. José Pablo Arellano et al., 205–7. Santiago: Editorial Aconcagua.

————. 1986. *Chile y su industrialización: Pasado, crisis y opciones.* Santiago: CIEPLAN.

————, ed. 1993. *Historias personales, políticas públicas.* Santiago: Editorial los Andes.

Muñoz, Oscar, and Ana María Arriagada. 1977. "Orígenes políticos y económicos del estado empresarial en Chile." *Estudios CIEPLAN* 16:34–62.

Navia, Patricio. 2004. *Las grandes alamedas: El Chile post Pinochet.* Santiago: La Tercera–Mondatori.

Nunn, Frederick M. 1970. *Chilean Politics, 1920–1931: The Honorable Mission of the Armed Forces.* Albuquerque: University of New Mexico Press.

————. 1976. *The Military in Chilean History: Essays on Civil-Military Relations, 1810–1973.* Albuquerque: University of New Mexico Press.

————. 2000. "Introduction." In José Victorino Lastarria, *Literary Memoirs,* xv–xxxvii. New York: Oxford University Press.

O'Brien, Philip, ed. 1976. *Allende's Chile.* New York: Praeger.

————. 1981. "The New Leviathan: The Chicago Boys and the Chilean Regime, 1973–1980." *IDS Bulletin* 13, no. 1: 38–50.

O'Brien, Philip, and Jackie Roddick. 1983. *Chile, the Pinochet Decade: The Rise and Fall of the Chicago Boys.* London: Latin American Bureau.

O'Donnell, Guillermo. 1973. *Modernization and Bureaucratic-Authoritarianism: Studies in South American Politics.* Berkeley: Institute of International Studies, University of California.

O'Donnell, Guillermo, Phillipe Schmitter, and Laurence Whitehead, eds. 1986. *Transitions from Authoritarian Rule.* Baltimore: Johns Hopkins University Press.

Ominami, Carlos. 1991. "Promoting Economic Growth and Stability." In *From Dictatorship to Democracy: Rebuilding Political Consensus in Chile,* ed. Joseph S. Tulchin and Augusto Varas, 21–28. Boulder, Colo.: Lynne Rienner.

Ortega, Luis, Carmen Norambuena, Julio Pinto, and Guillermo Bravo. 1989. *Corporación de Fomento de la Producción: 50 años de realizaciones, 1939–1989.* Santiago: CORFO.

Ouweneel, Arij. 1996. "The Germination of Politics Within the Directorio of the Institute of Chilean Engineers, 1910–1927." *Historia* 29:357–90.

Oxhorn, Philip D. 1995. *Organizing Civil Society: The Popular Sectors and the Struggle for Democracy in Chile.* University Park: Pennsylvania State University Press.

Petras, James. 1969. *Political and Social Forces in Chilean Development.* Berkeley and Los Angeles: University of California Press.

———. 1990. "Metamorphosis of Latin America's Intellectuals." *Latin American Perspectives* 172:102–12.

Pike, Fredrick B. 1963. *Chile and the United States, 1880–1962.* Notre Dame: University of Notre Dame Press.

Pinto, Aníbal. [1958] 1985. "Estado y gran empresa: De la precrisis hasta el gobierno de Jorge Alessandri." *Colección Estudios CIEPLAN* 16 (June): 5–40.

———. 1973a. *Chile, un caso de desarrollo frustrado.* Santiago: Editorial Universitaria.

———. 1973b. "Desarrollo económico y relaciones sociales en Chile." In *Chile, un caso de desarrollo frustrado,* 294–359. Santiago: Editorial Universitaria.

Portes, Alejandro. 1974. "Modernity and Development: A Critique." *Studies in Comparative International Development* 9, no. 2: 247–79.

Prebisch, Raúl. 1981. "Diálogo acerca de Friedman y Hayek, desde el punto de vista de la periferia." *Revista de la CEPAL* 15:161–82.

Puryear, Jeffrey M. 1994. *Thinking Politics: Intellectuals and Democracy in Chile, 1973–1988.* Baltimore: Johns Hopkins University Press.

Putnam, Robert D. 1977. "Elite Transformation in Advanced Industrial Societies: An Empirical Assessment of the Theory of Technocracy." *Comparative Political Studies* 10, no. 3: 383–412.

Rabkin, Rhoda. 1993. "How Ideas Become Influential: Ideological Foundations of Export-led Growth in Chile (1973–90)." *World Affairs* 156, no. 1: 3–25.

Ramírez, Pablo. 1921a. *Discursos Parlamentarios i Políticos, 1919–1920.* Santiago: Sociedad Imprenta i Litografía Universo.

———. 1921b. *Discursos Parlamentarios i Políticos, 1921.* Santiago: Sociedad Imprenta i Litografía Universo.

Ramírez Necochea, Hernán. 1958. *Balmaceda y la contrarrevolución de 1891.* Santiago: Editorial Universitaria.

Ramos, Joseph. 1986. *Neoconservative Economics in the Southern Cone of Latin America, 1973–1983.* Baltimore: Johns Hopkins University Press.

Rex Crawford, William. 1971. "Positivist Thought in Chile: Lastarria and Bilbao." In *Positivism in Latin America, 1850–1900: Are Order and Progress Reconcilable?* ed. Ralph Lee Woodward, 17–24. Lexington, Mass.: D. C. Heath.

Riz, Liliana de. 1989. "Política y partidos: Ejercicio de análisis comparado: Argentina, Chile, Brasil y Uruguay." In *Muerte y resurrección: Los partidos políticos en el autoritarianismo y las transiciones del Cono Sur,* ed. Marcelo Cavarozzi and Manuel Antonio Garretón, 35–78. Santiago: FLACSO.

Rojas, Darío. 1989. *El fenómeno Büchi.* Santiago: Editorial Santiago.

Rojas Flores, Jorge. 1993. *La dictadura de Ibáñez y los sindicatos (1927–1931).* Santiago: Dirección de Bibliotecas, Archivos y Museos.

Rostow, Walt Whitman. 1960. *The Stages of Economic Growth: A Non-Communist Manifesto.* London: Cambridge University Press.

Rowe, William, and Vivian Schelling. 1991. *Memory and Modernity: Popular Culture in Latin America.* London: Verso.

Rowney, Don K. 1989. *Transition to Technocracy: The Structural Origins of the Soviet Administrative State.* Ithaca: Cornell University Press.

Roxborough, Ian, Philip O'Brien, and Jackie Roddick. 1977. *Chile: The State and Revolution.* London: Macmillan.

San Francisco, Alejandro, and Ángel Soto. 2004. "El Gobierno del General Augusto Pinochet en Chile, 1973–1990." *Aportes* 19, no. 55: 98–123.

Sartori, Giovanni. 1984. *La política: Lógica y método en las Ciencias Sociales*. Mexico City: Fondo de Cultura Económica.

Schneider, Ben Ross. 1998. "The Material Bases of Technocracy: Investor Confidence and Neoliberalism in Latin America." In *The Politics of Expertise in Latin America*, ed. Miguel A. Centeno and Patricio Silva, 77–95. London: Macmillan, 1998.

Schneider, Cathy Lisa. 1995. *Shantytown Protest in Pinochet's Chile*. Philadelphia: Temple University Press.

Scott, Robert E. 1966. "The Government Bureaucrats and Political Change in Latin America." *Journal of International Affairs* 20, no. 12: 289–308.

Scully, Timothy R. 1992. *Rethinking the Center: Party Politics in Nineteenth- and Twentieth-Century Chile*. Stanford: Stanford University Press.

Sepúlveda Rondanelli, Julio. 1993. *Los radicales ante la historia*. Santiago: Editorial Andrés Bello.

Sheahan, John. 1987. *Patterns of Development in Latin America: Poverty, Repression, and Economic Strategy*. Princeton: Princeton University Press.

Sierra, Enrique. 1970. *Tres ensayos de estabilización en Chile*. Santiago: Editorial Universitaria.

Sigmund, Paul E. 1980. *The Overthrow of Allende and the Politics of Chile, 1964–1976*. Pittsburgh: University of Pittsburgh Press.

Silva, Eduardo. 1991. "The Political Economy of Chile's Regime Transition: From Radical to 'Pragmatic' Neo-Liberal Policies." In *The Struggle for Democracy in Chile, 1982–1990*, ed. Paul W. Drake and Iván Jaksic, 98–127. Lincoln: University of Nebraska Press.

———. 1996. *The State and Capital in Chile: Business Elites, Technocrats, and Market Economics*. Boulder, Colo.: Westview Press.

———. 2002. "Capital and the Lagos Presidency: Business as Usual?" *Bulletin of Latin American Research* 21, no. 3: 339–57.

Silva, Fernando. 1974. "Un contrapunto de medio siglo: Democracia liberal y estatismo burocrático, 1924–1970." In *Historia de Chile*, vol. 4, ed. Sergio Villalobos et al., 826–977. Santiago: Editorial Universitaria.

Silva, Patricio. 1983. "Intellectuals, Technocrats, and Social Change in Chile: Past, Present, and Future Perspectives." In *The Legacy of Dictatorship: Political, Economic, and Social Change in Pinochet's Chile*, ed. Alan Angell and Benny Pollack, 198–216. Liverpool: University of Liverpool, Institute of Latin American Studies.

———. 1987. *Estado, neoliberalismo y política agraria en Chile, 1973–1981*. Amsterdam: CEDLA.

———. 1991. "Technocrats and Politics in Chile: From the Chicago Boys to the CIEPLAN Monks." *Journal of Latin American Studies* 23, no. 2: 385–410.

———. 1992. "Intelectuales, tecnócratas y cambio social en Chile: Pasado, presente y perspectivas futuras." *Revista Mexicana de Sociología* 54, no. 1: 139–66.

———. 1993a. "Intellectuals, Technocrats, and Social Change in Chile: Past, Present, and Future Perspectives." In *The Legacy of Dictatorship: Political, Economic and Social Change in Pinochet's Chile*, ed. Alan Angell and Benny Pollack, 198–223. Liverpool: Institute of Latin American Studies Monograph Series.

———. 1993b. "State, Politics, and the Idea of Social Justice in Chile." *Development and Change* 24:465–86.

————. 1994. "State, Public Technocracy, and Politics in Chile, 1927–1941." *Bulletin of Latin American Research* 13, no. 3: 281–97.

————. 1995. "Intellectuals and Technocrats in the Third World: Towards a Convergency?" In *Designers of Development: Intellectuals and Technocrats in the Third World,* ed. Benno Galjart and Patricio Silva, 269–78. Leiden: Centre for Non-Western Studies.

————. 1997. "Going Asia: Economic Internationalization and Technocratic Empowerment in Chilean Foreign Policy." Paper presented at the Twentieth LASA Congress, Guadalajara, Mexico, April 17–19.

————. 1998. "Pablo Ramírez, A Technocrat Avant-La-Lettre." In *The Politics of Expertise in Latin America,* ed. Miguel A. Centeno and Patricio Silva, 52–76. Basingstoke: Macmillan.

————. 2000. "Politics Across Frontiers: The Pinochet Affair and Chilean Democracy." In *Fronteras: Towards a Borderless Latin America,* ed. Pitou van Dijck et al., 151–63. Amsterdam: CEDLA.

————. 2001a. "Forging Military-Technocratic Alliances: The Ibáñez and Pinochet Regimes in Chile." In *The Soldier and the State in South America: Essays in Civil-Military Relations,* ed. Patricio Silva, 87–108. London: Palgrave.

————. 2001b. "Towards Mass Technocratic Politics in Chile? The 1999–2000 Elections and the 'Lavín Phenomenon.'" *European Review of Latin American and Caribbean Studies* 70:25–39.

————. 2003. "Democratisation and State–Civil Society Relations in Chile, 1983–2000: From Effervescence to Deactivation." *Nordic Journal of Latin American and Caribbean Studies* 32, no. 2: 73–96.

————. 2004. "Doing Politics in a Depoliticised Society: Social Change and Political Deactivation in Chile." *Bulletin of Latin American Research* 23, no. 1: 63–78.

————. 2006a. "Lastarria, Letelier, and 'Scientific Politics' in Chile." *Revista Bicentenario* 5, no. 2: 85–114.

————. 2006b. "Los tecnócratas y la política en Chile: Pasado y presente." *Revista de Ciencia Política* 26, no. 2: 171–86.

Simón, Raúl. 1926. "The Kemmerer Mission and the Chilean Central Bank Law." *Chile,* January, 13–16, 19.

Sklair, Leslie. 1991. *Sociology of the Global System.* London: Harvester Wheatsheaf.

Soto, Ángel. 2003. *El Mercurio y la difusión del pensamiento politico económico liberal, 1955–1970.* Santiago: Centro de Estudios Bicentenario.

Spalding, Hobart, Lance Taylor, and Carlos Vilas. 1985. *SAREC's Latin American Programme: An Evaluation.* Stockholm: SAREC.

Stallings, Barbara. 1978. *Class Conflict and Economic Development in Chile, 1958–1973.* Stanford: Stanford University Press.

Subercaseaux, Bernardo. 1997. *Historia de las ideas y de la cultura en Chile.* 2 vols. Santiago: Editorial Universitaria.

Sunkel, Osvaldo. 1963. "El fracaso de las políticas de estabilización en el contexto del desarrollo latinoamericano." *El Trimestre Económico* 120:123–41.

Taller (Taller de Cooperación al Desarrollo). 1989. *Una puerta que se abre: Los organismos no gubernamentales en la cooperación al desarrollo.* Santiago: Taller de Cooperación al Desarrollo.

Tironi, Ernesto. 1982. *El modelo neoliberal chileno y su implantación.* Santiago: CED.

———. 1986. *El liberalismo real.* Santiago: Ediciones SUR.

———. 1988. *Los silencios de la revolución: Chile, la otra cara de la modernización.* Santiago: Editorial La Puerta Abierta.

———. 1990. *Autoritarismo, modernización y marginalidad: El caso de Chile 1973–1989.* Santiago: Ediciones SUR.

———. 2005. *El sueño chileno: Comunidad, familia y nación en el Bicentenario.* Santiago: Aguilar.

Toha, Carolina, and Ricardo Solari. 1996. "La modernización del estado y la gerencia pública." Santiago: Friedrich Ebert Stiftung.

UNDP (United Nation Development Program). 1998. *Las paradojas de la modernización.* Santiago: UNDP.

———. 2002. *Desarrollo humano en Chile: Nosotros los chilenos, un desafío cultural.* Santiago: UNDP.

———. 2005. *El poder: ¿Para qué y para quién?* Santiago: UNDP.

UP (Unidad Popular). 1969. "Programa de gobierno de la Unidad Popular." Santiago: Comando de la Unidad Popular.

Urzúa, Germán, and Anamaría García. 1971. *Diagnóstico de la burocracia chilena, 1818– 1969.* Santiago: Editorial Jurídica de Chile.

Valdés, Juan Gabriel. 1995. *Pinochet's Economists: The Chicago School in Chile.* Cambridge: Cambridge University Press.

Valdivieso, Patricio. 2002. "Leadership and Democracy: The Case of Chile." Instituto de Ciencia Política, Universidad Católica de Chile.

Valenzuela, Arturo. 1978. *The Breakdown of Democratic Regimes: Chile.* Baltimore: Johns Hopkins University Press.

———. 1989. "Chile: Origins, Consolidation, and Breakdown of a Democratic Regime." In *Democracy in Developing Countries: Latin America,* ed. Larry Diamond, Juan Linz, and Seymour Lipset, 159–82. Boulder, Colo.: Lynne Rienner.

Valenzuela, Arturo, and Alexander Wilde. 1979. "Presidential Politics and the Decline of the Chilean Congress." In *Legislatures in Development: Dynamics of Change in New and Old States,* ed. Joel Smith and Lloyd D. Musolf, 189–215. Durham: Duke University Press.

Van der Ree, Gerard. 2007. *Contesting Modernities: Projects of Modernisation in Chile, 1964–2006.* Amsterdam: Dutch University Press.

Veblen, Thorstein. 1965. *The Engineers and the Price System.* 1921. Reprint. New York: Sentry Press.

Venegas, Alejandro. 1910. *Sinceridad: Chile íntimo en 1910.* Santiago: Editorial Universitaria.

Vergara, Pilar. 1982. "Pasado y presente de la industria chilena." *Mensaje* 306:39–47.

———. 1985. *Auge y caída del neoliberalismo en Chile.* Santiago: FLACSO.

Vergara Vicuña, Aquiles. 1931. *Ibáñez: César criollo.* 2 vols. Santiago: Imprenta La Maestranza.

Vernon, Raymond. 1963. *The Dilemma of Mexico's Development.* Cambridge: Harvard University Press.

Vial, Gonzalo. 2001. *Historia de Chile (1891–1973).* 5 vols. Santiago: Zig-Zag.

Vial, Marisol. 1981. "Chicago boys: Cómo llegaron al gobierno." *Qué Pasa* 548:26–28.

Viera-Gallo, José Antonio. 1986. "Crisis y reafirmación del ideario democrático: Trayectoria de una generación." In *Democracia en Chile: Doce conferencias,* ed. Ignacio Walker et al., 41–55. Santiago: CIEPLAN.

Villalobos, Sergio. 1987. *Origen y ascenso de la burguesía chilena.* Santiago: Editorial Universitaria.

Wiarda, Howard. 2001. *The Soul of Latin America: The Cultural and Political Tradition.* New Haven: Yale University Press.

Woll, Allen. 1976. "Positivism and History in Nineteenth-Century Chile: José Victorino Lastarria and Valentín Letelier." *Journal of the History of Ideas* 37, no. 3: 493–506.

———. 1982. *A Functionalist Past: The Uses of History in Nineteenth-Century Chile.* Baton Rouge: Louisiana State University Press.

Woodward, Ralph Lee. 1971. *Positivism in Latin America, 1850–1900: Are Order and Progress Reconcilable?* Lexington, Mass.: D. C. Heath.

Würth Rojas, Ernesto. 1958. *Ibáñez: Caudillo enigmático.* Santiago: Editorial del Pacífico.

Zahler, Roberto. 1977. "La inflación chilena." In *Chile 1940–1945: Treinta y cinco años de discontinuidad económica,* ed. Roberto Zahler et al., 17–72. Santiago: ICHEC.

Zammit, J. Ann, ed. 1973. *The Chilean Road to Socialism.* Sussex: IDS University of Sussex.

Zea, Leopoldo. [1965] 1976. *El pensamiento latinoamericano.* Barcelona: Editorial Ariel.

———. 1970. *The Latin American Mind.* Norman: University of Oklahoma Press.

———. 1980. "Positivism." In *Pensamiento positivista latinoamericano,* ed. Leopoldo Zea, 2 vols. Caracas: Biblioteca Ayacucho.

Zeitlin, Maurice. 1988. *Landlords and Capitalists: The Dominant Class of Chile.* Princeton: Princeton University Press.

Index